The Anthem Companion to Niklas Luhmann

ANTHEM COMPANIONS TO SOCIOLOGY

Anthem Companions to Sociology offer authoritative and comprehensive assessments of major figures in the development of sociology from the last two centuries. Covering the major advancements in sociological thought, these companions offer critical evaluations of key figures in the American and European sociological tradition, and will provide students and scholars with an in- depth assessment of the makers of sociology and chart their relevance to modern society.

Series Editor

Bryan S. Turner – City University of New York, USA / Australian Catholic University, Australia / University of Potsdam, Germany

Other Titles in the Series

The Anthem Companion to Alexis de Tocqueville
The Anthem Companion to Auguste Comte
The Anthem Companion to C. Wright Mills
The Anthem Companion to Ernst Troeltsch
The Anthem Companion to Everett Hughes
The Anthem Companion to Ferdinand Tönnies
The Anthem Companion to Gabriel Tarde
The Anthem Companion to Georg Simmel
The Anthem Companion to Hannah Arendt
The Anthem Companion to Karl Mannheim
The Anthem Companion to Karl Marx
The Anthem Companion to Maurice Halbwachs
The Anthem Companion to Max Weber
The Anthem Companion to Philip Selznick
The Anthem Companion to Philip Rieff
The Anthem Companion to Pierre Bourdieu
The Anthem Companion to Raymond Aron
The Anthem Companion to Robert N. Bellah
The Anthem Companion to Robert K. Merton
The Anthem Companion to Robert Park
The Anthem Companion to Talcott Parsons
The Anthem Companion to Thorstein Veblen

The Anthem Companion to Niklas Luhmann

Edited by Ralf Rogowski

ANTHEM PRESS

Anthem Press
An imprint of Wimbledon Publishing Company
www.anthempress.com

This edition first published in UK and USA 2023
by ANTHEM PRESS
75–76 Blackfriars Road, London SE1 8HA, UK
or PO Box 9779, London SW19 7ZG, UK
and
244 Madison Ave #116, New York, NY 10016, USA

British Library Cataloguing-in-Publication Data
A catalogue record for this book is available from the British Library.

Library of Congress Control Number: 2022915194
A catalog record for this book has been requested.

ISBN-13: 978-1-83998-488-4 (Hbk)
ISBN-10: 1-83998-488-0 (Hbk)

This title is also available as an e-book.

CONTENTS

AUTHORS

Dirk Baecker He is Senior Professor for Sociology at Zeppelin University, Friedrichshafen, Germany. He studied systems theory with Niklas Luhmann and received his doctorate and habilitation at the University of Bielefeld. Professor Baecker published numerous books and articles on economic sociology, sociological theory, organisation research and form calculus. He edited the volume "Problems of Form" (Stanford University Press, 1999) and has been active in translating Niklas Luhmann's work into English, including Luhmann's 'Social Systems'.

Paul Buckermann He is postdoctoral researcher at Heidelberg University. Previously, he taught and researched at the Department of Sociology at the University of Lucerne. He uses Luhmann's social system's theory in analysing art in modern society with a specific focus on mechanisms of evaluating art and knowledge about the arts.

Klaus Dammann He is a Emeritus Professor of Sociology and Organisation Theory, University of Bielefeld. He previously taught at the Free University of Berlin and was for many years a a close colleague of Luhmann at Bielefeld University. Professor Dammann's publications include numerous works on Luhmann's theory as well as his biography; he owns one of the largest private archives on Niklas Luhmann.

Elena Esposito She is Professor of Sociology at the University of Bielefeld and Professor of Political and Social Sciences at the University of Bologna. She is a leading Luhmann scholar and was a key author of 'GLU', the glossary on Luhmann's Social Systems. In her research she has used Luhmann's social system theory in studying a variety of social phenomena, including social forgetting, paradoxes in fashion and the role of futures and derivatives in modern financing. Her current project analyses social consequences of algorithmic predictions.

Aldo Mascareño He is Professor of Sociology at the School of Government, Universidad Adolfo Ibáñez, Chile, senior researcher at Centro de *Estudios Públicos*, and general editor of the journal Estudios Públicos since 2019. His main research areas are sociological theory, sociology of law and complexity theories.

Kolja Möller He is postdoctortal researcher at the Institute of Political Sciences, Technical University Dresden. Before, he was a postdoctoral researcher in the project 'Transnational Force of Law' at the University of Bremen. He has been engaged for a while in developing a critical systems theory that seeks to combine Luhmann's social system theory and critical theory developed by the Frankfurt School.

Richard Nobles He is Emeritus Professor of Law at the Queen Mary University of London. Before, he held the position of Reader in Law at the London School of Economics and Political Science. He is the author (with David Schiff) of *A Sociology of Jurisprudence* (Hart 2006), and one of the four editors of the English Translation of Niklas Luhmann's *Law as a Social System* (OUP 2004). His latest book (with David Schiff) *Observing Law through Systems Theory* (Hart) was published in 2013.

Ralf Rogowski He is Emeritus Professor of Law, former Director of the Law and Sociology Programme and former Co-Director of the Social Theory Centre at the University of Warwick He has applied Luhmann's social system theory throughout his research in a variety of areas of modern law and policy. He is the author of *Reflexive Labour Law in the World Society* (Elgar 2015).

David Schiff He is Emeritus Professor of Law at the Queen Mary University of London. Before he held the position of reader in law at the London School of Economics and Political Science. He is the author (with Richard Nobles) of *A Sociology of Jurisprudence* (Hart 2006), and one of the four editors of the English Translation of Niklas Luhmann's *Law as a Social System* (OUP 2004). His latest book (with Richard Nobles) *Observing Law through Systems Theory* (Hart) was published in 2013.

Jasmin Siri She is research assistant at the Institute for Sociology at the Ludwig-Maximilians-University Munich. Before, she was fellow of the Institute for Advanced Study which is part of the Center of Excellence "Cultural Foundations of Social Integration", at the University of Konstanz. She is engaged in research in the areas of political sociology, social theory, political parties and gender studies.

Gunther Teubner He is Emeritus Professor of Law at Goethe Universität Frankfurt. Previously he was professor of private law, University of Bremen, 1977-1981; Professor of Law, European University Institute Florence, Italy, 1981–1993; Otto Kahn Freund Professor, London School of Economics, 1993–1998; and Professor of Law, Goethe Universität Frankfurt, 1998-2013. Professor Teubner is a leading Luhmann scholar with a particular interest in applying social sytems theory in analyses of modern law; he was the first scholar to coin the concept of reflexive law.

Chris Thornhill He is Professor of Law and Head of the School of Law at the University of Manchester. He was educated at Cambridge University, and he has previously held professorial positions in different disciplines at Kings College London and Glasgow University. He is a member of the Academia Europaea and has held Visiting Professorships in Law, Politics and Sociology in Chile, Brazil and Germany, where he occupied the Luhmann Chair at the University of Bielefeld in 2018. He has engaged with Luhmann's social system theory in many of his monographs and articles on the sociology of constitutional law and the sociology of democracy. His research is currently focused on processes of constitution-making in post-Imperial societies.

Raf Vanderstraeten He is Professor of Sociology at Ghent University, Department of Sociology where he is currently the Director of the Centre for Social Theory. He holds a PhD from Leuven University and a Habilitation in Sociology from the Bielefeld University. As a former student of Niklas Luhmann, he particularly draws on the tradition of systems-theoretical research. His fields of research are sociological theory, sociology of knowledge, sociology of religion and sociology of education.

Gert Verschraegen He is Professor of Sociology at the University of Antwerp. His research is concerned with numerical governance, Europeanisation, science and society, (social) innovation, cultural diversity in cities and the sociology of human rights and asylum. Before joining the University of Antwerp, Verschraegen was a postdoctoral fellow at the universities of Leuven and Luxemburg. He also held visiting positions at Harvard University and at the University of Alberta.

Chapter 1

INTRODUCTION

Ralf Rogowski

The Introduction consists of four parts. It starts with short remarks on the biographical details of Niklas Luhmann. The second part outlines the development of Luhmann's social theory in three stages and highlights a number of tenets of his social theory. In the third part, the Introduction offers concise summaries of the contributions contained in the Companion. And the last part provides a list of core monographs of Niklas Luhmann in English.

Brief Biographical Facts on Niklas Luhmann

Niklas Luhmann was born on 8 December 1927 in Lüneburg (in the North of Germany) and died 6 November 1998, in Oerlinghausen, near Bielefeld where he was Professor of Sociology for 30 years. He gained a worldwide reputation as a sociologist, philosopher of social science, and a prominent thinker in systems theory, who can be considered as one of the most important social theorists of the twentieth century.

Rather unusually for an academic sociologist, he worked during the first period of his adult life as a lawyer.[1] He gained his legal education in Freiburg in the late 1940s (first state exam in law), followed by an obligatory period of legal training at the appellate administrative court in Lüneburg (second state exam in law). From 1956 to 1962 he was a civil servant in the Ministry of Culture in Lower Saxony, Germany. During this time, he was able to be seconded to spend a year (1960–1961) at Harvard University where he encountered and studied with the leading U.S. sociologist and social system theorist Talcott Parsons.

In 1962 he gained a research position at the College (since 1997 University) of Administrative Sciences in Speyer and moved in 1965 to a social science research institute located in Dortmund. This research institute was associated with the University of Münster where he was awarded in 1966 within one year the obligatory two doctorates for an academic career (Ph.D. and Habilitation). Further details and analyses of Luhmann's early career can be found in Klaus Dammann's contribution to this Companion which also reflects on how to write a Luhmann biography.

In 1968, Luhmann became Professor of Sociology in the newly founded University of Bielefeld. In large part due to his writings, the new department in Bielefeld became the leading department in sociology in post-war West Germany and gained a worldwide reputation as the centre of a new beginning in sociology and, in particular, a new understanding of modern society based on ideas borrowed from general systems theory and other scientific traditions outside social sciences. Luhmann became emeritus professor in Bielefeld when reaching the official age limit for retirement in 1993.

The Development and Core Tenets of Niklas Luhmann's Social Theory[2]

Once Niklas Luhmann became a professor in the Department of Sociology at the University of Bielefeld, he saw it as his main task to work on a new systems theory that would revolutionise the sociological understanding of modern society. For this reason, he developed his own version of a theory of social systems that claims nothing less than to offer sociology a new universal theory for the discipline as a whole.[3] One of the major concerns guiding his approximately 700 publications[4] was to counter the trends, as he perceived them, of abandoning general sociological theory, confining sociological theory to exegeses of the classics, and dispersion of sociological research and thinking into sub-disciplines. In countering these trends, he devoted his energy to introducing a new general sociological theory that is able to provide an adequate understanding of the real challenges to modern society. He called his alternative approach autopoietic social systems theory. It borrows insights from general sciences, in particular general systems theory, epistemological constructivism, mathematical logic and the theory of communication.[5]

Luhmann's approach developed in three stages. In his early work, he formed his ideas in discussion with the systems-theoretical approach as expounded by Talcott Parsons, whom he encountered during his stay at Harvard University. He criticised Parsons for operating with a one-dimensional concept of functionalism that is preoccupied with system maintenance and proposed to replace causal relationships between structure and function with a notion of functional equivalence of structural solutions adopted by social systems. He elaborated this approach in numerous studies, including path-breaking analyses of formal organisations and administrations. In the second phase, Luhmann advanced his theoretical base by integrating the theory of autopoiesis into the study of social systems. The major publication of this period was his *Social Systems*.[6] The theoretical focus shifted from concerns with functions and structure to an analysis of self-reproduction of elements. The structure and the unity of a developed social system are seen as directly linked to operationally closed self-reproductive processes. In his late work, Luhmann used autopoietic systems theory to create a general theory of the modern society and its major function systems. He presented this theory in eight voluminous monographs, which include a general *Theory of Society*, published in 1997, a year before his death, and seven studies of major societal function systems covering the economy, science, law, art, politics, religion, and education, of which four were published between 1989 and 1995 and the last three posthumously.[7]

Five aspects can be highlighted in characterising Luhmann's theoretical approach.

First, Luhmann combines the three concepts of function, differentiation and evolution in order to analyse the development and dynamics of modern society. He distinguishes between three levels of analysis of autopoietic systems: general systems theory, the theory of social systems (as opposed to psychic systems, organisms and machines) and the level of concrete analysis of social systems. Similar to Parsons, Luhmann considers the development of social systems as a process of differentiation and evolution. However, in Luhmann's concept, the Parsonian ordering of society with just four primary subsystems is replaced by a polycentric view. Modern society replaces vertical stratification with horizontal functional differentiation as primary mode of social integration and thereby loses its centre.

The key concept in Luhmann's theory of society is functional differentiation.[8] Modern society consists of a number of function systems that operate next to each other. Major function systems of modern society are the economy, law, science, politics, religion, art and education. However, the list is not exhaustive and there is no fixed number of function systems.

Modern society is plural and there is no ranking of functions or function systems. For analytical purposes, Luhmann distinguishes between society and function systems. He considers society as a first-order social system, whereas function systems like the economic and the legal system are viewed as second-order social systems or societal subsystems. Society as a first-order social system differs from second-order social systems insofar as it has no other social system as an environment; society's environment consists only of natural and psychic systems (human beings).

In Luhmann's theory, functions are not derived from a fixed set of pattern variables (like in Parsons's approach), but are ultimately defined by the social systems themselves. Functions are represented by binary codes specific to each function subsystem of society. Binary codes are achievements of evolution and necessary requirements of a function system in order to define its boundary and select its elements, that is its specific communications. In applying the binary code, the function subsystems can distinguish between societal communications that belong to the system or the environment of the system. Examples of binary codes are true/false in the case of the science system, legal/illegal in the case of the legal system, and payment/non-payment in the case of the economic system. However, these codes do not guide the behaviour of the participants directly. They require programmes (like methods, statutes or invoices) that translate them into behavioural directives.

The second feature of Luhmann's theory concerns his understanding of elements and structures as key components of a system. Autopoietic systems theory develops a new understanding of structure and its relation to elements. Luhmann insists that it is not sufficient to define structure as relations of elements. In the general autopoietic conception of systems, structures result from the fact that only certain relations of elements are selected and held constant over time. Structure is thus defined as the limitation of possible combinations of elements within the system. In this sense Luhmann is not a structuralist but rather a post-structuralist.

The function of structures is not to translate environmental needs into the system, but to secure the autonomy of the system's self-reproduction, which is conceived as an operationally closed process. Structures of the system emerge both from self-reproduction of the elements and from selection of relationships. The system acquires properties in the evolutionary process that cannot be explained by the properties of its elements. The system instrumentalises the self-reproduction of the elements for its own self-reproduction, upon which in turn the self-reproduction of the elements becomes dependent. The structure of the system evolves in this process as a product of both the self-reproduction of the elements and the system itself. Furthermore, the system derives its complexity from its elements and their innumerable relations. System complexity is defined by a combination of selectivity, contingency and self-constitution of the system through specific selections. Complexity is the result of the relationship between the set of all possible relations between elements (contingency) and the selectivity achieved by the self-constituted structure of a system.

A third characteristic of Luhmann's approach refers to the processes of communication, self-reference and autopoiesis that constitute social systems. Probably the most radical departure from the Parsonian social system theory and, indeed, from conventional sociology, is Luhmann's assumption that the ultimate, non-decomposable elements of an autopoietic social system are communications and not human beings. For Luhmann, human beings constitute part of the environment of the social system and he views the individuality of human beings and their consciousness as separate, highly complex psychic systems. Furthermore, in Luhmann's theory, communications replace actions or interactions as the main elements of a social system. Communication consists of three components: information, utterance and understanding. Each component is described as a selection, and communication is accordingly characterised as the coordination of three selections. The important feature of communications is that they are related in self-referential processes. Thus, without linkage to other communications, no communication can happen.

Luhmann's theory of communication incorporates logical and mathematical approaches. In this respect, it has been elaborated by Dirk Baecker[9] into a general systems theory of communication. Baecker, in accordance with Luhmann, emphasises that communications as such cannot be observed but require specific forms in which they appear.[10] This is crucial for a social system because survival depends on its ability to observe and describe itself, which is a precondition for self-reference and autopoiesis. This requirement to become observable both for external observers and for self-observation is the main reason why, according to Luhmann and Baecker, a communication system generally ascribes itself as an action system.

Luhmann has demonstrated such ascription in his analysis of the emergence of structures in interaction systems. Structures reduce uncertainty and create trust relations.[11] In face-to-face interactions, the mutuality of expectations binds the actors through double contingency and thus becomes a self-referential circle. Luhmann merges the theory of self-reference and double contingency and thereby arrives at a concept of action and interaction without a subject.[12]

Interaction conceived as a self-referential circle is unstable and can cease to exist from one moment to the next. In order to survive, it needs a system which treats the self-referential circle as an element of its self-reproduction. Self-reference of the system means, in this respect, that the system produces and delimits the operative unity of its elements through the operation of its elements. It is precisely this process that Luhmann calls the autopoietic process, which lends its own unity to the system.[13]

Pre-autopoietic systems theory defined systems as open systems which are characterised by their exchange relations with the environment. Autopoietic systems theory conceives systems instead as closed systems which reproduce themselves not by variation of structure but by constant recombination of their elements. Recursive closure of the system, with respect to its elements, guarantees self-reproduction or autopoiesis. Luhmann constructs a theory of an operationally closed social system which is not dependent on other social systems or its environment for its core activity (i.e., autopoiesis). Only if autopoiesis is guaranteed can the system be open and relate to the innumerable events and conditions in its environment.

Fourth, a particularly pertinent problem for a theory of autopoietic social systems is the conceptualisation of the relationship of the system with its environment and with itself. A social system can logically develop three kinds of relationships. It can relate to society, it can relate to another social system or societal subsystem and it can relate to itself. Luhmann calls the relationship to society function, to another social system performance and to itself reflexion.[14]

In debates within systems theory, a number of concepts are used for the analysis of intersystem relationships. Originally, Parsons adopted the notion of interpenetration as the main concept in studying exchange relations between systems. However, Luhmann uses this concept only in a limited sense and reserves interpenetration, at least in his theory of social systems, for an analysis of the relationship between social systems and psychic systems.[15] The central concept that he uses in theorising relations between social systems is structural coupling. Luhmann adopted this concept from general systems theory and biological evolution theory in order to explain the emergence of mechanisms of coupling in co-evolutionary processes of social systems. Prominent examples of mechanisms of structural coupling in society are for Luhmann the semantic concepts of the constitution, contract and property that emerge in links between law, politics and the economy. Coupled systems increase the chances of structural variation of systems. However, they cannot determine structural changes. Structural coupling increases the chances of reciprocal irritation or perturbation of the coupled systems, to which each system can only respond with internal means that are limited by the autopoietic needs of the system.

A further concept of intersystem linkage has been proposed by Gunther Teubner.[16] His notion of interference tries to capture the special nature of communication, which is always at the same time general societal and special communication in the function system. The elements of function systems consist of the same material as in society at large. Indeed, the same communication is linked to the communication process or circle of society and of the function system. Teubner calls this societal context of communication the 'life world context'.

Efforts of one system trying to regulate affairs in another system constitute a particular case of intersystem relations. In an autopoietic social world, systems can only observe each other, and cannot regulate each other's self-reproduction. Any regulatory effort has to be compatible with the autopoietic requirements of the regulated system. Modern regulation has to become reflexive in order to be successful and understand that external regulation of self-reproduction can ultimately only be successful if it corresponds with self-regulation. Ultimately all regulation has to become regulation of self-regulation.[17]

A fifth feature of Luhmann's theory relates to the fact that society becomes global as an 'unavoidable consequence of functional differentiation'[18]. The concept of the world society that dominates Luhmann's late work was already conceptually developed in his early work. Function systems that have a high degree of autonomy 'detonate' societal boundaries. Most advanced in this respect are the economy, technology and science. In particular, science is said to have adopted universal intersubjectivity as its own structuring principle and criterion of performance. In contrast, law and politics remain backward by clinging to territorial boundaries.

The globalisation of function systems results from their very nature as systems of communications. It is difficult to prevent communications from flowing across territorial boundaries. It is this that makes it almost impossible to isolate function systems from world processes. All function systems are exposed to the pressure of globalisation that results from worldwide communications. Furthermore, worldwide communications produce new structures at the world level. In a systems-theoretical perspective, the world society can be conceived as a system characterised by specific emergent properties. New structures that transcend 'inter-nationalism' occur in the form of world law, world politics and world religions.[19]

Luhmann reveals nevertheless a certain pessimism for the future of the world society, a pessimism that bears resemblance to Max Weber's pessimistic outlook of modern society.[20] The world society is increasingly becoming itself the source of manifold regional, economic, cultural, climatic and ecological differences that create new challenges for the function systems.[21] Discrepancies between function systems as a result of functional differentiation become a source of conflict in the world society.[22] In particular, the legal system is confronted in the world society with specific challenges. Its performances for other social systems change, in the first place due to the changing role of the political system in the world society that is no longer organised by a state at the global level.[23]

For Luhmann, the role of law and politics as risk bearers of societal evolution decreases in the world society.[24] This does not mean that law withers away, but that we can expect a change of the legal form. However, in one respect Luhmann is optimistic. As a result of an increase in cognitive expectations, the economy, science and technology have begun to orientate themselves towards the future rather than the past. This cognitive transformation is gradually becoming true for all function systems and also for the world society at large.

The Contributions

In *Luhmann and Constitutional Sociology: Law and Functional Differentiation Revisited* Chris Thornhill discusses Luhmann's understanding of politics and law in modern society. He engages with Luhmann's core idea of functional differentiation in modern society which he backs but wants to enrich with historical accounts of 'underlying institutional forms of society'. Thornhill's aim is to generate 'more complex descriptions of empirical realities' that in his view should include analyses of processes of de-differentiation of which, he alleges, Luhmann was afraid. The main topic of Thornhill's chapter is an engagement with Luhmann's understanding of the constitution as structural coupling between the legal system and the political system. For him this idea contains vital insights for sociological analyses of constitutional law, including its foundations and impacts. At the same time, he detects blind spots in Luhmann's discussion of the constitution and emphasises in particular a neglect of the role of the military in the origin of constitutionalism in modernity.

In *Luhmann on Law and Legal Theory*, Richard Nobles and Paul Schiff analyse Luhmann's sociological theory of law based on Luhmann's two prominent books on this subject, namely *A Sociological Theory of Law* and *Law as a Social System*. They explain in detail how the legal system functions as an autopoietic system. They highlight that, in contrast to positivistic legal scholars (Kelsen and Hart) who consider the highest norm to constitute the unity of the legal system, Luhmann locates its unity in the autopoietic reproduction of legal communications and the application of the legal code legal/illegal. Nobles and Schiff also underline the importance of Luhmann's theory of legal argumentation that enables the production of redundancy and variety in legal communications which support the system to evolve autopoietically.

In *Niklas Luhmann on Politics and the Economy in Twenty First Century's World Society* Aldo Mascareño uses insights from Luhmann's two main books on politics and the economy, *Die Wirtschaft der Gesellschaft* and *Die Politik der Gesellschaft*, and tests them in analysing critical events in world society in the last two decades. He shows that for structural, semantic and technological reasons, politics and the economy have intensified their pace as world social systems, but that Luhmann's insights still hold true and can explain why levels of neglect have increased. In line with Luhmann's predictions on the reduced capacity of inclusion and increase in exclusion in social systems and in creating burdens for each other, politics and the economy have become highly unstable social systems and are prone to critical transitions and sudden regime shifts in the twenty-first century.

In *Epistemic Sociology: Luhmann's Theory of Science and Knowledge*, Gert Verschraegen analyses Luhmann's account of science as a social system in his important monograph *Die Wissenschaft der Gesellschaft*, which contains in his view an unrecognised treasure trove for science and technology studies. Verschraegen interests in particular connections between science and other function systems which Luhmann theorised as structural couplings. Verschraegen highlights linkages that exist between science and education (coupled via e.g., curricula content in textbooks), the economy (coupled via e.g., patents), politics (coupled through research policy as well as policy advice) and the medical system (coupled through scientifically tested medicinal knowledge and operative practices). However, the autopoietic closure of function systems means that scientific implications of social problems as well as environmental concerns must find internal 'resonance' within each function system (for example in the legal system via environmental legislation, or in the political system through ecological party programmes and in the economic system by internalising environmental externalities in prices). Science can no longer claim to have a privileged position for finding solutions in the functionally differentiated world society.

In *Niklas Luhmann on Religion and Secularisation*, Raf Vanderstraeten discusses Luhmann's various contributions to studying religion in society. While in his early works Luhmann focuses on organisational and role aspects, he is interested in his later work on the theory of society how the religious system contributed to the genesis of modern society. Vanderstraeten emphasises that Luhmann's work stresses especially the consequences of functional differentiation for the social system of religion and how it was forced to adapt to the consequences of differentiation. Religion, in particular Christianity, had to restructure and reconceive itself as a consequence of this transition. In his later works, Luhmann reveals both pessimism regarding maladaptation of religion to functional differentiation as well as the emergence of new opportunities for the system of religion to respond to consequences of individualisation within contemporary society. In Luhmann's posthumously published study of religion as a social system, he predicts in comparing world religions that individualised religions (for example Zen Buddhism) become more attractive in the future modern society.

In *How is Art Possible? Luhmann's Theory of Art*, Paul Buckermann examines Luhmann's specific sociological approach to study art as an autopoietic function system in society. He shows how Luhmann's functional method of analysis explores the way in which social processes and structures have shaped art to the present. Buckermann agrees with Luhmann that self-referential selections are the key to understanding how the art system produces art communications which, as chains and networks, can reproduce themselves. Following this approach, he reveals that the function of the modern art system lies in making visible possibilities of order that otherwise remain invisible. For

Buckermann, the art system unlike other function systems (legal, political economic, etc.) is characterised by polycontexturality, a combination and array of perspectives in different contexts. Buckermann criticises Luhmann, however, for lacking in his sociological account of art an adequate analysis of the institutional structures of the art world.

In *Niklas Luhmann and His Sceptical Notion of Culture*, Dirk Baecker analyses Luhmann's lifelong sceptical but also constructive engagement with the concept of culture, He reveals Luhmann's critical attitude towards Talcott Parsons' concept of a normative culture, which led Luhmann to abstain from granting culture a prominent role in his theory of modern society. Baecker claims that, nevertheless, Luhmann's fragmentary sociology of culture provides inspiration for what he calls a media theory of 'culture forms of society'. Baecker can show that in Luhmann's late work on the theory of society, culture reappears in historical analyses of forms of media and of memory of human society. Baecker claims that this was partly due to an acknowledgement on Luhmann's part of the emerging field of cultural studies.

In *Niklas Luhmann and Critical Systems Theory*, Kolja Möller and Jasmin Siri compare and show links between Luhmann's social systems theory and critical theory represented by the Frankfurt School. The authors consider themselves belonging to a specific strand called critical systems theory. In their portrayal of this approach, they discuss three dimensions of systems theory that in their understanding can contribute to a critique of modern society. First, Luhmann's assessment of voluntaristic approaches to social critique, second functional analysis as critical practice of comparison that focuses on alternatives, and third their interpretation of structural coupling of social systems as an approach to understand processes of social crisis.

In *Luhmann, on Algorithms, in 1966*, Elena Esposito shows that Luhmann was a man ahead of his time as well as a true visionary regarding the surprising amount of knowledge he had about digitisation and algorithms. Esposito discusses an early book of Luhmann *Recht und Automation in der öffentlichen Verwaltung* (Law and Automation in Public Administration). The key aspect of this work relates to a topic prominent in the ongoing debate on the spread of algorithms, that is, algorithmic accountability. It concerns the interrogation who is to be held accountable, for example for accidents involving self-driving cars. Esposito demonstrates that Luhmann's work may serve as a stepping stone in answering this question, for example with his suggestion that the responsibility should be shared between people and machines, just as in the case of the relationship between doctor and patient.

In *Niklas Luhmann Observed in a Luhmannian Perspective*, Klaus Dammann asks what kind of biography in writing about Niklas Luhmann is compatible with Luhmann's own theory. By adopting a Luhmannian perspective and using his theoretical distinctions the chapter introduces Luhmann as a divided person and comes to the conclusion that information on the individual is of limited value for an understanding of the academic and theoretician Niklas Luhmann. A central concern of the chapter lies in an effort to reconstruct a Luhmannian perspective on methodology and empirical research. It demonstrates the usefulness of Luhmann's theories, for example for empirical studies of Nazi violence.

In the final contribution *Three Encounters with Niklas Luhmann*, Gunther Teubner narrates his academic and personal experiences with Luhmann. His first encounter came from reading a short but brilliant article by a still unknown Luhmann that impressed Teubner because it offered a new radicalised critique of law. His second encounter was meeting Luhmann in person. Teubner describes Luhmann as a distant person, who, nevertheless, always kept a friendly smile. The third encounter describes the relationship Teubner had with the content of Luhmann's oeuvre and he uses a surprising parallel with music. He compares Luhmann's theory with Bach's music because both share formal rigour, remarkable expressivity and sober seriousness. Teubner argues that this has to do with both having experiences with the calamities of wars, for Bach the Thirty Years' War (1618–1648) in Europe, and for Luhmann the aftermath of the 30-year period of the two world wars in the twentieth century (1914–1945).

List of Core Monographs of Niklas Luhmann in English

Niklas Luhmann, *Differentiation of Society* (New York: Columbia University Press, 1980).

Niklas Luhmann, *Love as Passion* (Cambridge, MA: Harvard University Press, 1986).

Niklas Luhmann, *Ecological Communication* (Chicago: University of Chicago Press, 1989).

Niklas Luhmann, *Essays on Self Reference* (New York: Columbia University Press, 1990).

Niklas Luhmann, *Political Theory in the Welfare State* (Berlin, New York: de Gruyter, 1990).

Niklas Luhmann, *Social Systems* (Stanford: Stanford University Press, 1995).

Niklas Luhmann, *Observations on Modernity* (Stanford: Stanford University Press, 1998).

Niklas Luhmann, *The Reality of the Mass Media* (Stanford: Stanford University Press, 2000).

Niklas Luhmann, *Theories of Distinction. Redescribing the Transcriptions of Modernity* (Stanford: Stanford University Press, 2002).

Niklas Luhmann, *Law as a Social System* (Oxford: Oxford University Press, 2004).

Niklas Luhmann, *Risk: A Sociological Theory*. New ed. (New Brunswick, London: Aldine Transaction, 2005).

Niklas Luhmann, *Theory of Society*, 2 vols. (Stanford: Stanford University Press, 2012/3).

Niklas Luhmann, *A Systems Theory of Religion* (Stanford: Stanford University Press, 2013).

Niklas Luhmann, *Introduction to Systems Theory* (Cambridge: Polity, 2013).

Niklas Luhmann, *A Sociological Theory of Law*. Second edition. (Abingdon, New York: Routledge, 2014).

Niklas Luhmann, *Trust and Power*. Revised edition (Cambridge: Polity, 2017).

Niklas Luhmann, *Organization and Decision* (Cambridge: Cambridge University Press, 2018).

I would like to conclude this Introduction by acknowledging the support and assistance of my Ph.D. student Rafael Quintero Godinez in preparing *The Anthem Companion to Niklas Luhmann*.

Notes

1 Dirk Baecker, 'Niklas Luhmann: Der Werdegang', in *Luhmann Handbuch: Leben, Werk, Wirkung*, ed. Oliver Jahraus, Armin Nassehi, Mario Grizelj, Christinan Kirchmeier and Julian Müller (Stuttgart, Weimar: J.B. Metzler, 2012), 1–3.

2 Part II of the Introduction is an updated version of my entry on Niklas Luhmann for the *Blackwell Encyclopaedia of Sociology*. Second edition (online). Oxford: Blackwell 2016.

3 Niklas Luhmann, *Social Systems* (Stanford: Stanford University Press, 1995), XLV (Preface to the German Edition).

4 See 'Niklas Luhmann - Gesamtbibliographie (1958–2018)', 7 July 2022, https://niklas-luhmann-archiv.de/person/nl-bibliographie.

5 Luhmann, *Social Systems*, 1–11 (Introduction).

6 Luhmann, *Social Systems* (the German original was published in 1984).

7 Four studies of major function systems, covering the economy, science, law and art, were published between 1989 and 1995 and three, covering politics, religion and education, were published posthumously. His concluding Theory of Society (*Gesellschaft der Gesellschaft*) was published in two volumes in 1997. The monographs covering Luhmann's theory of society (plus Social Systems as an introductory volume) were published in German as a box (*Kassette*) in 2002: Niklas Luhmann, *Theorie der Gesellschaft*, 9 vols. (Suhrkamp: Frankfurt am Main).

8 See also Rudolf Stichweh, *Functional Differentiation of Society* (Bielefeld: transcript, 2022).

9 Dirk Baecker, *Form und Formen der Kommunikation* (Frankfurt am Main: Suhrkamp, 2005).

10 *Problems of Form*. Edited by Dirk Baecker (Stanford: Stanford University Press, 1999).

11 Niklas Luhmann, *Trust and Power*. Revised edition (Cambridge: Polity, 2017).

12 Luhmann, *Social Systems*, ch. 10.

13 Ibid., 33–4.
14 Niklas Luhmann, *Political Theory in the Welfare State* (Berlin, New York: de Gruyter, 1990), 73–8.
15 Luhmann, *Social Systems*, ch. 6.
16 Gunther Teubner, *Law as an Autopoietic System* (Oxford: Blackwell, 1993), 88–90.
17 Ralf Rogowski, *Reflexive Labour Law in the World Society* (Cheltenham: Elgar, 2013), chs. 4 to 6.
18 Niklas Luhmann, 'The World Society as a Social System', in Niklas Luhmann, *Essays on Self Reference* (New York: Columbia University Press, 1990), 191–214.
19 Rudolf Stichweh, *Die Weltgesellschaft. Soziologische Analysen* (Suhrkamp: Frankfurt am Main, 2001). On world religions see Niklas Luhmann, *A Systems Theory of Religion.* (Stanford: Stanford University Press, 2013), 199–200 and on world politics see Mathias Albert, *A Theory of World Politics* (Cambridge: Cambridge University Press, 2016).
20 See Ralf Rogowski, 'Recht und Industrielle Beziehungen in Luhmanns Weltgesellschaft (Law and industrial relations in Luhmann's world society)', *Zeitschrift für Rechtssoziologie*, Vol. 21, No. 2, 2000, 279–92.
21 On ecological communication, see Niklas Luhmann, *Ecological Communication* (Chicago: University of Chicago Press, 1989); on risk, see Niklas Luhmann, *Risk A Sociological Theory. New ed.* (New Brubswick, London: Aldine Transaction, 2005); on the mass media, Niklas Luhmann, *The Reality of the Mass Media* (Stanford: Stanford University Press, 2000); on modernity in general, Niklas Luhmann, *Observations on Modernity* (Stanford: Stanford University Press, 1998).
22 Niklas Luhmann, *Theory of Society*, Vol. 2 (Stanford: Stanford University Press, 2013), 309.
23 Luhmann, *A Sociological Theory of Law*, 255–64.
24 Niklas Luhmann, *Law as a Social System* (Oxford: Oxford University Press, 2004), ch. 12; Rogowski, *Reflexive Labour Law in the World Society*, chs. 1 and 10.

Chapter 2

LUHMANN AND CONSTITUTIONAL SOCIOLOGY: LAW AND FUNCTIONAL DIFFERENTIATION REVISITED

Chris Thornhill

Introduction: Constitutional Blind Spots and Theories of Differentiation

This chapter examines ways in which Luhmann's sociology can be used to enrich empirical understanding of institutional structures in contemporary global society.[1] In particular, it discusses how the formation of the institutions that typify modern societal order, both at the national and the transnational level, can be illuminated by his theory of functional differentiation. To achieve this, it proposes a counter-intuitive way of reading Luhmann. It argues that his sociology provides the most adequate construction of the institutional determinants of world society, not if it is simply employed a literal sociological lens, but if it is observed through a method that probes critically at its conceptual adequacy. Centrally, this chapter advances a dialectical engagement with Luhmann's theory of functional differentiation: it accepts his account of differentiation as a matrix for examining modern society, yet it argues that institutional organs with a central position in society have resulted from historical trajectories of differentiation that deviate from those imputed to society by Luhmann. It claims that Luhmann's theory has utility as a framework for distilling many social phenomena in broad terms, but many institutional phenomena come most sharply into focus as they jar against the terms of his systemic observation. As a result, his theory frequently illuminates social institutions in a rather unintended fashion. On this basis, this chapter claims that, more than any direct application of Luhmann's thought, it is through engagement with the aporia, blind spots and oversights in his work that we obtain the most accurate perspective for describing the underlying institutional form of society. In promoting this approach, this chapter aims to show, using a broadly Luhmannian method, how explanatory simplifications in systems theory hold clues for the comprehension of society, challenging us to think through the given categories of systems theory to generate more complex descriptions of empirical realities.

As its primary object, this chapter discusses Luhmann's understanding of the legal system and the political system and his interpretation of the processes by which contemporary society structures legal and political communications to produce and preserve its essential differentiated form. It explains how Luhmann's work falls short of providing a persuasive account of the conditions of law and politics in world society, and it sketches out ways in which an internal discussion of the lacunae in his thought might be used to account for contemporary legal and political forms. The key to understanding these aspects of Luhmann's sociology lies in a critical reconstruction of his theory of the constitution. The constitution has particular standing in Luhmann's analysis of the emergence of modern society, and the constitutional ordering of procedures for generating political power, resulting from a structural coupling between the legal system and the political system, is proposed as a defining institutional precondition for modern social organisation.[2] This chapter examines how his theory of the constitution contains insights that are vital to constitutional inquiry, and it underlines ways in which his thought can contribute to sociological observation of constitutional law, its foundations and its broad consequences. At the same time, however, it examines blind spots in his discussion of the constitution, isolating material complexities and historical variations in the emergence of modern politics and modern law that Luhmann himself did not perceive. In so doing, it develops the claim that his inquiry into the constitutional fabric of modern society remains unfinished, and it outlines how systems-theoretical reflections on the constitution could be revised to create a more accurate sociological model for describing constitutional functions.

The Differentiation of Politics and the Necessity of the Constitution

In Luhmann's broader theory of functional differentiation, his analysis of the political system has a distinctive character, and it reflects a sharply bipolar understanding of politics. The distinctive quality accorded to the political system lies at the core of his discussion of the constitution.

At one level, Luhmann's theory of modern society contains a starkly anti-political tone. Indicatively, he argues that observers of modern society attach excessive importance to the political system, and the widespread assumption that society in its entirety is in some way centrally determined by its political system reflects a distortion of the essentially differentiated fabric of society.[3] This claim is supported by an argument based on the historical sociology of concepts. He explains that original reflections on processes of functional differentiation in early modern Europe often projected inflationary conceptual images of the political system, condensed à la Hobbes or à la Bodin in classical theories of the state as sovereign entity, and these self-descriptions still imprint an exaggerated or inflationary form on understandings of the political system.[4] On this basis, he presents the modern political system as a system which is marked by a deep tendency towards unproportioned societal expansion, possessing dangerous propensities for functional overreach. Such propensities, which he sees as exemplified in contemporary societies by authoritarian governments and by elaborate welfare systems, contain the risk that they may unsettle society as a whole, leading, potentially, to the politicised distortion of communications in other systems.[5] Both normatively and functionally, in short, Luhmann argues that the political system needs to be defined in more limited terms, accurately attuned to the intricately differentiated structure of society as a whole. Expansive *de-differentiation* of the political system, caused by its original reflection as the state, appears as a prominent check both on adequate comprehension of modern society and on adequate institutional organisation.[6]

At a different level, Luhmann's theory is coloured by the sense that, uniquely among other systems, the political system is – intrinsically – a weakly differentiated system, which does not, on its own, form a fully autonomous domain in society. As set out later in the chapter, his account of the political system implies a distinctive co-dependency in the relation between the political system and the legal system. Of course, in general terms, the legal system always possesses an unusual position in the differentiated systemic order that Luhmann construes as characteristic of modern society. For Luhmann, each social system shows a distinctive reliance on law; the positive form of modern law is vital for translating decision-making functions in each system into societally transmissible communications. However, the political system is defined by a sui-generis connection with law, and each functional attribute of the political system presupposes an integral relation with law. At different points in his analysis, Luhmann characterises the political system as a system with the following attributes: (1) its function is to make and communicate *collectively binding decisions* through society;[7] (2) its essential reference is *legitimacy*, which it manufactures to circulate its decisions through society in a form likely to be met with acceptance;[8] (3) it transmits decisions in the code of power, so that exchanges properly classifiable as pertinent to the political system are exchanges that can be observed as *subject-to-power* or *not-subject-to power*.[9]

In each determinant, the essential operations of the political system are sustained by the fact that it is structurally interlocked with law. First, the collectively binding decisions produced by the political system can only be circulated through society to the extent that they are mediated into legal form, and they are enforced throughout society as legally authorised decisions. Second, the basic resource of legitimacy that is fabricated within the political system depends on the fact that the political system is able to signal that its decisions are compliant with the law, so that the mediation of political power into legal form becomes fundamental to the societal recognition and acceptance of political decisions.[10] In addition, third, the defining code of the political system, the code of power, is also, rather anomalously, determined by its intersection with law. At different points in his work, Luhmann states that, uniquely amongst systems, the political system operates on the premise of a *double code*. In the first instance, societal exchanges are observed as political if they can be aligned to the code: *subject-to-power/not-subject-to-power*. Yet, political decisions can only be radiated through society if they are subject to a process of second-coding (*Zweitcodierung*),[11] in which they are also mediated through the legal code: *legal/illegal*.[12] In other words, the political system only functions as an effective system of communication if it communicates via law, and if it translates pure political contents into the communicative medium of law. The 'pure code of power', Luhmann explains, is insufficient for the effective distribution of political decisions, and power only becomes effective and usable – that is, it undergoes an 'enormous expansion' – if it is translated into the code of law.[13] In each respect, although inclined to semantic over-inflation or trans-systemic expansion, the political system is distinct from other systems in that it is not an entirely differentiated system, and it is structurally interdependent with the legal system.

It is in the context of this ambiguous analysis of the political system that Luhmann proposes his theory of constitutional law, and his interpretation of the societal effects of constitutional government is strongly determined by the uncertain differentiation of politics qua system. He explains that constitutions originally developed in modern society as normative documents, in which the intricate co-dependency of politics and law is reflected and ordered in mutually beneficial fashion. Constitutions emerge at the legal boundary of politics as a form that simplifies exchanges in both systems, expanding systemic autonomy in each domain, and ultimately allowing each system to operate effectively in a societal environment defined by advanced functional differentiation. On one hand, he defines the constitution as an instrument of legal–political supervision and self-control that helps to transform political power into a legally accepted medium, legitimated by formally acceded principles.[14] In addition, he argues that the constitution spells out collectively binding norms to authorise the use of law, and, by conferring higher-order authority on law, it heightens the communicative capacity of the legal system, making it possible for political institutions to transfer functions into the legal system.[15] Where a political system takes constitutional form, therefore, law begins to explain (and positivise) itself and its decisions as *politically enforced*, and power acquires the capacity to explain (and positivise) itself and its decisions as *legally determined*.[16] Both systems experience heightened differentiation and inclusivity because of their attachment to a constitution. On the other hand, he explains that the constitution makes it possible for the political system to solidify the differentiation of society in general terms, which again acts to simplify its own functions. This wider role of the constitution is associated with the fact that most constitutions contain guarantees for basic rights for particular persons, as legal subjects, in society. These rights normally include, for example, rights sanctioning economic autonomy (e.g., rights of ownership, contractual independence, freedom to move residence for employment), rights supporting religious and aesthetic freedoms, and rights underpinning liberty of inquiry and expression in science, public media, education and the arts. The constitutional protection of such rights, Luhmann argues, creates an objective legal framework, positioned in the interstices between law and politics, in which the political system identifies, delineates and places limits on the functions that require express political regulation.[17] By concretising such rights in hard constitutional form, the political system materialises the boundaries between itself and other social function systems, it imposes legal checks on its potential tendency towards uncontrolled functional expansion, and it curtails any over-extended use of political power in spheres of society that are not eminently political, or to which the simple application of power is not appropriate.[18] On these separate counts, Luhmann examines the constitutional state as a defining legitimational order for the political system. The constitution is deeply shaped by processes of differentiation at the centre of modern society, and it creates a legal/political order that is distinctly capable of preserving legitimacy and supporting general political functions in an acentric modern society.

In each of these respects, Luhmann's theory of the political system contains striking ambiguities. As discussed, he views the modern political system as defined by the inherent risk that it promotes an inflationary idea of its functions. At the same time, he indicates that, intrinsically, the political system is less strongly differentiated than other systems, as it relies on the legal system for the social circulation of power. In this analysis of modern law, then, he suggests that the legal system plays a twofold co-constitutive role for the political system: the political system presupposes the legal system to sustain its basic functions, and it relies on law to countervail its proclivity to blur the lines of its interaction with other systems– this is the basic sense of his analysis of second coding.[19] The legal system, in other words, is never categorically differentiated from the political system, yet it also acts as a prerequisite for the effective differentiation of the political system. In each respect, the analysis of the political system shapes Luhmann's theory of the constitution. He observes the constitution as a vital component of the modern political system, as the constitution helps to correct both the weak differentiation and the excessive expansion that afflict the political system. The constitution emerges as the central element in this aporetic argument, serving to tie the political system to the legal system and objectively to articulate the differentiated functional boundaries of politics. In this way, the constitution is constructed, auto-genetically, within the political system itself, as a primary determinant of its adequate differentiation.

Empirical Observation 1: The Missing Military Citizen

In some respects, Luhmann's discussion of the political system and its constitution forms a cipher through which primary institutional features of modern society become interpretable. As examined later in the chapter, the representation of the constitution as a normative order, in which the systems of law and politics are both integrally interlocked and finely differentiated, throws light on the basic institutional shape of society. Accordingly, sociological analysis of constitutional law can hardly proceed without deep reflection on Luhmann's thought. In some ways, however, this account of constitutional law clarifies modern society in a manner not immediately foreseen by Luhmann himself, and empirical observation of constitutional functions in the context of societal differentiation necessitates a revision of his theory.

Luhmann's understanding of the constitution as a text that both structurally connects and promotes the differentiation of law and politics is clearly supported by inquiry into the origins of modern constitutional law. Prior to the constitutional revolutions of the eighteenth century, most national societies had experienced long, embedded processes of functional differentiation, in which, through the protracted dissolution of feudalism, they had begun to construct political institutions as centralised foci of legitimational authority and to promote generalised legal norms as elements of social integration. Before the revolutionary period, however, the capacity of national societies to construct politics and law as centralised, generally inclusive system had been checked by the residual authority of local families and powerful sectoral organisations. This long trajectory of differentiation was dramatically accelerated through the emergence of modern constitutions, and the essential inclusive form of modern society resulted, at this time, from the deep articulation of law and politics in the form of the constitution.

The initial formation of modern constitutions, beginning in the American Revolution (starting in 1775–1776) and intensified through the revolutionary period in France (1789–1795), occurred as a process in which legal institutions and political institutions entered a relation of increased interdependence, and the relative distinction of both systems was consolidated by their interpenetration. Notably, early constitutions articulated ideas of legitimacy, based on generally acceded norms and principles of popular authority, which meant that institutions assuming constitutionally defined powers were able to propose themselves as possessing higher authority than other institutions, and as claiming a relative monopoly of authority and legitimacy in society. In this process, political institutions were able to establish a generalised account of their authority to legislate. On this basis they were able to produce laws that could assume legitimacy in all parts of society and to remove the traces of older, more localised or less systematically justified legal orders. As a result, associations that had traditionally been able to arrogate public authority, such as families, estates, guilds, and churches, lost much of their capacity for asserting powers of legal and political obligation. In each respect, the rise of constitutional constructions of legitimacy consolidated the political system as a distinctive and socially abstracted set of institutions, and it established principles to demarcate the legal system as a single normative order.[20]

The effective codependency in the relation between law and politics at the core of modern society was strongly reflected in the fact that many early constitutions contained catalogues of rights, which marked out spaces of subjective autonomy for social agents in their religious, economic, communicative, educational and scientific practices. Visibly, the modern political system took form in the eighteenth century as a functional order that depended on the clear distinction between political and non-political functions in society, and the concentration of political power in the polity was linked to the protective individualisation of personal liberties outside the polity.[21] Indeed, the promotion of subjective individualisation across society meant that legal and political institutions were able to remove accretions of power traditionally attached to religious and economic bodies and other corporations, intensifying their ability to impose uniform obligations on society. The protection of rights in modern constitutions clearly helped to promote a general reality of societal differentiation as a precondition of the differentiation of the legal system and the political system.

In analysing the social dynamics emanating from constitutional law, however, Luhmann's descriptions show a lack of sensitivity to some sociological dimensions of constitutional law. In some ways, the emphasis placed on the constitution as the externalisation of the boundary between politics and law closes his analysis against wider evaluation of constitutional functions, and it obstructs reflections on material sources of constitutional norms. This limits the explanatory value of his theory as a whole.

The original growth of constitutional law in the eighteenth century cannot be simply interpreted as the result of a linear process of functional differentiation in the legal and political systems of society. In some ways, in fact, the growth of early constitutional law was an occurrence reversed, or at least attenuated, by patterns of differentiation that were already pronounced in the eighteenth century, before the period of constitutional revolution. Before the last decades of the eighteenth century, most European societies had witnessed the partial differentiation of institutional systems with legal and political functions. In the political dimension of society, this was reflected in the rapid rise of centralised administrative bodies, which gathered pace after the religious wars of the seventeenth century. In society's legal dimension, this was manifest in the processes of legal codification and in the systematic ordering of legal norms that characterised many regions in the middle and latter stages of the eighteenth century. The accelerated process of social integration and functional differentiation that occurred in the wake of later constitutional revolutions had clearly been foreshadowed by lines of legal systematisation and political institution building that occurred during the era (so-called) of European 'absolutism'. By the later eighteenth century, most European states already possessed increasingly centralised political institutions and legal institutions capable of imposing a shared normative order on society.

In most European societies, the relative differentiation of law and politics that culminated in the eighteenth century had been driven by a quite distinct institutional process, which Luhmann's theory does not bring into focus. Indeed, the patterns of legal and political differentiation that preexisted the rise of modern constitutions were shaped by forces for which Luhmann's sociology shows a marked and very surprising blindness. These processes were determined, namely, by the fact that early modern legal and political institutions resulted from the progressive differentiation of law and politics from actors in society defined by their discharge of military functions. In fact, the differentiation of the *military system* formed a distinct line of differentiation in early modern Europe, on which the parallel differentiation of the legal and the political system was structurally dependent. The centralisation of political institutions and the codification of legal norms at this time were both sustained by the fact that authority for legal and political functions was withdrawn from actors and social groups that had traditionally obtained constitutional influence as providers of military force. By the eighteenth century, persons attached to the old military class (the nobility) were increasingly placed in constitutionally subordinate roles within the state and subject to the law as an autonomous, integrated system of norms.[22] This meant that the modern legal/political system evolved as executive elites within emerging nation states found ways to give authority to political decisions and legal ordinances without relying on the external constitutional consent of the nobility, who had historically assumed socially protected positions, in which they influenced the direction of the polity and controlled aspects of the law because they had used supply of military power as a constitutional bargaining tool. The reduction in the constitutional role of the nobility in the eighteenth century entailed a strict differentiation of authority to make law and authority to make war, and the positive form of the modern administrative state and the modern legal system developed as functional elites within the governmental order separated their activities from military power.[23]

What this means, in essence, is that, before the advent of modern constitutional law, most modern societies had reached a certain level of functional differentiation in their legal and political systems. This differentiation was premised, centrally, on the fact that both law and politics had developed a crude constitutional apparatus, in which legal and political institutions were able to derive legitimacy from relatively stable internal definitions of their functions, distinct from persons, organisations and corporations with historical responsibility for providing military capacity to support the government. To be clear, the level of differentiation reached by national legal and political systems in the pre-revolutionary period was always restricted. In fact, the limits to differentiation in early modern Europe were closely connected to the shifting conjuncture between law, politics and the military. Before the emergence of modern constitutions, defined by their extraction of legitimacy from ideas of popular sovereignty, members of the old military class still preserved some of their original status in society. The political structure of much of *ancien-régime* Europe remained formatively dependent on a complex bargain between the functional elites attached to centralised states and members of the nobility, in which the aristocracy accepted constitutional exclusion from core legal and political roles because its members received, as compensation, an expansion of their privileges in their private lands and their professional trajectories.[24] As a result of this, in much of Europe, society was defined by a delicate balance between legal and political differentiation at the national level and the preservation of pre-modern private monopolies at the local level. The persistent privileging of the nobility meant that differentiated patterns of legal and political authority did not fully penetrate into aristocratic estates, and noble families were able to establish jurisdictional powers that were partly closed to public authority, typically reflected in the persistence of serfdom. The terms in which the differentiation of law and politics from military agency was negotiated thus militated against the full integration of society in the same legal/political system. Nonetheless, the original basis of modern legal and political institutions was defined – tentatively – by the creation of a socio-constitutional order, in which military agents were not directly incorporated in law-making functions.

What this means, further, is that the accelerated transformation of law and politics that occurred in the era of revolutionary constitution making entailed both occurrences that promoted and occurrences that reduced existing modes of systemic differentiation. The lines of functional differentiation that first shaped the form of modern society had been promoted through the diminution of the constitutional relevance of military actors. In contrast, the emergence of modern constitutions after the 1780s had the result that legal and political institutions were once again integrally attached to the military system, and they became reliant on constructs of legitimacy formed by needs of war. Indicatively, in all states that experienced constitutional revolution or radical semi-constitutional reform in the period beginning in the late 1780s, constitution-making processes were driven by military motivations, and constitutions were created, at least in part, as instruments to facilitate the levying of troops, usually by mandatory conscription, for newly emergent regimes.[25] More importantly, in each newly created constitutional regime after the 1780s, the basic constitutional rights that were accorded to citizens – that is, rights enabling the participation of individual persons in law-making procedures – were strongly tied to the assumption of military obligations, and constitutions conferred citizenship on persons, in essence, in return for their willingness to act as soldiers. Early constitutional rule, in other words, took shape as a system of integration, in which legal and political institutions were authorised and legitimated by social agents assuming military roles, as *soldats-citoyens*.[26] These institutions integrated persons by drawing them into the military system, and by justifying their actions in terms likely to sustain the concerted mobilisation of citizens for war. In each respect, the emergence of modern constitutions occurred as a process that both intensified and deeply transformed the patterns of functional differentiation that define modern society. Through the growth of constitutional law, the ancient feudal linkage between military roles and constitutional roles was partly re-established, and the legitimacy of law was defined in terms designed to satisfy, qua public-legal contract, the interests of persons obliged to act as military combatants.

On balance, we can see two prominent weaknesses in Luhmann's analysis of the constitution as a normative order promoting legal/political and broader societal differentiation. On one hand, his theory of social systems does not contain an account of the military as a distinct system in society, and this diminishes the tenability of his wider historical and theoretical analysis of systemic differentiation.[27] In reality, if modern constitutions intensified the integrational force of law and politics, they did so precisely because they tied both the production of legal authority and the production of political legitimacy to the military system. From the 1780s on, basic functions of legitimation for both law and politics depended on the consent of citizens, whose assumption of constitutionally formative roles was inextricably connected to their role in assuming combat duties. The differentiation of law and politics as separate social systems presupposed the deep interpenetration of both these systems with the military system, which was ordered through early constitutional law. On the other hand, his analysis of the constitution, designed to account for the differentiation of the political system, adopts a strictly legalistic comprehension of constitutional law. Throughout his theoretical career, Luhmann proposed a remarkably formalistic analysis of constitutional functions, reducing the constitution to a simple legal document securing the separation of powers in the state, giving protection to basic rights, establishing normative principle for the exercise of power, and deflating the basic emphasis of political functions.[28] This approach was essentially determined by his construction of the political system, and by the role attributed to the constitution in the stabilisation of the political system. Owing to this determinacy, however, his theory of the constitution does look beneath the normative lines of constitutional texts to trace the material processes reflected in them and the principles, bargains, and contracts, which they establish. This is one reason why he lacks appreciation of the military emphases of constitutional law.

The legitimational principle that appeared at the core of modern constitution-making situations was the construction of the citizen (*citoyen*, *Staatsbürger*) as a holder of objective rights, whose exercise engaged the citizen in acts of law making and legitimacy production. Indeed, modern constitutionalism in its entirety can be seen as a doctrine of political legitimacy and legal organisation, in which the sovereign active citizen was placed at the core of the legislative apparatus of government.[29] In key respects, the expansion and differentiation of the legal system and the political system attached to the emergence of modern constitutional law were integrally linked to, and propelled by, this concept of the citizen. As mentioned, the rise of constitutional law had the material outcome that both systems experienced an expansion of their integrational force across society, as, in referring to constitution norms for their legitimacy, both systems acquired a higher-order normative diction to authorise their functions. The fact that the authority for all legal or political decisions could be traced to acts of politically implicated citizens, such that all legal and political decisions were backed by the original legitimating figure of the citizen, played a crucial role in establishing law and politics as stable authoritative systems. The modern figure of the citizen, however, was primarily constructed as a reaction to military pressures, and the constitutional definition of the citizen as a holder of rights of participation and consultation in legislative matters served, as discussed, to place citizens in a role in which their utility as soldiers was protected. The citizen became a foundation for both law and politics by linking these systems directly to military imperatives, and it constructed the legitimacy of law and politics in reference to military recruitment. This basic conceptual shift underlying modern constitutionalism is not reflected in Luhmann's thought.

As explained, Luhmann's claim that, in mediating between law and politics, the constitution intensifies the autonomy and inclusivity of both systems clearly encapsulates the impact of constitutional norms at the origins of modern society, around 1789. However, the formalistic emphasis of his interpretation of constitutional norms means that his theory simplifies the actual normative content of constitutions, and it simplifies the form of the modern political system. Through a slight refocusing of Luhmann's theory, it becomes evident that the constitution first evolved as a corpus of norms that enacted, not a simple coupling between law and politics, but a complex, triadic coupling between law, politics and the military. In fact, the essential functions of the modern political system and the modern legal system – the production of legitimacy, the translation of political power into socially transmissible form and the construction of universally acceded legal norms – originally depended on the existence of a hard functional nexus between the polity and the army, which acquired condensed expression in the modern figure of the sovereign citizen. Constitutions thus originally took shape by interrupting processes of differentiation that were already strongly articulated in society.

Empirical Observation 2: The Absent War

The deep linkage between constitutional law and the military system influenced the development of modern constitutional law from its origins in the 1780s and 1790s to the twentieth century. At all junctures in the early history of constitutional government, military pressures played a key role in shaping constitution-making processes and in defining the legitimacy of constitutional law. Indeed, through the nineteenth century and beyond, the constitutional organisation of national political systems reflected a deepening interaction between the polity and the military system, and the constitutional construction of legitimacy for national processes of legal and political integration depended on the intensification of the responsiveness of national political institutions to military imperatives.

A short survey of constitution making since the early nineteenth century shows that, until very recently, constitutions were typically either created by highly militarised political actors, or they were drafted or fundamentally revised in conditions in which citizenship was defined by military pressures. For example, many constitutions that came into being after the first revolutionary period were established or at least deeply modified through wars, either interstate wars or civil wars, in which the army assumed status as the basic constituent power. Cases of this are found in France in 1848, in Prussia in 1848–1850, in the USA around 1865, in Colombia in 1886, in Russia in 1906, in Brazil in 1891, in Poland in 1919–1921 and in many postcolonial states after 1945. In parallel, many constitutions were created or substantially elaborated in the aftermath of protracted military conflicts, in which electoral rights of citizenship were extended to previously marginalised social groups, in order to reward and/or motivate them for military service and to tie them more directly to the state. This process drove electoral reforms and constitution making in Germany, Austria, France and Italy between the 1860s and the 1870s; it impelled the process of widening enfranchisement in much of Europe and North America around the time of World War I; it then shaped the extension of citizenship to excluded ethnic groups in many polities, most notably the USA, after 1945. In each instance, the basic functions of constitutions in providing legitimacy for national legal and political system have been acutely sensitive to warfare, and the constitutional rights granted to social agents to participate in the legitimation of law have been constructed through war.[30]

Visible in this recurrent articulation between the legal, political and military systems of society is a further phenomenon of great relevance for Luhmann's theory of differentiation. As examined, Luhmann argues that the modern constitution underpins the differentiation of the legal system and the political system, maximising the inclusivity of both legal and political communications. In some ways, however, if the constitutional significance of the army is brought into view, it becomes apparent that, owing to their commitment to military mobilisation as a source of legitimacy, constitutions frequently had an outcome diametrically opposed to that imputed to them in systems-theoretical descriptions. Although originally acting to expand the systemic integrity of both systems, in most national contexts, the constitutional design of the polity rapidly brought both the legal system and the political system to acute functional crisis.[31] In most national societies, the construction of political legitimacy articulated through constitutional law instilled deeply debilitating potentials in institutions responsible for producing law and power, and it unsettled the basic procedures for stabilising legal and political exchanges. This tended to occur because legitimational constructions of citizenship established in national constitutions promoted patterns of integration and obligation very closely linked to warfare, tending to replicate external patterns of conflict at the legitimational core of national legal and political systems.

There are many empirical examples to illustrate this phenomenon. It can be observed, for instance, in early democratic experiments in France and Germany in the late nineteenth century. In these polities, the exercise of electoral rights was clearly sanctioned as a mechanism for integrating male citizens as military conscripts. In fact, increasing democratisation was not obviously distinct from rising inner-societal militarisation, as statutory and constitutional legislation in both polities was profoundly determined by bilaterally generated, and sharply symmetrical, military pressures. In both societies, the creation of legitimacy for the political system was eventually transposed from the political system to the military domain.[32] By 1914, war itself, leading to devastating socio-political collapse, replaced political functions as the primary source of institutional legitimacy. After 1918, this phenomenon often became more acute, as most constitutions established patterns of citizenship that were intensely determined by international ideological conflicts, caused by the Bolshevik Revolution of 1917. Most new constitutions designed at the end of World War I were intended to placate conflicts between groups of citizens (classes) in national society that were defined, politically, by divergent attitudes to Bolshevism, and they were expected to produce legitimacy for legislation by mediating between different positions in the global conflict emanating from Russia.[33] As a result, most new constitutions quickly transposed global conflicts into domestic inter-group antagonisms, and they conferred on national state institutions a daunting responsibility for regulating or mollifying such conflicts and for binding all societal actors by general legal norms. Through such commitments, most interwar constitutions led to the deep militarisation of citizenship, and they eventually resulted in the overthrow of the polity by those groups able to reject the force of formal law and to assume dominant positions in the conflicts which they inflamed. Such groups typically used military instruments to take control of political institutions and forcibly to control the production of legitimacy. By 1940, virtually all European democracies were subject to some kind of anti-Communist military regime, established through domestic regime formation, foreign occupation or some combination of the two processes. At each stage in the early development of mass-democratic constitutionalism, the basic constitutional nexus between the legal system, the political system and the military system led, over a longer period, to the construction of a deep thread between national citizenship (legitimacy) and global conflict, leading to the unmanageable militarisation of all three systems.

For these reasons, Luhmann's account of the constitution as a primary guarantor of the differentiation of law and politics has very significant, yet also curiously selective and limited explanatory value. Constitutions surely provide a normative premise to stabilise the basic distinction and integrational traction of modern law and modern politics. However, in tying both systems to a third system, the system of military force, most national constitutions ultimately destabilised the systems whose differentiation they were expected to uphold, typically leading to the catastrophic loss of autonomy by these systems. In each respect, analysis of constitutional law through the prism of Luhmann's systems theory reveals that constitutions do not enact a smooth legal logic of systemic differentiation and institutional balance. Instead, they instil an extremely precarious source of legitimacy in different systems. Most national constitutions were originally phrased in categories, focused on military expressions of citizenship, which were not adequate for the construction of political legitimacy and the finely mediated transmission of power through society. An inversion of the Luhmannian perspective is required to capture the historical formation of constitutional law.

Empirical Observation 3: The Global Institutional Dimension

Even where his analysis requires deep empirical revision, however, Luhmann's theory of constitutional law need not be abandoned in its entirety, and it retains a certain heuristic importance. Indeed, over a long period of time, Luhmann's claim that constitutions evolved as texts sustaining functional differentiation in politics and law re-acquired a certain plausibility, and its value as a construction of constitutional functions was ultimately renewed. However, the eventual role of constitutions in sustaining functional differentiation became evident in ways that Luhmann himself had not anticipated.

In the decades after 1945, constitutions finally acquired a shape in which, as Luhmann imagined, they began to heighten the autonomy of political institutions and to solidify a basic legal order for society. At this time, the number of polities designed as constitutional democracies increased steadily, and constitutional models were promulgated that proved able to secure the relative autonomy of the legal and political system, consolidating democratic institution building.

Of course, this did not occur in a simple linear fashion. Many constitutional democracies created or re-created immediately after 1945, for example those in Japan, Italy, Austria, India and the Federal Republic of Germany (FRG), remained incomplete, with weakly institutionalised procedures for governmental rotation and systemic autonomy, until the 1960s, or later. The USA, which retained its pre-1945 constitution, remained only selectively democratised until electoral reforms were implemented in 1964–1965, which allowed all ethnic groups to participate equally in elections. Many polities in Latin America and Africa experienced intensified democratisation in the decades after 1945 only then to collapse into dictatorship or authoritarian rule.

Despite this, in the years after 1945, constitutional democracy was consolidated as a governmental order in a growing number of politics, mainly in northern Europe; by the 1960s, it was promoted as an international political ideal; by the 1980s, the entitlement to live in a democracy was increasingly perceived (although clearly not enforced) as a universal personal right.[34] The longer aftermath of 1945 thus witnessed the gradual globalisation of constitutional rule. Compared with pre-1939 democratic experiments, constitutional systems established after 1945 were increasingly defined by the fact that they supported political institutions and legal organisations capable of imprinting a solid integrational form on national society, in which the capacity of actors outside these systems to extricate themselves from formal inclusion was reduced. This was also not a simple development. Yet, the basic telos of post-1945 constitutionalism reflects a process in which political institutions were able to consolidate increasingly universal patterns of legal/political integration. Evidence of this can be found, by way of example in the reduction of variable political authority in the FRG, in the eradication of private power enclaves in the USA in the 1960s, and in the weakening of extra-systemic political actors in Argentina and other polities in Latin America in the 1980s. To this extent, Luhmann's claims about the role of constitutions in promoting the differentiation of law and politics were, ultimately, strongly vindicated.

Several aspects of the incremental global reproduction of constitutional democracy after 1945 have relevance for Luhmann's theory of constitutional rule.

First, compared with earlier constitutional models, constitutions promoted after 1945 adopted a construction of citizenship that was much less strongly focused on the active, implicated exercise of national citizenship rights as the foundation for legal and political legitimation. Most post-1945 constitutions were centred around a concept of the citizen in which the factual engagement of the citizen in the production of legitimacy was curtailed. In most polities, the original premise for the construction of legitimacy to support institutions and to authorise particular legal norms was attached to human rights law, and legitimational practices of citizens were circumscribed by provisions for basic rights with high constitutional protection. Notably, most constitutions put into effect after 1945 provided for the institution of powerful constitutional courts or supreme courts, with authority to check legislative acts in accordance with basic rights provisions. In many cases, the integrational force of legal and political institutions was directly caused by their provisions for individual rights, as the emphasis on the protection of single legal persons tended to heighten the uniformity of legal order in society.[35]

Second, in contrast to earlier constitutional systems, most post-1945 constitutions were shaped by a deep interaction with a normative system that was acquiring constitutional force outside the confines of national societies. Notably, the first constitutions created after 1945, for example those in the FRG and India, replicated aspects of the corpus of international human rights law that was in the process of consolidation, under the auspices of the United Nations. Constitutions that survived from before 1945, such as that of the USA, also saw an amplification of provisions that reflected international constitutional consensus about the standing of basic rights; the catalogue of rights in the Federal Constitution acquired greatly extended effect in state law in the years between 1945 and the 1960s.[36] By the 1980s, most constitutions internalised core elements of international human rights law, and they gave recognition to principles contained in regional human rights systems. The spread of democracy in Europe, Latin America and Africa after the mid-1980s was accompanied by the increasing domestic penetration of regional human rights instruments. In each respect, the basic emphasis of national constitutions was altered, and the most essential legitimating focus of constitutional law was transferred to the transnational plane, so that the figure of the constitutionally implicated active citizen was supplanted, in part, by the transnationally constructed rights holder as the original source of legitimacy for law and political institutions.[37]

One striking outcome of these transformative processes, third, was that national constitutions showed a decreasing propensity to attach legitimational processes to war or to military practices. Self-evidently, the decades after 1945 were marked by an intensification of the patterns of international polarisation that characterised the interwar period. After 1945, most states defined their legitimacy as connected to their position in the global ideological dichotomy resulting from the Cold War. Some states, especially in Latin America, experienced a rapid militarisation of their domestic political interactions because of this, and, in the 1960s and 1970s, they often fragmented into rivalries between groups supporting, and supported by, the USA and their adversaries. In Brazil, for example, the overthrow of the elected left-leaning President João Goulart in 1964 was expressly justified by military actors, who imagined their actions as justified by the fact that they were engaged in a global revolutionary war against the Soviet Union and its infiltrators.[38] Over a longer period, however, the fact that state institutions constructed their legitimacy around the recognition of individual rights-holding subjects tended, gradually, to insulate national polities against pressures caused by global polarities. In many societies, the recognition of persons as single rights holders weakened the incorporation of citizens in collective associations, overtly attached to class affiliation, and it tended to imprint an individualising emphasis on society as a whole. By the 1980s, many democratising states actively promoted recognition of single human rights as a focus of legal/political legitimation that was designed to supplant class affiliation as the basis for legal entitlement and to detach persons in society from class-determined organisations.[39] As a result, many societies were able to establish institutions that were less likely to internalise inter-group conflicts, and many societies witnessed a correlated growth in their integrational capacities. The rise of international human rights law was thus frequently promoted as a legitimational framework for the demilitarisation of national citizenship and the correlated differentiation of legal and political institutions.

In key respects, the transformation of constitutional law after 1945 enacted a process in which Luhmann's vision of the constitution began to acquire real meaning. In many societies, constitutions began to support enduringly autonomous legal and political systems, which promoted individual-subjective inclusion and broad societal differentiation. However, Luhmann's sociology displays a curious inability to isolate the empirical reasons why constitutions eventually assumed the characteristics that he predicted. Importantly, Luhmann did not interpret constitutional law in a global-legal perspective. In most societies, constitutions only acquired the functions that he imputed to them because they acquired support from a global body of human rights law, which was strong enough to project overlying individualised norms to underpin the legitimacy of legal and political exchanges in national societal contexts. The capacity of national constitutions to perform differentiatory functions presupposed, in effect, the *hyper-differentiation of the legal system* at the global or transnational level, which allowed global norms to cut deep into national legitimation processes. One key result of this was that the original constitutional nexus between power, law and war was severed, or at least reduced in its inflammatory force. In the decades after 1945, constitutional law was finally able, as Luhmann expected, to sustain the political system at a high level of differentiation. But this only occurred when national constitutional law was bolstered by its attachment to a global legal system. This general fact of modern constitutionalism does not come into view in Luhmann's thought. His claim that constitutions are required to intensify the differentiation of the political system obliquely implies that some hyper-differentiation in law is necessary to sustain a separate political system. Yet this claim was never thought through to its implicitly globalist conclusion.

Conclusion

Luhmann's reflections on constitutional law provide a vital starting point for sociological inquiry into constitutionalism. His explanation of the growth of constitutional norms as part of a process of systemic differentiation and legal and political integration can hardly be omitted from consideration in any serious legal-sociological inquiry. However, the role assigned to the constitution within Luhmann's construction of the political system over-determines his constitutional analysis. To comprehend the role and functions of constitutions in contemporary society, Luhmann's approach requires some corrective supplements.

First, his understanding of the constitution remains curiously un-sociological, and his investigation into the actual production of legitimacy by constitutions is superficial. This aspect of his thought reflects a lack of awareness of the *constitutional role of the citizen*, which is required to identify the legitimational link that attaches constitutional law to societal communications more widely. Consideration of the constitutional role of the citizen then indicates a second hiatus in Luhmann's thought. His understanding of constitutional law is weakened, in part, by the fact that he did not discuss the military as a distinct system in society. This meant that he was not able to comprehend the societal forces that originally dictated the constitutional terms of national citizenship; he did not notice linkages between constitutional law and other systems that pulled against legal and political differentiation; he did not account for the more pathological aspects of constitutional formation. Consequently, *a theory of military differentiation* is essential to make sense of Luhmann's constitutional intuitions. A necessary starting point in analysis of constitutions based on differentiation theory is to show awareness of constitutions as documents that form a triadic nexus between law, politics, and war, often generating uncontrollable patterns of legitimational conflict through this attachment. Luhmann's bracketing out of the military from systemic analysis meant that he did not understand the problem of legitimational militarisation, and he did not see how a global demilitarisation of citizenship was required, after 1945, to bring leverage to support the differentiation of national polities. The constitutional process that ultimately secured democratic constitutionalism might be best observed through the addition, third, of *a theory of global legal hyper-differentiation* to Luhmann's basic constitutional analysis.[40] It was only through the intensified differentiation of the law in the transnational dimension of society that the full differentiation of law and politics in the national dimension of society was realised. Constitutions usually only acquired genuinely constitutional force as they locked national legal/political systems into a transnational legal/political system. This is visible today in the fact that, wherever national constitutions weaken their linkage to the global normative order, they tend immediately to reduce the autonomy of the institutions which they are supposed to support. Where this occurs, we frequently also see a re-militarisation of citizenship.[41]

Notes

1 This chapter has benefited from discussions with the editors of this volume and with Ulisses Schwarz, Hening de Vries and Atina Krajewska.

2 For Luhmann, simply, it is not possible in a functionally differentiated society 'to attribute a central responsibility to politics that might possibly destroy its present boundaries': Niklas Luhmann, *Political Theory in the Welfare State* (Berlin: de Gruyter, 1990, 1981), 32–3.

3 Amongst its other consequences, this assumption forms the premise for Luhmann's repeated critique of the welfare state. See Niklas Luhmann, *Politik der Gesellschaft* (Frankfurt am Main: Suhrkamp, 2000), 364.

4 Niklas Luhmann, 'Staat und Politik. Zur Semantik der Selbstbeschreibung politischer Systeme', *Politische Vierteljahresschrift*, Sonderheft 15 (1984): 99–125.

5 Luhmann, *Political Theory in the Welfare State*, 4850.

6 Luhmann wrote extensively about the risk of political *de-differentiation*. This concept contains the most important clues about his political stance. See Michael King and Chris Thornhill, *Niklas Luhmann's Theory of Politics and Law* (Basingstoke: Palgrave, 2003), 115.

7 Ibid., p. 72.

8 Luhmann states that the 'production of legitimacy' is performed by politics in the strict sense, and 'the usage of legitimacy' is the basis for the operations of the administrative aspects of the political system, which include parliamentary legislation: Niklas Luhmann, *Politische Planung: Aufsätze zur Soziologie von Politik und Verwaltung* (Wiesbaden: Springer, 1971), 62. On this account, politics creates legitimacy ex nihilo, as a symbolic resource; it generates this resource by proposing plans or politicians to the public, or by filtering themes from the public which might find some degree of popularity.

9 Luhmann, *Die Politik der Gesellschaft*, 98.

10 In this respect, Luhmann explained that the 'use of politics for purposes of the shaping of society' is likely to give rise to 'ineffective decisions': Niklas Luhmann, 'Selbstlegitimation des Staates', *Archiv für Rechts- und Sozialphilosophie* (Beiheft: Legitimation des modernen Staates, 1981), 65–83 at 82–3. Consequently, he implied that the legitimacy of politics depends, not on the representation of encompassing norms in all parts of society, but on the legal self-restriction of political functions. See Luhmann, *Political Theory in the Welfare State*, 31–32.

11 Niklas Luhmann, *Theory of Society*, Vol. 1 (Stanford, CA: Stanford University Press, 2012), 213.

12 Niklas Luhmann, 'Verfassung als evolutionäre Errungenschaft', *Rechtshistorisches Journal* 9 (1990): 176–220; 201; Niklas Luhmann, *Law as a Social System* (Oxford: Oxford University Press, 2004), 371.

13 Niklas Luhmann, 'Widerstandsrecht und politische Gewalt', *Zeitschrift für Rechtssoziologie* 5 (1984): 36–45, 41.

14 Ibid., 40. It is only in the medium of law that power becomes 'effective power':

15 Luhmann claimed that the organisation of the political system as a legal-constitutional state leads to an 'increase in the freedom' of both the legal system and the political system: Luhmann, *Politik der Gesellschaft*, 391.

16 Luhmann, 'Verfassung als evolutionäre Errungenschaft', 202.

17 The idea in classical constitutional theory that the constitution and the rights that it contains in some way place limits on state power is reflected in the reality that the

constitution helps to counteract society's tendency to converge around its political power. Constitutions formalise acts of self-restriction, or the 'renunciations and indifferences', which enable a political system to avoid exceeding its functional reach and prevent a society from reliance on simplistic or over-emphatic expressions of political power. See Niklas Luhmann, *Grundrechte als Institution. Ein Beitrag zur politischen Soziologie* (Berlin: Duncker und Humblot, 1965), 182–3.

18 Ibid., 135.

19 For a related discussion see Gorm Harste, *The Habermas-Luhmann Debate* (New York: Columbia University Press, 2021), p. 215.

20 See my discussion of this process as the basis for a sociology of constitutions in Chris Thornhill, *A Sociology of Constitutions: Constitutions and State Legitimacy in Historical-Sociological Perspective* (Cambridge: Cambridge University Press, 2011), Chapter 3.

21 This was reflected paradigmatically in the French Revolution in the *Le Chapelier* law of 1791. This law abolished corporations, denouncing them as imposing 'seditious' restrictions on individual liberties. The author of this law, Jean Le Chapelier, chairman of the Constitutional Committee, justified it in the following terms: 'There are no corporations in the state; there is only the particular interest of each individual and the general interest': Philippe Joseph Benjamin Buchez and Pierre Celestin Roux-Lavergne, *Histoire parlementaire de Révolution française*, vol. 22. (Paris: Paulin, 1834), 194–5. One historian explains that 'politics in the modern sense of the word did not exist' in pre-1789 France: Michael Sonenscher, *Work and Wages. Natural Law, Politics and the Eghteenth-Century French Trades* (Cambridge: Cambridge University Press, 1989), 46.

22 See my analysis in Chris Thornhill, *Democratic Crisis and Global Constitutional Law* (Cambridge: Cambridge University Press, 2020), Chapter 2.

23 See my analysis in Chris Thornhill, 'Global Sociology and the Sociology of Law', *Zeitschrift für Soziologie* 47, no. 6 (2018): 375–401. One historian explains that this period was characterised by a 'division of labour' between civil and military office holders: Martin Rink, 'Preußisch-deutsche Konzeptionen zum »Volkskrieg« im Zeitalter Napoleons', in *Reform-Reorganisation-Transformation. Zum Wandel in deutschen Streitkräften von der preußischen Heeresreform bis zur Transformation der Bundeswehr*, ed. Karl-Heinz Lutz, Martin Rink and Marcus von Salisch (Munich: Oldenbourg, 2010), 65–87.

24 See analysis of this in different contexts in Karl Grünberg, *Die Bauernbefreiung und die Auflösung des gutsherrlich-bäuerlichen Verhältnisses in Böhmen, Mähren und Schlesien, I: Überblick der Entwicklung* (Leipzig: Duncker und Humblot, 1894), 91; Heinrich Kaak, *Die Gutsherrschaft. Theoriegeschichtliche Untersuchungen zum Agrarwesen im ostelbischen Raum* (Berlin: de Gruyter, 1991), 3–6; Guy Lemarchand, *Paysans et seigneurs en Europe. Une histoire comparée. XVI-XIX siècle* (Rennes: Presses universitaires de Rennes, 2001), 101; Richard Evans, *The Making of the Habsburg Monarchy, 1500–1700* (Oxford: Clarendon Press, 1979), 88–91.

25 On this process in revolutionary America see Harry M. Ward, *The War for Independence and the Transformation of American Society* (London: Routledge, 1999), 111. Art 109 of the Jacobin Constitution of 1793 declared, simply: 'Tous les Français sont soldats; ils sont tous exercés au maniement des armes'.

26 See Annie Crépin, *La conscription en débat. Ou le triple apprentissage de la nation, de la citoyenneté, de la République (1798–1889)* (Arras: Artois Presses Université, 1998); Thomas Hippler, *Soldats et citoyens. Naissance du service militaire en France et en Prusse* (Paris: PUF, 2006).

27 See commentary and attempts to rectify this in Barbara Kuchler, 'Krieg und gesellschaftliche Differenzierung', *Zeitschrift für Soziologie* 42, no. 6 (2013): 502–20; Gorm Harste, *Kritik af Krigens Fornuft. Et perspektiv på selvreferentielle systemer fra 11. - 21. Århundrede* (Aarhus: Aarhus University Press, 2016).

28 Luhmann, *Das Recht der Gesellschaft*, 424.

29 See Carl Schmitt, *Constitutional Theory*. Translated by Jeffrey Seitzer (Durham, NC: Duke University Press, 2007); Dieter Grimm, 'Entstehung und Wirkungsbedingungen des modernen Konstitutionalismus', in *Die Zukunft der Verfassung*, ed. Dieter Grimm (Frankfurt am Main: Suhrkamp, 1991), 31–66.

30 This is a common claim in historical sociology. See its paradigmatic expression in Max Weber, *Economy and Society, An Outline of Interpretive Sociology*. Vol. 2 (New York: Bedminster Press 1968 [1921]), 1022; Brian Downing, *The Military Revolution and Political Change. The Origins of Democracy and Autocracy in Early Modern Europe* (Princeton: Princeton University Press, 1992), 25; Margaret Levi, 'The Institution of Conscription', *Social Science History* 20, no. 1 (1996): 133–67; Charles Tilly, 'Where do Rights Come From?', in *Democracy, Revolution, and History*, ed. Theda Skocpol (Ithaca: Cornell University Press, 1999), 55–72.

31 See my analysis of this point in Thornhill, *Democratic Crisis*, Chapter 3.

32 See historical discussion in Markus Ingenlath, *Mentale Aufrüstung. Militarisierungstendenzen in Frankreich und Deutschland vor dem Ersten Weltkrieg* (Frankfurt: Campus, 1998).

33 For instance, the German Constitution of 1919 contained a section that addressed the 'organization of economic life'; it was designed to create modes of regulation for employment and professional relations able to soften class antagonisms. The Polish constitutions of 1919 and 1921 were flanked by land reallocation schemes to facilitate social integration (especially of ex-soldiers). See Polish legislation regarding land occupancy in U. 1921 nr 4 poz. 18. For comments on these processes see Zbigniew Landau and Jerzy Tomaszewski, *W dobie inflacji 1918–1923* (Warsaw: Książka i Wiedza, 1967), 164. Land reallocation was commonplace in post-1918 constitutional systems in Eastern Europe.

34 Thomas M. Franck, 'Democracy as a Human Right', in *Human Rights: An Agenda for the Next Century*, ed. Louis Henkin and John L.H. Hargrove (Washington, DC: American Society of International Law, 1994), 73–101.

35 See Chris Thornhill, *A Sociology of Transnational Constitutions. Social Foundations of the Post-National Legal Structure* (Cambridge: Cambridge University Press, 2016), 364.

36 Tinsley E. Yarbrough, 'Justice Black, The Fourteenth Amendment, and Incorporation', *University of Miami Law Review* 30, no. 2 (1976): 231–75.

37 See my discussion in Chris Thornhill, *The Sociology of Law and the Global Transformation of Democracy* (Cambridge: Cambridge University Press, 2018), Chapter 4.

38 See Bilac Pinto, *Guerra revolucionaria* (Rio de Janeiro: Forense, 1964), 57.

39 The classic example of this is transitional Argentina in 1983.

40 See my claims in Thornhill, *Sociology of Transnational Constitutions*, 428.

41 See my discussion in Chris Thornhill, 'Constitutionalism and Populism: Global Legal Integration and National Political Integration', *International Theory* 12, no. 1 (2020): 1–32.

Chapter 3

LUHMANN ON LAW AND LEGAL THEORY

Richard Nobles and David Schiff

Introduction

To appreciate how Luhmann distinctively approached law, we have to consider how law understands itself. As he says in the revised conclusion to the second edition of *A Sociological Theory of Law*:

> Today we do not think solely of the self-programming of computers and the problems of self-organisation which could be compared with, for example, positivisation in the area of law. In other words, we are talking about self-reference not only at the level of system structures. Rather we are speaking of self-referential systems which *themselves produce every type of unity* that they require and employ: even the unity of the system itself as well as the unity of those elements (e.g. actions) of which the system consists.[1]

Similarly, legal theories have unfailingly attempted to account for the unity and autonomy of law. They ask themselves questions about what gives law its unity and distinguishes it from the rest of society. Even those legal theories which challenge claims that law exhibits unity or autonomy take such accounts seriously, if only to refute them. However, within legal theory, the principal attempts to explicate law as unified and autonomous have not offered themselves as sociological explanations, relying instead on forms of philosophical analysis. The two leading twentieth-century legal theorists offering such accounts of law as, and operating within, separate autonomous systems are Hans Kelsen and H.L.A. Hart. For Kelsen, law is, or operates within, a system of positive (non-moral) norms which authorise coercive action, unified by a constitution whose own authority is presupposed. Sociology is not relevant or necessary for the identification of this system. The empirical requirement is limited to a sufficient congruence between the norms authorising coercion and their occurrence to justify the conclusion that the identified system of norms is generally effective.[2] For Hart, law's existence as operating within a system of positive (non-moral) rules is achieved through the adherence by officials to a common standard when identifying those 'legal' rules: the rule of recognition. This standard is a socio-psychological fact, evidenced by the limited but common sources of law acknowledged by legal officials. Hart claimed that his approach is an example of 'descriptive sociology', but its sociological content is extremely constrained. Having asserted that law's identification arises through a conventional shared attitude by officials (especially judges) he felt no need to analyse the nature of that convention – how it might arise, and how it might be maintained, except as a thought experiment pertaining to pre-legal societies and the emergence of the characteristics necessary for a developed legal system. There is a similar absence of sociology in Hart's version of the requirement that law must have a minimal level of efficiency. The rules imposing duties and conferring powers on a population must be generally obeyed or at least recognised, but there is no further analysis of what might generate this level of obedience or recognition.[3]

Luhmann's contribution to our understanding of law, and legal theory as it addresses such understanding, lies in his sociological account of the basis on which law could take the autonomous, positive, and systematic form claimed within most positivist legal theory.[4] It is fitting to explore this contribution by reference to two of the books he wrote on law[5] – *A Sociological Theory of Law* (*STL*)[6] and *Law as a Social System* (*LSS*)[7] – as these embody the shift in his general sociological approach from an understanding of systems within the tradition advanced by Talcott Parsons, to the autopoietic version of systems theory with which he is now associated.[8]

A Sociological Theory of Law

In *STL*, Luhmann explored a problem central to much positivist legal theory – what is the nature of the normative posture that accompanies contemporary nation-state legal systems? Positivist legal theory rejects claims associated with Natural Law theorising: that law's normativity arises through its incorporation of values identified as moral, consistent with a focus on moral philosophy, or by reference to a moral consensus shared by the general population.[9] Despite this rejection, an element of normativity is invariably conceded: at a cognitive level (the awareness of the presence of standards with a normative meaning); and through significant congruence between actual behaviour and behaviour required by legal norms. Luhmann offers an account that links the evolution of this kind of normativity with the evolution of society. His account commences with a sociological reformulation of what is being referred to, within society, when we speak of normativity. Norms are expectations that are maintained despite disappointment. They should be distinguished from cognitive expectations, which are altered in response to disappointment. This immediately takes us outside the forms of argument utilised within much philosophical discussion of law, as the distinction cognitive/normative expectation has replaced the more usual one of fact/norm. In addition, it is experience, rather than language, or deontic logic, which is the primary determinant of normativity.

With this reformulation of normativity, Luhmann begins an account of law that connects legal and social theory. Building on Parsons, he seeks to show how orientation toward action is achieved through the mutual integration of normative expectations[10] held by interacting individuals, and evolves into that offered through nation-state legal orders. At the level of human face-to-face interaction, many expectations can only be classified retrospectively, by reference to how an individual chooses to react to disappointment – by abandoning or modifying the expectation (cognitive – involving learning) or insisting on the expectation (normative – not learning).[11] Many unstated expectations (he gives the example of the distance between people during face-to-face conversations) remain at this level.[12] But other expectations can be regulated, by being institutionalised. *A* can expect that *B* will expect both of them to meet the expectations of *C*. But to understand the possibilities of institutionalising normative expectations one needs also to consider how individuals can be motivated not to choose to learn from disappointment. This is a particular problem for contemporary positive law – which is transparently contingent – both in the sense that laws are frequently changed through, principally, legislative choices, and in the sense that the constitutions that enable and constrain those changes are peculiar to each legal order. Disappointment will occur through the changing of law, through breaches of law, and through the inability of law to activate sanctions in many, if not most, cases where law is breached. The kinds of expectations that need to be maintained also raise problems as many laws will be unknown to a good number of the population. So the expectation to be maintained is not an expectation of third parties' concrete expectations, but *A*'s and *B*'s mutual expectations that third parties will adopt normative expectations, both at the level of selecting norms to become law (legislation) and deciding what laws are currently in force (adjudication). At the same time, those deciding cannot simply give effect to the expectations of parties (*A* and *B*). First, because there is an overproduction of norms within society, requiring some expectations to be selected as law and others rejected. And secondly, because as law increases in complexity, expectations arising from the lived experience of individuals do not offer an adequate basis for adjudication. Instead, those deciding must address norms to themselves to identify what is expected, whilst *A* and *B* simply expect that this will be the case.[13]

Luhmann combines functional and evolutionary analysis. Positive law is the appropriate form of law for a functionally differentiated and constantly changing society, since it is able to change rapidly and frequently in response to changes within its environment. But the kind of normative expectations required to be generated by positive law (as described earlier) are, as Luhmann observes, highly improbable evolutionary achievements when considered from the starting point of how two individual actors can establish common expectations of each other's behaviour. The concept through which he traces this evolutionary process is also his definition of law:

> We can now define law as *structure of a social system which depends upon the congruent generalisation of normative behavioural expectations.*[14]

This is not to claim that the content of laws expresses a societal/cultural consensus. Rather, it is directed towards the functionality of three dimensions of normative expectations: temporal, social and material. Temporal refers to when, in time, expectations are directed. In particular, whether expectations are directed towards future behaviour. Archaic societies do not communicate about the future as an unknown but alterable state. Functionally differentiated societies do. Thus, they need norms that do not simply stipulate how deviants should be treated, but norms directing future behaviour. The social dimension refers to the institutionalising of expectations. Towards whom are they directed? A complex society not only needs expectations to be directed towards third parties, it needs this to occur even in situations where the third party has no personal interest which might motivate them to become involved in a dispute – pointing to the need for remunerated judges. It also needs clear indications as to when law is changed, pointing to the need for an expectation that identifiable procedures will alter the law. The material dimension requires us to consider the form in which norms are generalised. Within archaic societies norms could be directed towards concrete situations. With increased complexity, one has an amplified need for abstraction. Norms must transcend the particularities of situations and be greatly enhanced when law itself is structured in terms of a distinction between facts and norms. In addition, one needs to consider how this process of abstraction is organised – what is the constancy within the particular that one is seeking to stabilise as an expectation? Is it the behaviour of specific individuals, or the behaviour of persons acting within particular roles, or identified behaviour without reference to actors' roles, or abstract values? The first is inappropriate for a complex society, and whilst values play a part in directing the selection of norms, they do not offer the level of precision required to support behaviour in a society with a high degree of division of labour. So, modern society relies on norms addressed to the behaviour of occupants of roles or, and even more so, behaviour identified through rules – if behaviour *x* occurs, *y* will follow. The latter, which Luhmann terms conditional programmes, are the dominant material form of law in a functionally differentiated society.

These dimensions are co-dependent. For example, conditional programmes are linked to both temporality, and institutionalisation. Rules that stipulate 'if x happens y follows' can be decided by judges at the time by reference to facts which have arisen in the past, by contrast with norms that direct actors to pursue future conditions (purposive programmes) where the expectation is tied to predictions of future facts. The latter would alter in meaning whenever the expectation of future events changes, making it difficult to integrate these norms with others within the system. Conditional programmes are also easier to integrate if the status of a statute as law does not depend on the date when it was introduced (for example, with newer laws having higher status than older ones). Thus, conditional programmes are compatible with both of the other two dimensions of normativity and the complexities of a functionally differentiated society.

It is useful at this point to take stock of the difference between Luhmann's analysis of positive law and much positivist legal theory. Positivist legal theories, with their philosophical approaches, focus on the current characteristics of positive legal orders and attempt to identify their essential structures. Here, by contrast,[15] Luhmann is analysing what problems needed to be solved for positive law operating in legal systems to come into existence, beginning with the basis on which simple interactions can give rise to order (integrating his account with classical sociological theory) and then tracing the evolution of law, within the evolution of society, from archaic societies to High Cultures (particularly Roman and Anglo-Saxon) through to functionally differentiated society. This does not lead to a different description of what currently exists, so much as a different understanding of its status. Luhmann's functionalist approach, with its focus on structures as contingent solutions to problems, offers a new understanding of law's current features. This is not only because law has been different in the past, but because one can identify functional equivalents – the fact that problems were solved in a particular way does not mean that they had to be solved in that manner, or will continue to be solved in that manner (assuming that the problem(s) still exists).[16] In addition, this approach directs us to the kinds of problems that must continue to be solved if law is to continue to generate normative expectations appropriate to our functionally differentiated society. Will law offer expectations appropriate to systems such as science and the economy which, in contrast to the current predominantly regional institutionalisation of law, are operating globally? Can law continue to combine a reduction of consensus and a trivialising of the esteem consequences of unlawfulness with sufficient motivation for individuals to pursue the cases that provide courts with their opportunities to generalise and integrate normative expectations? Is the specificity and purpose orientation of much regulatory legislation a serious obstacle to congruent generalised behavioural expectations?

Law as a Social System

Between publishing the German versions of *STL* and *LSS* Luhmann underwent, as outlined in the Introduction to this Volume, his autopoietic 'turn', drawing on cybernetics, evolutionary biology and the mathematics of form of George Spencer-Brown. This 'turn' is not a rejection of his previous functional analysis or its implications for our understanding of law. In the chapter within *LSS* devoted to function, the primary function of law, at the level of society, remains that of the provision of normative expectations. However, as Luhmann himself acknowledges in the first conclusion to *STL*,[17] his functional definition of law does not address the issue, central to legal theory, of the unity of law. Defining law in terms of a single function allows different structures to be brought into an *analytical* relationship of identity. But the multi-functionality (or dysfunctionality) of any empirical system undermines any claim that the identity ('being') of that system is established and maintained through the execution of a single function,[18] and in particular 'because the indication of the function of law is not generally an adequate criterion by itself for the judgment of the individual norms' membership to law'.[19] In his conclusion to the second edition of *STL*, published in German the year before the German version of *Social Systems*,[20] Luhmann maps out the possibilities of understanding law's unity and autonomy on the basis that it is an autopoietic system, and therefore one of those:

> [...] self-referential systems which *themselves produce every type of unity* that they require and employ: even the unity of the system itself as well as the unity of those elements (e.g. actions) of which the system consists.[21]

As he makes clear in *Social Systems,* he is no longer using the term 'systems' as a purely analytical concept: 'the concept of system refers to something that is in reality a system and thereby incurs the responsibility of testing its statements against reality.'[22]

LSS is Luhmann's fullest statement of this understanding of law and the legal system and its implications for legal theory, addressing law's autonomy (its operative closure), its function, conditional programmes and code; justice, the evolution of law, the role of courts, legal argument, law's relationship with politics and other social systems, the nature of its claim to unity, and its possible future within world society. Here we focus on the issue central to legal theory: his account of the unity of law.

Luhmann draws a distinction between the unity of the legal system as this is developed within legal operations (its self-description) and the external observation of how law creates itself. Beginning with the latter: there is no unity as such, but only a distinction that makes a difference.[23] One can observe (secondary observation) how different systems draw distinctions, and the difference that this makes within society. This includes the differences which result from the applications of laws' distinctions compared to those of other sub-systems (religion, politics, mass media, etc.) and the difference between the legal system's (and other social sub-system's) application of distinctions and those occurring within organisations and interactions. At the level of society's subsystems, including law, these distinctions involve a combination of code and programme. Law's coding, which is implicitly or explicitly applied by all legal communications, is legal/illegal, with the results of that coding (output) providing the input for further coding. Sub-system codes have no inherent meaning, being only positive/negative distinctions. Meaning arises through the system's observation on its own application of its own code: self-observation. When the legal system observes on its own application of its code it selects features from the particular situation for abstraction and generalisation. If these generalisations are reused and thereafter stabilise, they offer structures which limit the possibilities of further applications of the code – conditional programmes (if *x*, then *y*). These structures prevent the application of the code from being arbitrary. Their creation increases the internal complexity of the legal system. In this manner law 'transforms a tautology into a sequence of arguments and makes something that is seen as highly artificial and contingent from the outside appear quite natural and necessary from the inside'.[24]

The self-referential continuation of the legal system, in which the changes to the system which follow from the application of the code are then selected as the basis for further communications, produces a distinction within society (what is legal and what is not) that can be observed, and described. When observing from an external point of view, 'validity' (that ubiquitous phrase operating within legal discourse) is nothing more than the endless connection between legal communications, linking past applications of the code to events in ways that both enable and seem to limit the possibilities of future applications of the code. It is this, but also more than this for the legal system which 'provides itself with a symbol [validity] that marks the unity of the system in the interactive sequence of its operations [...]'.[25]

Self-observation always involves the distinction between self-reference and hetero reference. In law, this involves the evolutionary achievement acknowledged in *STL*: the distinction between law and fact. There is also a norm/fact distinction in legal communication, which identifies itself as a system of norms, and its environment as the facts given relevance through its norms. Luhmann described law as 'normatively closed but cognitively open'.[26] Law is normatively closed, in the sense that it uses its own communications to identify itself, and it identifies itself as its norms:

> No environmental meaning as such is normatively binding for the legal system [...] If the legal system refers to extra-legal norms, such as loyalty and belief or good practice, these norms attain legal quality only with this reference.[27]

These norms not only identify relevant facts within law's environment, they also allow law to identify what facts constitute its operations, allowing it to understand itself as a system of action, with actors. Systems not only apply their code (first-order observation) and observe (communicate about) their applications of their code (second-order observation), they also engage in self-observation at a third level on those occasions when they describe themselves as a unity. This Luhmann terms 'self-description' which itself changes the system 'through that description'. However, in presenting self-description in that form, what is involved is a 'paradoxical enterprise, because it deals with the internal description as if it were an external description'.[28]

Luhmann claims that systems theory is better placed (i.e., more capable of offering meaningful explanation or 'being scientific') than other theories (sociological or philosophical) to identify law as an object, because it starts from the premise that law (along with all other functioning social systems – the economic, the political, etc) is a system that identifies itself to itself. What Luhmann is advancing here is that the kinds of communication that are the object of legal theory – attempts to describe the legal system as a whole, as having a unity – exist autologically. They are general communications about the system which belong to the system. They form part of what they attempt to describe. They are one of the operations of law. And, like self-observation, they constrain (but do not determine) the application of the code: legal/illegal. At the same time, they are paradoxical, while attempts to understand them outside the system are necessarily self-contradictory.

Despite being parts of the systems that they describe, self-description does not routinely guide their everyday practice. Luhmann makes this point humorously, using a quotation referring to natural law: '[...] it is hard to imagine many JPs thumbing through the *Summa Theologiae* after a hard day at the sessions.'[29] Despite that, self-descriptions do operate within legal systems: because they are presupposed within more mundane legal operations: '[Legal] practice presupposes that the fundamental questions of the meaning of the system can be answered';[30] and because communications about the system as a whole facilitate legal operations that would not occur without them. To develop Luhmann's own example, whilst Aquinas may not have been read by the judges, the idea within Medieval Europe that positive law was only law (at his time) to the extent that it expressed a higher natural law was not simply an idealistic critique. Such communications allowed positive law to evolve whilst still claiming that the real law (the universal law evidenced by, but not synonymous with, positive law) remained unchanged. Prior to the reciprocal developments within the political and legal systems that now make frequent and particular legal change possible by detailed legislation, subordinate legislation and regulation, natural law self-description (communications describing the law in terms of its connections to reason and a natural order) were clearly both important, and autological.[31]

Luhmann warned that '[…] sociological theory[…] [should] not be confused with such self-descriptions'.[32] This is arguably what happens within analytic and/or philosophical legal theory in its positivist, natural law and even realist and critical versions. Such legal theories ignore the particularities of much legal communication and can do so because abstraction and generalisation are part of what it means to undertake such analysis/philosophy. In reaching levels of higher abstraction, these theories are also mirroring what occurs within the legal system with the move from decision, to self-observation, to self-description. But not being part of the legal system, they can make connections between communications that are not, and often simply could not, be duplicated by the operating legal system. To quote one of Luhmann's own observations: 'There are a number of typical approaches which, however […] never achieved any particular impact on legal practice.'[33] In order to see what constitutes law's self-description, one cannot simply borrow general communications from law and subject them to analytic/philosophical examination. Rather, one has to identify how such communications are used or reused within the legal system, and thereby establish the difference between self-description and critique.[34]

As self-descriptions are generated by, and play a role within, law's operations, law is resistant to theoretical descriptions that are incompatible with those operations. The most important example of such incompatibility is law's inability to incorporate systems theory's observation that its code is simply a positive/negative distinction, without inherent meaning. If admitted within operations, the system would be paralysed. This is what Luhmann called asking 'The Third Question'.[35] For law to incorporate into its communications, the admission that there is no objective basis for applying the legal code would contradict the use of the system's past history as a basis for current decisions, and undermine the potential for any current decision to operate as a basis for future decisions. (A loss of the temporal basis for congruently generalised expectations). This need to have regard to the function of self-description within the system has implications for some versions of deconstruction. Pointing out the arbitrariness of law's distinctions, including its presentation of itself as an objectively identified unity, offers little reason to believe that this will result in law reforming or reformulating itself. Instead, taking Luhmann's approach, one would need to consider what operations could not occur, or no longer take their current form, if the criticised communications were to cease.[36] Similar criticisms apply to some versions of Marxist theory which treat law's self-observations and self-descriptions as 'ideological', failing to engage with self-descriptions as solutions to the system's internal problems.

Modern Positivist and Realist legal theories have struggled with law's self-descriptions. Bentham and Austin sought to re-interpret law's claimed normativity as a reference to a factual power matrix: the ability of rulers to command obedience from a particular population. Some Realist theories have sought law's unity in the psychological commitments of actors. These attempts to reject law's description of itself as a unity of norms suffer (as a means to understand law sociologically) from their incompatibility with law's continuing and evolving existence. If law communicated about itself as power, or the psychological commitment of its actors, it could not exist at its current level of complexity – it would lack the normative meanings necessary to achieve this. As Hart observed, judges would lack the means to understand themselves as judges in the absence of communications with normative meanings; reducing law to the anticipation of coercion renders the normative statements that accompany legal rules and operations meaningless.[37]

Rather than re-interpreting law's self-description in purely factual terms, Hart and Kelsen accepted law's self-description as a system of rules or norms and sought to explain the conditions that make this description possible. In *The Concept of Law*, Hart offered the 'rule of recognition' as something which established the unity (within space and over time) of a particular legal order. Hart argues with philosophical rigour that legal rules could not be a system, but only a set, unless there was a standard identifying which rules belong to that system and which do not. And the standard that identifies which rules belong to a particular system of rules is not itself a rule within that system. Following this logic, and seeking a foundational basis for the unity, systematisation and autonomy of law, Hart looked outside the system of communication to an 'unstated' official/judicial convention.[38] As noted at the beginning of this chapter, the sociological basis for such a convention is unexplored. Whilst Hart addresses problems that need to be solved for a positive national legal order to have come into existence, he does not adequately address the barriers to further evolution presented by the foundation he has identified. According to his legal theory, all responses to law's environment that cannot be achieved through the existing legal rules for change (legislation and contract being the principal current mechanisms) must either not occur or await a shift in the common commitments of the judiciary/officials. This is clearly a problem for legal orders that have written constitutions restricting the validity of specified kinds of legislation and subjective rights. But even the UK legal order, which was clearly the one most within Hart's contemplation, has experienced two forms of evolution that Hart's theory cannot accommodate. The rule of recognition, as he conceived of it, has no application to a judicial overruling of settled law by courts with the same hierarchical status as those who established the law at an earlier stage. And what he considered to be the ultimate source of UK law identified by the rule of recognition (the supremacy of the latest statute over all other kinds of law) was altered judicially in favour of the supremacy of European law in the *Factortame* case [1991] 1 AC 603, again without any clear judicial/official consensus in favour of this change. A third difficulty with his theoretical account of law's unity is that it requires him to attribute improbable commitments to the judiciary. Judges have a commitment in common to uphold specified sources of law when deciding settled law but are engaging in subjective moralising disguised by a common (and therefore consensual) rhetorical deceit when they claim to find existing law in novel situations where the law is unclear. The difficulties of confining the subjective preferences of judges to situations where the law is unsettled remain unexplored.[39] Hart's theorisation of the unity of law is, in at least these respects, self-contradictory.[40]

Kelsen's *Pure Theory of Law*, like Hart's, attempts to account for law's self-description as a system of norms. Kelsen accepts the inevitable lack of normative foundation for positive law, and considers how, nevertheless, law can be understood as a system composed of a hierarchy of norms. Philosophical rigour dictates that the highest norm in such a system cannot be a positive norm, as this would require normative meanings to be derived from facts (the naturalistic fallacy). He identifies the highest positive norm authorising the creation of further norms as the constitution, and the normativity of that constitution in a logical presupposition, or fiction[41] which enables the norms within the system to be connected through deontic logic. But the self-description of law as a hierarchy of norms, which has a function within the system in terms of stabilising the application of its code, does not describe its unity as autopoietic reproduction. The self-continuity of law is established from event to event, with hierarchy as a 'secondary structure':

> [...] the autopoiesis is a *strictly symmetrical-recursive event*, and in this respect all hierarchies are circular structures: legal decisions are valid on the basis of legal rules, although (even because!) rules are valid on the basis of decisions.'[42]

We have here a reason for the self-contradictions that are represented by legal theories as they approach self-description, namely they seem unable 'to give up the idea of a unitary solution'.[43]

In *LSS* Luhmann goes beyond self-description, to consider how the legal system achieves its ongoing recursivity. We cannot explore every one of the problem solutions he discusses. However, it is worthwhile considering how he approaches a topic that has particular relevance for attempts to theorise law's self-description: legal argumentation.[44] Legal argumentation occurs in cases where opposing parties offer conflicting interpretations of the norms applicable to their factual circumstances. As such, it is largely located within appeal courts, where argument forms the precursor to appeal court decisions; normally, a selection from parties' arguments reappears within appeal court judgments as they purport to justify their decisions. Hierarchies of authority (that of the legislature vis-à-vis the courts, and that of different courts vis-à-vis each other) do not in themselves explain decisions reached in particular cases, including ones that have considerable political, economic and (in terms of required reconfiguration of legal doctrine) legal significance. Hart tries to explain such cases within his hierarchy of rules, as those where judges may be authorised to make new law (though he cannot explain why judges fail to admit to this in their judgments). The Realists and Critical Legal Scholars claim that legal arguments may disguise the fact that the decisions they support are actually the outcome of the political, moral or other commitments of judges. They see the form of argumentation (claiming to identify existing law) as ideological in nature.

In *LSS* Luhmann re-describes the functional concern with congruently generalised expectations in terms of systems' needs for sufficient levels of both variety and redundancy. These terms are taken from communication theory and refer to the manner in which a communication generates information. Information is the difference made by the communication – the difference between what is new and what has already been generated within the system. The latter is a communication's redundancy. The information content of a communication is identified by subtracting the message's redundancy. With individual communications, the greater the amount of any message that is redundant (repetition), the more consistently its information can be extracted. In advance of a communication, variety is the range of information that could meaningfully be conveyed against the background of existing levels of redundancy. Whilst the accuracy of information extraction with an individual communication is a factor of the degree of redundancy that accompanies it, the evolution of complexity within a system requires an increase in both redundancy and variety. In the case of law, even more technically complex distinctions have to be depicted. This is the particular function of the courts, who steer the legal system by creating congruent generalised expectations which, expressed within communication theory, offer sufficient variety (in terms of law's response to its environment) whilst retaining sufficient levels of redundancy to allow technical and specific distinctions to be drawn.

Utilising this analysis, the hierarchical structures often exploited by positivist legal theories to account for law's unity can be examined in terms of the redundancies which they offer, and the loss of redundancy (and corresponding variety/complexity) that would result if they were discarded.[45] So, for example, a legal argument premised on the wholesale rejection of the doctrine of legislative authority to make new laws would be difficult to incorporate into legal doctrine without a huge loss in law's ability to draw complex distinctions (including those which establish the hierarchical authority of judges deciding cases). But whilst hierarchies may represent important redundancies within legal orders, this also means that they do not in practice operate in a top-down manner assumed within many positivist legal theories. The redundancy of the hierarchy is a factor of the redundancy and variety that it generates throughout the system (including rules with lesser formal status). So hierarchies are 'tangled' (and to repeat): 'legal decisions are valid on the basis of legal rules, although (even because!) rules are valid on the basis of decisions'. What matters is to understand how the legal system achieves both sufficient consistency (through redundancy) and sufficient (and ever-increasing) variety in the operations that it can execute in response to the increasing complexity of its environment.[46] Whilst redundancy and variety are usually thought of as conflicting qualities (an increase in one results in a decrease in another) this is not the case when systems evolve. There are forms of redundancy which, if achieved, can increase a system's ability to respond to its environment. Again, the structures regarded as foundational within positivist legal theories are examples of this. Hierarchies which allow rules to be altered by decisions are a redundancy which has hugely increased law's variety. But hierarchies can, through legal argument (and as shown by the *Factortame* case) be offered opportunities to evolve, in circumstances where that does not represent a loss of redundancy.[47] But alongside hierarchy, one also finds legal concepts – generalisations from the specifics of particular cases that are available to be reused in future cases. Legal 'concepts compound information, thereby producing the redundancy required in the system'.[48] And their critique requires the problems solved by those concepts to be re-visited, and 'functionally equivalent constructions'[49] to be formulated. Concepts immunise the legal system from having simply to rely on interests or general values.

Conclusion

We have used legal argumentation as an example of Luhmann's palpably well-informed understanding of law. One can see how his discussion is in substance, even though not in its discourse, reminiscent of many intricate debates on the meaning of particular laws that fill law review journals, and also much of the reasoning underpinning appeal court judgments of the highest courts, with their self-observations and self-descriptions. What this indicates is that Luhmann's understanding of law as an autonomous and unified system, together with all of that system's potential self-contradictions, encouraged by its recursive operations, is a companion to at least prevailing positivist theories of law, if not other legal theories that theorise law's unity, and try to represent its self-description. This is not surprising. The extensive juridification of the modern world has profound consequences not only for the world addressed, society in general, but also law as it operates in society, in other words, for itself. Luhmann's account of law is a sociological account of how law understands itself as a unity which understanding, in a functionally differentiated society, is a precondition for its operation and further evolution. The full import and potential of this profound understanding have however yet to be fully realised.

Notes

1 Niklas Luhmann, *A Sociological Theory of Law*. Second edition in English, edited by Martin Albrow, with the new conclusion (Abingdon: Routledge, 2014,), 281 (first edition in English, London: Routledge and Kegan Paul, 1985, translated by Martin Albrow and Elizabeth King-Utz). Originally published in German: Niklas Luhmann, *Rechtssoziologie* (Reinbeck bei Hamburg: Rowohlt Taschenbuch, 1972); 2nd German edn Opladen: Westdeutscher, 1983, with a new conclusion.

2 His full argument is presented in many writings, but concisely in Hans Kelsen, 'On the Pure Theory of Law', *Israel Law Review* 1 (1966): 1. However, even this short statement contains the seeds of Kelsen's self-criticism of his own argument about the 'presupposition of', or 'fiction' concerning the basic norm: see Neil Duxbury, 'Kelsen's Endgame', *Cambridge Law Journal* 67 (2008): 51. This complex argument is pertinent; it indicates why even sophisticated philosophical attempts at theorising law's unity need a means to understand their own self-contradictions, which is where Luhmann's approach to legal theory, and law more generally, steps in. Our standard approach to Kelsen's 'pure theory' here, excluding the possibility of treating it as an example of realism or empiricism, is challenged by some: see, for example, the essays in Part II of Luis Duarte d'Almeida et al. (eds.), *Kelsen Revisited: New Essays on the Pure Theory of Law* (Oxford: Hart Publishing, 2013), 'Law's Empirical Existence'.

3 Most of Hart's analysis is captured in his book H.L.A. Hart, *The Concept of Law* (Oxford: Clarendon Press, 1961, 2nd edition with a 'Postscript' reply to criticisms, 1994). The critique presented here, of the absence of sociology, is tellingly constructed by Peter Fitzpatrick in his *The Mythology of Modern Law* (London: Routledge, 1992) especially 192–210.

4 Luhmann offered observations concerning other approaches to law, including in particular those of Natural Law theorising, but as one would expect in relation to contemporary law, a positivist focus is predominant.

5 Following the publication of the first of these, Niklas Luhmann, *Rechtssoziologie* in 1972, and the second edition in 1983, he also published a number of other books focused on law; see Niklas Luhmann, *Rechtssysteme und Rechtsdogmatik* (Stuttgart: Kohlhammer, 1974) and Niklas Luhmann, *Ausdifferenzierung des Rechts* (Frankfurt am Main: Suhrkamp, 1981).

6 Luhmann, *A Sociological Theory of Law*.

7 Niklas Luhmann, *Law as a Social System*. English edition translated by K.A. Ziegert (Oxford: Oxford University Press, 2004). Originally published in German: Niklas Luhmann, *Das Recht der Gesellschaft* (Frankfurt am Main: Suhrkamp, 1993).

8 A shift acknowledged by Luhmann himself, Luhmann, *A Sociological Theory of Law*, 281–8.

9 Though the reasons for that rejection differ according to different theories, beyond the simple rejection offered by John Austin in the 19th century: 'The existence of law is one thing; its merit or demerit is another …' *The Province of Jurisprudence Determined* (originally published in 1832, London: Weidenfeld and Nicolson, 1995), 184–5.

10 Luhmann, *A Sociological Theory of Law*, 17.

11 Ibid., 38–40.

12 Ibid., 34–6.

13 '[…] those decisions are legitimate where one can assume that any third parties expect normatively that the directly affected persons cognitively prepare themselves for what the decision-makers communicate as normative expectations.' Ibid., 201.

14 Ibid., 82. And it is this, rather than other characteristics offered by other positivist legal theorists, that Luhmann highlights, for example: 'Law is in no way primarily a coercive order, but rather a facilitation of expectation.' Ibid., 78.

15 Hart, for example, as mentioned in our earlier text, focused (as a thought experiment) on problems that needed to be solved for law to reach its current form within nation state orders, and then defined the structures which he found there as a central case of legal rules within a legal system.

16 Gradually Luhmann's analysis moves from that of Parsons. Whilst Parsons sought to identify the functions executed for society by existing structures (structural functionalism) Luhmann gave priority to the identification of functions (functional structuralism), treating structures as possible and contingent solutions to the problems that needed to be overcome for society to achieve greater complexity. (For a fuller account, see Hans Joas and Wolfgang Knöbl, *Social Theory: Twenty Introductory Lectures* (Cambridge: Cambridge University Press, 2004), ch.XI).

17 Luhmann, *A Sociological Theory of Law*, 276–7.

18 In *LSS* Luhmann distinguishes between the function of law and its performances. The function of law (generating symbolically generalised normative expectations) accompanies every performance and remains law's primary contribution to the evolution of functionally differentiated society. But 'mere' performances are not uniform. Sometimes law performs a dispute resolution role, but at other times it creates conflicts that would not otherwise exist. Law manages risks, but also creates risks (e.g. bankruptcy) that would not otherwise exist, etc.

19 Luhmann, *A Sociological Theory of Law*, 281.

20 Niklas Luhmann, *Social Systems* (Stanford: Stanford University Press, 1995). Originally published in German as Niklas Luhmann, *Soziale Systeme: Grundriß einer allgemeinen Theorie* (Frankfurt am Main: Suhrkamp, 1984).

21 Luhmann, *A Sociological Theory of Law*, 277.

22 Luhmann, *Social Systems*, 12.
23 '[...] the validity of law is founded not on unity but on difference. It cannot be seen, it cannot be "found"– it is the ongoing reproduction of law's difference.' Luhmann, *Law as a Social System*, 262.
24 Ibid., 445. The tautology being that law is law, or perhaps that the legal is not illegal, etc.
25 Ibid., 122.
26 Ibid., 106.
27 Luhmann, *A Sociological Theory of Law*, 2nd edition conclusion, 284.
28 Luhmann, *Law as a Social System*, 458 and 459 – a fuller account is found throughout chapter 11, 'The Self-Description of the Legal System'.
29 Luhmann, *Law as a Social System*, 425.
30 Ibid., 425. An assumption that drives law's continued evolution, through productive attempts to disguise and defer the underlying paradox that law has no ultimate foundation for the application of the legal code.
31 We have explored more fully elsewhere how the introduction of detailed and frequent legislation represented a stage at which self-description in the form of law as an unchanging entity ceased to facilitate the orderly evolution of the legal system, but operated instead to block everyday legal operations, viz. statutory interpretation. At this stage, self-description evolved into communications about legal sources as authoritative rather than evidence of reason. Within the common law system, precedent changed its nature, becoming described, like legislation, as communication that binds through authority, not reason. And with these changes, the object of general jurisprudence altered, and natural law theories lost some of their explanatory power and substantially gave way to positivist legal theories that sought to explain law in terms of authoritative sources. This corresponds with the move toward societal functional differentiation. See Richard Nobles and David Schiff, *A Sociology of Jurisprudence* (Oxford: Hart Publishing, 2006), ch. 3.
32 Luhmann, *A Sociological Theory of Law*, 2nd edition conclusion, 286.
33 Luhmann, *Law as a Social System*, 62. He cites Locke and Hobbes as two examples of this, and Grotius and Pufendorf as two exceptions.
34 The sociological aspects of such an endeavour require an awareness of the possibilities of different relationships between philosophical jurisprudence and self-description in different jurisdictions. In particular, one needs to look at the different role played by the universities on the continent in comparison with the UK and other common law jurisdictions. Just as doctrine, as developed within continental universities was routinely re-incorporated into the legal system, so too jurisprudence developed within the universities finds more of its way back into the legal system.
35 Niklas Luhmann, 'The Third Question: The creative Use of Paradoxes in Law and Legal History', *Journal of Law and Society* 15, no. 2 (1998): 153.
36 'Hence a critique of [legal] conceptions requires the return to the problems to be solved, and this leads to the question of functionally equivalent constructions.' Luhmann, *Law as a Social System*, 342.
37 Hart sets out this argument in Hart, *The Concept of Law*, particularly chapters IV and VII.
38 As Ronald Dworkin rightly observed in his criticism of the rule of recognition, a statement that most or all judges hold to a common standard when identifying legal rules is not a normative claim or even a recognised legal argument. See Ronald Dworkin, *Taking Rights Seriously* (Cambridge, MA: Harvard University Press, 1977).

39 See our article Richard Nobles and David Schiff, 'Why do Judges Talk the Way They do?', *International Journal of Law in Context* 5, no. 1 (2009): 25, 49.

40 And, as pointed out by many, circular, as the officials whose internal attitudes identify the sources of law are themselves identified as officials by the laws which they identify.

41 See Kelsen, 'On the Pure Theory of Law'.

42 Luhmann, *A Sociological Theory of Law*, 2nd edition conclusion, 285.

43 Luhmann, *Law as a Social* System, 431. That said, Luhmann refers to McCormick's institutional theory of law as doing exactly that. But, as a warning about the limits of conceptual analysis, and support for the critique offered here about self-contradiction in so much positivist legal theory, see Brian Leiter, 'Legal Realism, Hard Positivism, and the Limits of Conceptual Analysis', in *Naturalizing Jurisprudence*, ed. Brian Leiter (Oxford: Oxford University Press, 2007), 121–36.

44 Disagreement on the importance and nature of legal argumentation lies at the heart of Dworkin's criticism of both Hartian positivism and the critical legal studies movement, but also Hart's criticism of the US Realist movement. It is, in other words, a substantial ground for critique and often takes the form of the potential self-contradictions within each theory. For our critique of self-contradiction within Dworkin's legal theory, see Richard Nobles and David Schiff, 'The Emperor's New Clothes', *The Modern Law Review* 70 (2007): 139–60.

45 Redundancies (which Luhmann also described as 'attractors'): 'organize the processing of information. [...] [they] function as "values". One prefers to be guided by them because otherwise the loss of order, the "chaos" would be unbearable'. (Luhmann, *Law as a Social System*, 317–8).

46 Luhmann, *Law as a Social System*, 318–9.

47 Considering the implications for a system's redundancy provides a potentially more telling basis for understanding issues arising when courts decide on the meaning of rules (including the rule of recognition) than Hart's suggestion, reliant as it is on linguistic philosophy, of a core and penumbra of linguistic usage.

48 Luhmann, *Law as a Social System*, 340.

49 Ibid., 342.

Chapter 4

NIKLAS LUHMANN ON POLITICS AND THE ECONOMY IN TWENTY-FIRST CENTURY'S WORLD SOCIETY

Aldo Mascareño

Niklas Luhmann died in 1998. For illustrative purposes, it is an interesting exercise to remember what the world's concerns were at that time. These were the days of the raw conflict in Kosovo, of the discussions on banning human cloning particularly in Europe. It was also the era of the Clinton–Lewinsky affair, the planning of attacks on Saddam Hussein's Iraq for violations of peace agreements, and the long and winding trip of weapons inspectors through Iraq. India and Pakistan, countries that tested nuclear weapons and threatened each other, while US embassies in Tanzania and Kenya were bombed, presumably by Osama bin Laden. The 1997 Asian economic crisis hit Latin America strongly in 1998; with massive capital outflows and sharp currency depreciations, plunging the region into a crisis that lasted until 2003. In 1998, the Rome Statute was adopted by 120 States (and later ratified by 60 countries giving birth to the International Criminal Court in 2002), and 1998 was also the year in which the former Chilean dictator Augusto Pinochet was indicted and arrested by a Spanish magistrate in London for human rights violations committed during the military dictatorship that ruled Chile between 1973 and 1989. In 1998, Hugo Chávez was elected president in Venezuela, introducing the 'socialism of the twenty first century' to the world, a populist political system with ramifications relevant for Latin America even today. And if all that were not enough, Google was officially launched in 1998.

Turbulent and critical times *far from equilibrium*, as we may say in the language of complex systems.[1] The chronological end of the twentieth century is closer to the entangled and contradictory dynamics of the twenty-first century than to the Cold War deflationary bloc politics that prevailed since 1945.

Historically, it can be said that the twentieth century came to an end with the fall of the Berlin Wall, the disintegration of the Soviet Union, and the rise of the internet in the early 1990s. With this, politics and economy were released as world social systems in a twofold sense. First, they were freed from the structural and semantic forces that had contained their expansion, namely, the compulsion to understand every political operation as either supporting communism or capitalism and every economic operation as a question of capital or work. And second, through the quantum leap of the internet, both systems were finally released from the constraints of geography; not only were commercial and financial transactions now possible without face-to-face interaction but also the discovery of the immediacy of political communication affected the very foundation of representation and democracy as we had known it in previous decades. The financial crisis of 2008 and the political upheavals around the world in 2011 count as the first crises of the new political and economic world order; the massive migratory flows into Central Europe in 2015 and from Central America to USA and South America in 2018, created the conditions for the second one, while in 2020, the COVID-19 pandemic confirms that in the twenty-first century we are living close to the edge.

In one of his last articles on the topic of world society written in the mid-1990s, Niklas Luhmann accurately perceived the *Zeitgeist* of the coming century. The general impression is that the die is cast:

> If, on the other hand, we see functional differentiation, our description will point to the autonomy of the function systems, to their high degree of indifference, coupled to high sensitivity and irritability in very specific respects that vary from system to system. Then, we will see a society without top and without centre; a society that evolves but cannot control itself. And then, the calamity is no longer exploitation and suppression but *neglect*. [...] Today, the problem is much worse than before. We may continue with our habits and resort to moral claims that are as justified as ever. But who will hear these complaints and who can react to them, if the society is not in control of itself? And what can we expect when we know that the very success of the function systems depends upon neglect?[2]

By drawing on central books of Luhmann on politics and the economy as social systems and by confronting key concepts present in these works with some critical events in world society in the last two decades, I argue that for structural, semantic, and technological reasons, politics and the economy have intensified their pace in twenty-first century as world social systems, but in so doing, their levels of neglect have increased – namely, their unintended inattention to external demands – so that they are not in a position to control the consequences of their own success. As a result, politics and the economy have become highly unstable social systems, working far from being in equilibrium and are prone to critical transitions and sudden regime shifts.

In order to unfold this argument, in the next two sections, I present Luhmann's fundamental concepts used in his analyses of politics and the economy. For this, I follow the lines of two of his major books: *Die Politik der Gesellschaft* (2000) and *Die Wirtschaft der Gesellschaft* (1988).[3] In a third section, I then critically assess the capacity of Luhmann's concepts by applying them in an account of three major events in the twenty-first century: the 2008 financial crisis, the political upheavals in 2011, and the COVID-19 pandemic in 2020, and supplementing this analysis with new theoretical insights from complexity theories. As I will try to show, while neglect is crucial for the functioning of systems, it increases the political and economic instability of world society, so that, as Luhmann himself points out, one of the consequences of functional differentiation is that 'we even have to expect more or less permanent crisis in some of the subsystems'[4] in twenty-first century.

Luhmann's Analysis of Politics

The basic concept of politics as a social system in Luhmann's account is power. Power is neither defined with reference to causality (*A*'s effect on *B*) nor comprehended in relation to the intention or will of the 'power holder'. There are no ontological assumptions in Luhmann's conception of power so that 'something like "power" must first exist in order to create a power-based system'.[5] Power is rather a *medium* that offers an answer to the question of how to transform uncertainty into certainty, and loosely coupled elements into tightly coupled forms (influence, decisions, orders).

Influence is a general form of power. Luhmann distinguishes three forms of influence: absorption of insecurity (communication of inferences from evidence), positive sanctions (e.g., payments in money), and negative sanctions, from which political power as a symbolically generalised medium of communication arises. Negative sanctions are communicated by means of threats, yet it is crucial that threats are not realised, for their factual execution cancels out power. This is precisely the role of the medium political power: to presuppose the threat as a constantly absent presence in the communication process in order to realise the power. In Luhmann's words, the sociological reference problem of power reads as follows:

> An alternative is construed which the power holder does not wish to realise but which is less unpleasant for him than for the person subject to power, such

> as the exercise of physical violence, the disclosure of unpleasant information, or dismissal. The medium power only functions if both sides understand the alternative and want to avoid it. Power therefore only functions based on fiction, an unrealised second reality.[6]

The most universally generalisable form of threat is physical violence, and this is crucial for the differentiation of modern politics and the territorial state. Through power, the political system can operationally close itself and accomplish its modern *function*, namely, to produce collectively binding decisions. This means that the political system communicates decisions (forms) that work as a premise for new decisions (they are binding) in a manner (collectively) that can only be achieved through organisation. In modern democracies, this process is codified into the form government/opposition and organised by means of elections wherein the public of the system decides who occupies the corresponding positions.

Another central concept of modern politics is that of the *state*, which Luhmann conceives as a self-indication of political orders, that is, when political communication refers to the state, it refers to the unity of the political system.[7] Other concepts that accomplish a similar role are representation, sovereignty, democracy, and the welfare state,[8] yet the concept of state is crucial to understand the form of politics in contemporary world society. While the political system is a functionally differentiated world system, it is in turn internally differentiated into territorial states. States are equal segments of the functionally differentiated system of politics. They produce regional differences in the functioning of social systems, but at the same time they allow for the inclusion of world perspectives into regional contexts. In Luhmann's view: 'the segmentation of the global political system into states protects the dynamics of other functional systems without ruling out regional effects of different political trajectories and constraints'.[9]

Finally, there is a set of *structural couplings* (stabilised interdependencies between systems) that, in its evolution politics develops with other functional systems. Structural couplings are relevant for functional systems because they allow for adaptation to environmental conditions. By bringing to the fore the relevant environment for the focal system, they avoid that autopoietic operations turning into a solipsistic autarchy. One important structural coupling (it deserves special attention according to Luhmann) is *public opinion*. It is a coupling of politics with the system of the mass media and works for politics 'as a medium for a second order observation',[10] that is, as observation of observations. Through public opinion, politics can observe and re-create political communication, refer to political publics, assess political actions, differentiate themes and contributions, process consensus and dissensus, attribute communication to specific sources and continuously cope with the unity of the system – namely, with its boundaries. To that extent, public opinion is not the opinion of individuals, but a medium for political operations.

Other couplings of politics have been historically developed with systems that contribute to an informed accomplishment of the political function. These include structural couplings with the economy through taxes, with law through the constitution, and with science through counselling.[11]

Luhmann's Analysis of the Economy

In the Preface to *Die Wirtschaft der Gesellschaft* Luhmann explains that, since every economic operation is part of society, it makes no sense to speak of economy *and* society as if they were separate entities. Hence the title of the first volume in the series of books on the theory of society: The Economy of Society. Luhmann expresses the intention of bringing second-order cybernetics into a theory of self-referential systems, thereby breaking with the traditional perspective of observing the economy as 'political economy'. He begins his analysis of the economy with the concept of prices. Prices are information on which payments unfold; they are the form of communication that in the evolutionary process differentiates an economic system. Prices change over time; they are unstable yet temporarily fixed, so they allow for price formation and payments. To that extent, an operationally closed economic system is not characterised by an equilibrium (it works rather *far from equilibrium*); but controls its own instability through instability.[12]

Self-referential economic communication operates with a binary code payment/non payment, which allows for the specification of the function of the economy as the connection between present distribution and future provision of goods, services and money. It enables the economic system to deal with scarcity of goods and services, on the one hand, and to operate with money, on the other. In Luhmann's theory, this is called 'duplication of scarcity'.[13] The classical concept of 'satisfaction of needs' is in his view an outcome of the system, not its function. The circular flow of goods and services in one direction while money flows in the opposite direction is reinterpreted in terms of capacity and incapacity of payments, which characterises the operative closure of the system and its openness: the environment is assessed in terms of payments, for which a radical de-moralisation of the system is historically required.[14] Scarcity is, according to Luhmann, a *contingency formula* which he defines as a concept that allows the economy to observe the unity of the system. Thus, the problem the economy confronts 'is the social problem of the suffering that arises from the scarcity caused by others'.[15] The economy manages scarcity in the temporal dimension by connecting present scarcity with future provision.

While for classical theories the concept of *market* is considered a synonym for the economy or economic system, for Luhmann, the market is a communicative device that provides for an internal environment of the economic system wherein participants can mutually observe each other with the help of prices.[16] The market is different for every participant (there are different markets) yet the same for everyone (the market as internal environment of the economy). It is a tool for the second-order observing of the economy, the equivalent of public opinion in politics.

The complexity of the modern economy shows why for Luhmann it is insufficient – if not mistaken – to observe the system with old schemes such as rich and poor or capital and labour. In so doing, there is always an excluded third (labour in the case of the rich/poor distinction, and consumption in the case of capital/labour) that remains outside the equation, who (or what) is relevant to the operation.[17] Through the concept of money as a symbolically generalised medium of communication (the equivalent of power to politics), the economy can be conceived differently.

Money improves the success of communication with its capacity for symbolisation: it makes it possible for the ego to accept (or reject) the premises of alter's behaviour, just because alter pays (or not) the price.[18] For this to happen, money has to produce a strong connection between motivation and social selectivity. It has to turn people to prefer money instead of the independent use of their goods or work. Only if money succeeds in motivating towards money, exchange emerges in the form of a monetary economy. For the one who pays (alter), the action of buying allows for the satisfaction of needs; for the one who sells (ego), the reception of money means freedom of future use in the satisfaction of needs. But money does not only involve these two; symbolic generalisation also implies that all those who observe this relationship (the excluded third), accept it (they are included) – that is, they accept their exclusion of the possibility of using a good just because others pay for it. The symbolic generalisation of money constitutes, therefore, a form of social pacification: it makes the social selectivity of others tolerable. But money also separates, it is not only symbolic but also diabolic,[19] that is, it produces multiple differences, inequalities, asymmetries and criticism. For Luhmann, such exclusions and differences characterise the functionally differentiated world society in general. In the economic system differences, risks and dangers associated with the use of money are part of the everyday experience when dealing with economic affairs.

Finally, a relevant consideration for the relationship between economy and politics is what Luhmann calls 'the limits of steering'.[20] Since politics and the economy are functionally differentiated social systems, with their own organisations and decision-making processes, external regulation is a difficult endeavour, even as a programme for the reduction of differences. The self-regulation of the economy confirms this, and it is further confirmed by the fact that when politics seeks to regulate it, it can only create contextual conditions that then appear as economic self-regulation. There are structural couplings, but external regulation is either rejected or results in self-regulation, or, in the worst case, it leads to the collapse of systems' autonomy.

Discussion

Are these conceptual descriptions adequate to understand the initial decades of the twenty-first century? Are these technical terms such as symbolically generalised media of communication, structural coupling, operationally closed system, second-order observing, control of instability through instability or duplication of scarcity, to name a few, up to the task? How much has changed the 'world' of the world society, considering that in the 1990s politicians, entrepreneurs and even scholars still were talking about the First, Second and Third World?

In the Introduction, I made the proposition that the twenty-first century began in 1990. The end of the Cold War, with its heavy semantic and structural burdens and the rise of the internet, had a liberating impact on many political and economic operations that were semantically and technologically constrained in the constitution of functional systems. Functional differentiation at the world level intensified its pace under these conditions. In my view, Luhmann's announcement in 1997 that 'the problem is much worse than before' and that the contemporary 'calamity is no longer exploitation and suppression but *neglect*'[21] perfectly match with this intensification of functional differentiation in the last decades – namely, with an increase in globalisation and the *mondialisation*[22] and instability of social systems, as well as with their tendency to produce sudden regime shifts.[23]

While considering three major critical events in the twenty-first century, the 2008 financial crisis, the 2011 political upheavals, and the 2020 pandemic, I argue that Luhmann's descriptions of politics and the economy as social systems are suited well in giving a general account on the global behaviour of these systems, yet the descriptions need to be supplemented by an analysis of the relationship between the digital matrix of the world society (networked digital technologies and AI) and the increase in unpredictability of communication dynamics.[24]

The financial crisis in 2008

There is no doubt that Luhmann knew the risks of financial markets. Certainly, all the descriptions about the instability of prices, the connection between present distribution and future provision of goods, services, and money, the paradox resolution of the problem of scarcity, the market as a second-order observation and the symbolic and diabolic generalisation of money are adequate to illuminate that contemporary financial markets are a part of the economic system.

Financial markets deal with the instability of the price of money through the instability of risks. They connect the present scarcity of money with the future provision of it by producing promises of future money. They also constitute a communicative space of mutual observation – namely, the financial market – composed of traditional banks, financial banks, insurance and reinsurance institutions, and multiple financial instruments (derivatives). Financial markets even became a centre of the contemporary economic system 'in relation to which all other activities such as production, services, labour, exchange occur on the periphery'.[25] And finally, they produce a connection between motivation and social selectivity that is so successful that it is difficult to resist the magic of creating money out of nothing – which, in turn, is the very same basis for the diabolic effects of the crisis. Put in other words, at this general level, Luhmann's theory of the economy can perfectly cope with the form of this crisis. And yet, his description of the dynamics of risks in this system seems to be somewhat insufficient after the critical events in 2008:

> The banks assume and mitigate this risk. It thus becomes a risk of their own decisions. They have to check the creditworthiness of their debtors and may make mistakes. They invest their own money, often in productive investments, and expose themselves to the corresponding risks. They can speculate in financial markets – and whether they do it or not: in both cases it is possible to regret the decision.[26]

Organisationally, there are not only 'banks', but credit banks, investment banks, insurance and reinsurance companies, investor companies, rating agencies, brokers and an indefinite number (indefinite because the system permanently creates more) of investment tools, the derivatives, that are electronically construed and managed. Technically, it is not that banks 'may make mistakes' in assessing the creditworthiness of their clients. As we know from the risk management techniques of the crisis, non-creditworthy clients are included in triple *A* CDOs so that their risk becomes distributed.[27] And operatively, even though 'speculation' is part of the old semantic tradition of the economy – a figure devoid of the materiality of goods and labour[28] – it is a semantic device for designing the *modus operandi* of financial markets.

It seems, therefore, that the logic of contemporary financial markets does not change the basic principles of the functioning of the economy, but rather radicalises them. At the centre of this radicalisation are the electronic derivatives. As Elena Esposito has argued, derivatives 'are the extreme implementation of economic rationality'.[29] They do not refer to goods, but to the risk of a transaction which will be executed in the future. Dealing with risk intensifies, thus, instability: 'It produces a "leverage" that multiplies profits and damages, because it allows one to "free" oneself from a reference to the world. When risking on risk, one only has to deal with uncertainty and its trends'.[30] A market that only copes with risk, that distributes and exchanges them electronically in the form of future prices is a new development of this century. As Haldane and May have argued, there is no major risk when the supply of derivatives meets true hedging demand, however, beyond this point derivatives become unbounded:

> so long as there is an incentive to supply new instruments – a positive premium to trading – banks will continue to expand gross positions, independent of true hedging demand from non-banks. Such trades are essentially redundant, increasing the dimensionality and complexity of the network at a cost in terms of stability, with no welfare gain because market completeness has already been achieved.[31]

The consequence is that each bank is safer, but the systemic risk increases. Depending on the topology of the network, the whole system may collapse, particularly if risks models and operations are homogenous.[32] In this case, positive feedback deviations accumulate and result in a critical transition or a sudden regime shift in which 'the dynamics of the system accelerate dramatically to cause a runaway change'.[33] The sociological tradition has called this *crisis*; in the language of contemporary complexity theories, they are theorised and empirically analysed as *critical transitions*.[34] The most relevant message of these theories for sociology is that collapse and regime shifts in social systems – such as the 2008 financial crisis – do not come from the outside, but from the very same logic of functioning that distinguishes them.[35] Jacques Derrida ascribes *autoimmunity* to this self-destructive yet immanent logic of neglect of different social systems.[36]

Political upheavals in 2011

Possibly, future historians will observe 2011 as the year of the first reaction of the new *normative consciousness* of modernity in the twenty-first century. Of course, there were warning signals before that point, such as the Colour Revolution in several countries of the former Soviet Union starting with Yugoslavia in 2000, and the riots in the Parisian periphery in 2005.

But 2011 saw a dynamic wave of social movements reacting against systemic neglect worldwide: the Occupy Wallstreet, the Indignados, riots in Central Europe and Latin America, and certainly the Arab Spring were the decentred expressions that surpassed the threshold. The massive migrations from Middle East to Europe in 2015, from Central America to the United States in 2018, and the exodus from the collapsed states of Haiti and Venezuela to different countries in Latin American was the corollary of this political regime shift. In a nutshell, people did not find motivation only in survival, but in the fulfilment of normative expectations that modernity itself had first promised and then neglected.[37]

As in the case of the economy, I see no major difficulties in understanding contemporary politics in light of Luhmann's basic political concepts. States have not renounced negative sanctions; they have probably increased the use of physical force to quell riots, thereby degrading their own power, but threats remain as a 'civilised' substitute for violence. They still make collectively binding decisions, even with renewed enthusiasm during the COVID-19 pandemic, and draw the distinction between government and opposition, at least in democratic countries. States also remain being segments of the world political system, and despite efforts to build supranational political regions – democratically as in Europe, violently as in the Islamic State – classic states continue mediating between regional and world perspectives. Finally, regarding structural couplings, we still pay taxes, have a constitution, deal with the counselling technocracy and suffer from irrelevant public opinions. But then again, where is the basis for the synchronic intensification of social and political movements in the last years? While for Luhmann in the 1990s, television is the most relevant mass media for politics, digital social media are nowadays at the centre of the new developments:

> If one wants to assess the function and meaning of 'states' at the end of this millennium, it is advisable to start from the concept of world society. The fact of a worldwide communication system cannot be denied. The new communication technologies and *especially television* have a political impact. The place where one is located loses its role as a condition of possibility of seeing and hearing.[38]

If in Luhmann's quotation, the term 'television' is replaced by 'digital social media', the argument does not change at all, but the social and political consequences of depending either on unilateral communication technologies such as the television, on the one hand, or on the multidirectional social networks, on the other, are sociologically significant. When it comes to social media, political events intensify, accelerate, move far from equilibrium, are unpredictable, and are prone to sudden changes.

The upheavals in Egypt and Tunisia in 2011 are a good example of the significant role of social media in contemporary politics. YouTube, Facebook, Twitter, Google Maps, bloggers and activists, even online-dating sites, mobile phones and SMS networks were used to inform the people what national television did not show and to organise political actions and resistance: 'social media have become the scaffolding upon which civil society can build, and new information technologies give activists things that they did not have before: information networks not easily controlled by the state and coordination tools that are already embedded in trusted networks of family and friends'.[39]

Of course, this is not the only case. BlackBerry Messenger and Twitter were important in the 2011 UK in organising and supporting riots,[40] as in the Chilean case in the same year, when SMS, emails, Twitter, Facebook, Instagram, Fotolog, were used for coordination, convening and organisation of political actions.[41] The mentions can multiply for the following years and events, for example, the Catalunya referendum in 2017,[42] the Syrian refugee crisis[43] and Brexit.[44] Digital social media do not change the nature of the coupling between politics and diffusion media, but they include new second-order observers into the realm of public opinion who, in turn, introduce random communicative variations into the system, thereby increasing its unpredictable dynamics. The 'public' of the Luhmannian distinction between politics, administration and public[45] takes a more active role. It is no longer only visible in elections and can be conceived of as the butterfly that finally pushes the system beyond the critical threshold into the slippery slope of a critical transition or regime shift.

The COVID-19 pandemic

Undoubtedly, the experience of the COVID-19 pandemic is relevant for every social system. However, for politics, economy and the digital matrix of world society, it is a kind of social 'natural experiment' wherein some aspects of the functioning of these systems are brought to the fore and others are pushed into the background. The consequence is the re-entry of instability into instability, that is, the regular instability of every operationally closed social system is disturbed and reordered by the instability coming from the environment.

In the case of politics, the function of making collectively binding decisions has been continuously accomplished by politics and became overt to everyone. Yet, decisions made by states in the early stages of the pandemic such as physical distancing, reclusion, limits on public meetings, restrictions on mobility and commerce, and the closing of borders as well, affected directly interaction systems and organisations in every functioning system, from sports and tourism to economy and law. Following the imperative of saving lives, only the minimum was allowed to function.[46] This minimum had a name: the essential workers. The essential workers are the paradox of the decision, that is, to protect lives, some lives could be sacrificed. The essential workers are the included-excluded-third of the equation.

Perfectly visible is also the intermediate role of the state between regional communication and world perspectives. This role has become highly relevant, because the process of deciding on lockdown measures relies, first, on the mutual observation among states in public opinion, and second, on the coupling with the world system of science in activities of counselling. The geographic chronology of the contagion (from the East to the rest) made it possible for states to observe prior reactions in far regions, process them in regional public opinion and adapt them to local circumstances considering the structural and semantic landscape of each political *milieu*. Yet, at the same time, the social and demographic structures of every country change the dynamics of contagion, so that the imitation of measures taken in other regions may also introduce instability and produce unexpected consequences in the ways of dealing with the pandemic in local contexts. Through counselling, in turn, the state couples with the system of science to produce useful knowledge to make decisions – or at least to create the fiction that lockdown measures were taken on a solid basis. However, since Popper, we know that science works with provisional truths, so that counselling may change its recommendations every day according to the results of scientific conjectures and refutations.

As a consequence of the state-led lockdown measures, every social system was affected, but while politics could accomplish its function, it was increasingly difficult for the economy to connect the present distribution of goods, services and money with its future provision, that is, scarcity got completely out of hand. According to experts, the recession that is now underway could be greater than the crisis in 2008.[47] The legal system begins to be overloaded with claims of all kinds, from the termination of national and international contracts due to *force majeure*, to labour claims of varying scope.[48] And because complex crises are crises without solution, no government or political system can get it right, so the deflationary trend of trust in systemic politics remains – despite the sublime efforts of New Zealand's prime minister Jacinda Ardern.

Another form of reintroducing instability through lockdown measures derives from the paradox of their claim: they require to rule out physical interaction and physical presence in organisations, but functional communication is expected to continue.[49] From one day to another, everyone – with the exception of the essential workers – has to move online. However, connectivity, as any other opportunity for social inclusion in world society,[50] is not equally distributed. Economy, education, arts, law, intimacy, even politics transform the physical presence of interaction systems and organisations into digital presence. That this was possible without the entire collapse of society, shows that the digital matrix of world society has reached high levels of development and technological sophistication, but at the same time it adds another layer to the production of systemic neglect: world zones of inclusion and exclusion are now not only real, but they are even more real, that is, digital.

Conclusions

In this chapter, I presented Niklas Luhmann's basic concepts on politics and the economy and assessed the capacity of Luhmann's theory to deal with new developments in these social systems in the twenty-first century. I have argued that structural, semantic and technological transformations that started in the last decades of the twentieth century, such as the end of the Cold War and the rise of the internet, have intensified the unpredictable dynamics of politics and the economy in the world society. These systems increased their levels of neglect, namely, their unintended inattention to demands beyond their particular modes of observation and become unstable social systems prone to critical transitions and sudden regime shifts. Several conclusions emerge from my analysis.

First, Luhmann's account of politics and the economy as social systems accurately describes the functioning of these systems in the present century. Because it is based on fundamental concepts such as complexity, contingency, uncertainty, and risk, social systems theory is highly sensitive to the unpredictable dynamics of the contemporary world society. This is supplemented by basic concepts at the level of sociological theory to describe social dynamics – such as symbolically generalised media of communication, self-reference, function, second-order observation, internal environment, semantics, structural couplings – that construe a highly flexible theoretical framework to comprehend the continuities and discontinuities of social systems today.

Second, while Luhmann's theory perfectly captures instability in the functioning of modern social systems, his historical analyses take into consideration social processes and events until the end of the twentieth century. Therefore, it is worth asking whether new events, such as the end of the Cold War and the rise of the internet, the digital matrix of world society, have an impact on both the conditions of political and economic instability in contemporary world society, as well as on the ability of systems theory to provide a plausible interpretation of novel situations. A relevant consequence for politics of the end of the Cold War is the intensification of mutual state observation. The end of bloc politics increases the diversity of states and, therefore provides politics with new regional perspectives for observing world events. The internal segmentary differentiation of functionally differentiated world politics, as proposed by Luhmann, becomes denser and less semantically robust than in the ideological divide of the Cold War. The connection of this with the rise and diversity of social and protest movements in the twenty-first century is rather obvious.

Third, less obvious for systems theory is the form in which the digital matrix of world society affects politics and the economy. Although Niklas Luhmann was fully aware of the increasing importance of electronic media for contemporary world society, the stage of development of those media in the early 1990s was radically different from today's sophistication. Luhmann's references to this topic are related to growing storage capacity, some reflections on data processing, and a rather thin concept of artificial intelligence.[51] As Elena Esposito has shown, the world of derivatives in financial markets can be decoded using Luhmann's fundamental concepts, but the intensity and complexity of financial dynamics is a new boundary condition for the contemporary world economy.[52] Something similar can be said about the coupling of digital social media with politics and other social systems, as the political upheavals of 2011 and the sudden online migration of almost every functional system due to the COVID-19 pandemic have shown.

Fourth, because there are no ontological foundations, instability is a trademark of social systems. Since social systems are communication systems, the dislocation of communication as a result of the introduction of a set of new media, such as the numerous platforms contained in the digital matrix of world society, intensifies its unpredictable dynamics. Immediacy, de-centrality, volatility, interactivity, ubiquity and the mobility of social media reintroduces instability into the immanent instability of communication. Not every aspect, but relevant dimensions of the 2008 financial crisis, of the 2011 political upheavals and the fears and burdens of the 2020 pandemic are related to this increasing instability of world communication.

Finally, instability in systems far from equilibrium is a result of diversity and increasing connectivity. Since the 2008 financial crisis, the economy has learnt that homogeneity – all the banks applying the same risk models – combined with high connectivity is a recipe for disaster. In 2011, world politics learnt that by means of rising diversity the robustness of state-induced homogeneity can be overcome. And in 2020, all social systems realised that it is not impossible to coordinate the functioning of diverse social systems under the imperative of saving lives; however, they also realised that this deferral of their own operations cannot last too long. Put in other words, when diversity rules, systems have to control instability through their own instability. This is the irony of politics and the economy as social systems in contemporary world society.

Notes

1 Ilya Prigogine, 'Time, Structure, and Fluctuations' (Nobel Lecture), *Science* 201, no. 4358 (1978): 777–85.
2 Niklas Luhmann, 'Globalization or World Society: How to Conceive of Modern Society?', *International Review of Sociology* 7, no. 1 (1 March 1997): 67–79 at 74–5.
3 There is a significant difference between the works written by Luhmann on politics and those addressing the economic system. While the former amounts to eight books, there is only one book on the economy Niklas Luhmann, *Die Wirtschaft der Gesellschaft* (Frankfurt am Main: Suhrkamp, 1988), which, moreover, is largely based on published articles plus a few additional contributions. For Luhmann's basic concepts on economy, I shall rely on this book, while for his concepts on politics, I shall rely on Niklas Luhmann, *Die Politik der Gesellschaft* (Frankfurt am Main: Suhrkamp, 2000). The latter is a posthumous edition published in 2000, as explained by the editor of this book André Kieserling: 'A first version of the text was available in the early 1990s. The publication presented here is based on a computer printout from October 1996' (André Kieserling, 'Editorische Notiz', in *Die Politik der Gesellschaft*, ed. Niklas Luhmann (Frankfurt am Main: Suhrkamp, 2000), 435, translation AM). While there is evidence (notes and references) that the text was to be supplemented by Luhmann, this is the most advanced version on politics as a social system offered by the author. His other books on politics are Niklas Luhmann, *Legitimation durch Verfaren* (Darmstadt: Hermann Luchterhand Verlag, 1969); Niklas Luhmann, *Politische Planung* (Opladen: Westdeutscher Verlag, 1971); Niklas Luhmann, *Macht* (Stuttgart: Ferdinand Enke Verlag, 1975); Niklas Luhmann, *Politische Theorie im Wohlfahrtsstaat* (Wien: Günter Olzog Verlag München, 1981); Niklas Luhmann, *Politische Soziologie* (Berlin: Suhrkamp, 2010); Niklas Luhmann, *Macht im System* (Berlin: Suhrkamp, 2013); Niklas Luhmann, *Protest* (Frankfurt am Main: Suhrkamp, 1996). For further readings on Luhmann's conception of politics in English, see Niklas Luhmann, 'Politics as a Social System', in Niklas Luhmann, *The Differentiation of Society*, trans. Stephen Holmes and Charles Larmore (New York: Columbia University Press, 1982), 138–65; Niklas Luhmann, *Political Theory in the Welfare State* (Berlin: de Gruyter, 1990); Lena Hilkermeier and Mathias Albert, *Observing International Relations: Niklas Luhmann and World Politics* (London: Routledge, 2004); Michael King and Christopher J. Thornhill, *Niklas Luhmann's Theory of Politics and Law* (Basingstoke: Palgrave, 2003); and as regards the economy, see Niklas Luhmann, 'The Economy as a Social System', in Niklas Luhmann, *The Differentiation of Society*, trans. Stephen Holmes and Charles Larmore (New York: Columbia University Press, 1982), 190–226; Ivan A. Boldyrev, 'Economy as a Social System: Niklas Luhmann's Contribution and Its Significance for Economics', *American Journal of Economics and Sociology* 72, no. 2 (2013): 265–92.
4 Niklas Luhmann, 'The Self Description of Society: Crisis Fashion and Sociological Theory', *International Journal of Comparative Sociology* 25, no. 1–2 (1984): 59–72 at 64.
5 Luhmann, *Die Politik der Gesellschaft*, 28. All translations from German into English are by the author of this chapter.
6 Ibid., 47.
7 In Luhmann's words and with a significative emphasis on political action: 'The state, then, is not a subsystem of the political system. It is not the public bureaucracy. It is not only the legal fiction of a collective person to which decisions are attributed. It is the political system reintroduced into the political system as a point of reference for political action' (Luhmann, *Protest*, 166).

8 Luhmann, *Die Politik der Gesellschaft*, 319 et. seq.
9 Ibid., 223.
10 Ibid., 287.
11 Ibid., 382 et. seq.
12 Niklas Luhmann, *Die Wirtschaft der Gesellschaft*, 25; Dirk Baecker, 'Die Wirtschaft der Gesellschaft (1988)', in *Luhmann-Handbuch: Leben–Werk–Wirkung*, ed. Oliver Jahraus et al. (Stuttgart: J.B. Metzler, 2012), 219–23.
13 Luhmann, *Die Wirtschaft der Gesellschaft*, 197.
14 Ibid., 131 et. seq.
15 Ibid., 65.
16 Ibid., 91 et. seq.
17 Ibid., 151 et. seq.
18 Ibid., 230 et. seq.
19 Ibid., 257 et. seq.
20 Ibid., 324.
21 Luhmann, 'Globalization or World Society', 74.
22 Jacques Derrida, 'The "World" of the Enlightenment to Come (Exception, Calculation, Sovereignty)', *Research in Phenomenology* 33, no. 1 (1 January 2003): 9–52.
23 Marten Scheffer, *Critical Transitions in Nature and Society* (Princeton: Princeton University Press, 2009).
24 Dirk Baecker, *4.0 oder Die Lücke die der Rechner lässt* (Berlin: Merve Verlag, 2018). See also Pierpaolo Donati, 'The Digital Matrix and the Hybridisation of Society', in *Post-Human Institutions and Organizations*, ed. Ismael Al-Amoudi and Emmanuel Lazega (London: Routledge, 2018), 67–92.
25 Niklas Luhmann, 'Politics and Economy', *Thesis Eleven* 53 (1998): 1–10 at 3.
26 Luhmann, *Die Wirtschaft der Gesellschaft*, 269.
27 Conghui Hu, Xun Zhang, and Qiuming Gao, 'Synthetic CDO Pricing: The Perspective of Risk Integration', *Applied Economics* 47, no. 15 (28 March 2015): 1574–87.
28 Urs Stäheli, *Spektakuläre Spekulation* (Frankfurt am Main: Suhrkamp, 2007), 363.
29 Elena Esposito, *The Future of Futures: The Time of Money in Financing and Society* (Cheltenham: Edward Elgar, 2011), 94.
30 Ibid., 107.
31 Andrew G. Haldane and Robert M. May, 'Systemic Risk in Banking Ecosystems', *Nature* 469, no. 7330 (2011): 351–5 at 352.
32 Battiston Stefano et al., 'Complexity Theory and Financial Regulation', *Science* 351, no. 6275 (19 February 2016): 818–19.
33 Egbert H. van Nes et al., 'What Do You Mean, "Tipping Point"?', *Trends in Ecology & Evolution* 31, no. 12 (2016): 902–4 at 903.
34 Scheffer, *Critical Transitions in Nature and Society.*
35 Aldo Mascareño, 'Critical Transitions in Ecosystems and Society. The Contribution of Sociological Systems Theory to the Analysis of Socio-Environmental Transformations', *Frontiers in Sociology* 6 (24 January 2022), https://www.frontiersin.org/articles/10.3389/fsoc.2021.763453/full.
36 Jacques Derrida, 'Autoimmunity: Real and Symbolic Suicides', in *Philosophy in a Time of Terror: Dialogues with Jürgen Habermas and Jacques Derrida*, ed. Giovanna Borradori (Chicago and London: The University of Chicago Press, 2003), 85–136.
37 Luhmann addressed this topic as follows: 'We have at any rate to abandon an idea that long dominated in modernization research after World War II, the notion that modernization trends in the individual functional systems, namely, political democracy, the

market-oriented money economy, the rule of law, dogmatically unhampered scientific research, uncensored mass media, school education for the entire population according to individual aptitude, and so on would trigger a wave of development in which the achievements of the various functional systems would mutually support and confirm one another. The contrary is more probable' (Niklas Luhmann, *Theory of Society*, Vol. 1 (Stanford: Stanford University Press, 2012), 343). When promises are not kept, expectations are disappointed, and this in turn produces increasing political tensions that turn into protest against 'the system'. Peter Sloterdijk has expressed this with particular precision: 'Wherever manifestations of the extreme were encountered in the course of the twentieth century, there was always an uprising against complexity, that is, against the formal law of the real as conceived in contemporary terms' (Peter Sloterdijk, *What Happened in the 20th Century?* Translated by Christopher Turner (Cambridge: Polity Press, 2018), 57–8). The twenty first century represents an intensification of this dynamics.

38 Luhmann, *Die Politik der Gesellschaft*, 220.

39 Philip N. Howard and Muzammil M. Hussain, 'The Upheavals in Egypt and Tunisia: The Role of Digital Media', *Journal of Democracy* 22, no. 3 (2011): 35–48 at 48.

40 Paul Lewis et al., *Reading the Riots: Investigating England's Summer of Disorder* (London: The London School of Economics and Political Science and The Guardian, 2011).

41 Violeta Montero Barriga, Carlos Muñoz Labraña, and María Inés Picazo Verdejo, 'Estrategias y Recursos Empleados por el Movimiento Estudiantil en el 2011', *Universum* 32, no. 1 (2017): 137–57.

42 Gonzalo A. Ruz, Pablo A. Henríquez, and Aldo Mascareño, 'Sentiment Analysis of Twitter Data during Critical Events through Bayesian Networks Classifiers', *Future Generation Computer Systems* 106 (2020): 92–104.

43 Nazan Öztürk and Serkan Ayvaz, 'Sentiment Analysis on Twitter: A Text Mining Approach to the Syrian Refugee Crisis', *Telematics and Informatics* 35, no. 1 (1 April 2018): 136–47.

44 Miha Grčar et al., 'Stance and Influence of Twitter Users Regarding the Brexit Referendum', *Computational Social Networks* 4, article 6 (2017), https://computationalsocialnetworks.springeropen.com/articles/10.1186/s40649-017-0042-6#citeas.

45 Luhmann, *Die Politik der Gesellschaft*, 253 et. seq.

46 Rudolf Stichweh, 'Simplifikation des Sozialen', in *Die Corona-Gesellschaft*, ed. Michael Volkmer and Karin Werner (Bielefeld: transcript-Verlag, 2020), 195–206.

47 Adam Tooze, 'Is the Coronavirus Crash Worse than the 2008 Financial Crisis?', *Foreign Policy* 18 (2020): https://foreignpolicy.com/2020/03/18/coronavirus-economic-crash-2008-financial-crisis-worse.

48 Seng Hansen, 'Does the COVID-19 Outbreak Constitute a Force Majeure Event? A Pandemic Impact on Construction Contracts', *Forum. Journal of the Civil Engineering* 6, no. 2 (2020): 201–14.

49 Mauro Basaure, Alfredo Joignant, and Aldo Mascareño, 'Between Distancing and Interdependence: The Conflict of Solidarities in the COVID-19 Pandemic', *Sociological Perspectives* 64, no. 5 (October 2021): 706–25.

50 Niklas Luhmann, 'Inklusion und Exklusion', in Niklas Luhmann, *Soziologische Aufklärung 6. Die Soziologie und der Mensch* (Wiesbaden: VS Verlag für Sozialwissenschaften, 2005), 226–51.

51 Luhmann, *Theory of Society*, Vol. 1, 180 et. seq.

52 Esposito, *The Future of Futures.* See also Elena Esposito, *Artificial Communication. How Algorithms Produce Social Intelligence* (Cambridge, MA: The MIT Press, 2022).

Chapter 5

EPISTEMIC SOCIOLOGY: LUHMANN'S THEORY OF SCIENCE AND KNOWLEDGE

Gert Verschraegen

Introduction

Modern science enjoys an extraordinary authority in explaining 'reality', as well as in looking for solutions to the world's problems. Anyone who does not observe scientific insights and its standards of justification is thrown into defence. Even the Pope must make concessions to scientific thinking, for example, by actively supporting alternatives for using embryos in stem cell research.[1]

In his lengthy book, *Die Wissenschaft der Gesellschaft* (*Science as a Social System*),[2] Niklas Luhmann affirms the exalted prestige and the amazing accomplishments of science, yet at the same time stresses the severe limitations of its perspective and questions its ability to simply dictate rules to other parts of society. Science is just one of the function systems of modern society and hence cannot claim priority over any other fields, including law, politics, economy or religion. While many would like to see politicians developing policies based on scientifically sound facts, or religious leaders wising up and acknowledging scientific realities, the tasks of politics are simply not that of science, and neither are the issues of religion. Each of them requires specific solutions, which cannot just be transferred to other systems. While science can identify problems for politics (e.g., severe nitrogen pollution) and suggest solutions (e.g., reducing livestock production), it cannot tell politics how to find majority support for the latter, just as law cannot instruct the economy how to gain profit.

Throughout his career, Luhmann has emphasised this disappearance of a hierarchy in the structure of society. There is no 'grand narrative' anymore, no worldview, no philosophy and no system that can provide binding references for acting in the world. This also goes for science. Its customarily privileged position over other function systems, for instance in the Enlightenment project or twentieth-century modernist technocracy, can no longer be guaranteed. A common reality, as Enlightenment philosophers envisaged it to emerge out of the proper use of 'reason', is replaced by 'heterarchical' multiple realities, which are subject to continuous change and contingent upon constantly evolving social conditions. Notwithstanding its traditional prestige, scientific knowledge, within this constellation, is thus perceived to be 'only one form of social potency among others', Luhmann writes

> Whether it is economically advantageous, whether it is supported politically, or whether it is suitable for educational purposes, these questions are decided elsewhere [...]. To be sure no one seriously doubts the descriptions of the world furnished by science, insofar as science itself trusts them. Nonetheless, the effect is ultimately non-binding as far as other systems of communication are concerned.[3]

Not even science can provide common ground. Coordination between function systems can only be achieved at the level of second-order observation, given that each observer (whether economic, political, educational, mass media) can observe the observation of others and the differences between them, and this without the possibility or need for mutual references.[4]

It will not surprise avid readers of Luhmann that the systems theoretical formulae, such as functional differentiation and second-order observation, are also applicable to science. Indeed, at one level, Luhmann regards science merely as an area to test the basic premises and concepts of his systems theory. Yet, at another level, science constitutes a special case among the important function systems, because it is an observation position upon which Luhmann's theory itself is conditioned. Being a major sociological description of modern society, his work is firmly positioned within the modern science system. As a scientific observation of society, it is comparable to other descriptions of society (economic, political, religious), yet it is also different in the sense that it is not just 'a position *within* society, it is also a position *about* society. If one wants to know society, one first has to understand the preconditions under which one can develop knowledge *about* society. And where is this position to be found, if not *within* society?'[5]

Hence, it becomes understandable why Luhmann develops a theory of science with a clear sociological and epistemological focus. A sociological theory of science can only be performed within society and is itself a product of one of the systems, namely science, which it analyses, so Luhmann emphasises. An adequate theory of science must hence imply itself, so to speak; it must be able to account for its own observation position within its object of investigation. Luhmann further develops this argument by connecting the functional differentiation of society with the constructivist self-understanding of science.[6] While modern society's form of differentiation enables the emergence of purely scientific description of reality – including the reality of society – science understands itself as but one possible construction among others. Contemporary science's self-understanding thus corresponds to the structure of modern society as functionally differentiated: it is not the ultimate realisation of truth, but a social system with its own specific forms of communication, just like all other social systems. Its 'truth' is not a result of rational deliberation or enlightenment (not a 'Truth' with capital 'T'), but a communicative construct among many. Luhmann acknowledges that this self-understanding has developed only gradually throughout the process of functional differentiation. While the science system's reflection on its own 'identity' initially emphasized the correspondence between the knowing system and the known world (theory of knowledge or 'epistemology'), in the twentieth century the scientific self-reflection started emphasising that scientific knowledge is a historically situated and social construction, which differs from other types of knowledge.

Interestingly, Luhmann started outlining this basic position already in the late 1960s, in an essay called 'The Self-Steering of Science'.[7] Here, science is seen as a system that autonomously steers the production and validation of knowledge, in a way that can be clearly distinguished from the production of meaning and knowledge within politics, economics, the family, and so on. In the late 1970s and early 1980s, consecutive essays appeared on general and interdisciplinary systems science and on the role of scientific theories. Yet, it is only in the late eighties and the nineties that Luhmann really started focusing on the topic of science, first with his famous study on ecological problems,[8] followed by his most comprehensive treatment of science in *Die Wissenschaft der Gesellschaft* – unfortunately not (yet) translated into English – and concluded by the *Sociology of Risk*, which dealt with, among others, the problem of risk and uncertainty in science.[9] Prolific writer as he was, Luhmann also published a number of short essays concerning the university as an everyday working environment, and as the main organisational structure on which science relies.[10]

Important to mention here is that several of Luhmann's students have been greatly inspired by his views on science. Particularly, the work of Rudolf Stichweh deals extensively – and in a more empirically grounded way – with the historical differentiation and evolution of the modern science system and the emergence of scientific disciplines. The work of other sociologists connected to the University of Bielefeld, such as Peter Weingart, Wolfgang

Krohn or Elena Esposito, has also been influenced by Luhmann's writings on the science system and constructivist epistemology. This reception of Luhmann's ideas on constructivism and science within German-speaking sociology is in clear contrast to the neglect of this part of Luhmann's work in the Anglophone – or, for that matter, Francophone – sociology of science and, more broadly, the 'social studies of science'.

In this chapter, I present the main tenets of Luhmann's theory of science and knowledge and how they relate to other views on science. In the first section, I outline Luhmann's understanding of the emergence of the modern science system, highlighting how he applies his concepts of functional differentiation, autopoiesis and self-reference to modern science. I then discuss Luhmann's constructivist epistemology, and subsequently turn to the interrelations between science and other societal systems.

The Emergence of the Modern Science System

Science is a modern category. The birth of scientific reasoning is sometimes located in Ancient Greece, yet terms such as *episteme* (knowledge), *theoria* (contemplation, speculation) and *peri physeos historia* (inquiry concerning nature) meant something quite different than our modern term 'science'.[11] While Greek, Egyptian and Mesopotamian civilisations developed important mathematical, medical, and astronomical theories and expertise, this was usually intertwined with religious, magical, economic and political concerns.[12] The emergence of modern science, understood as the methodologically controlled pursuit of knowledge for its own sake, has to be situated in the long early modern period of the seventeenth and eighteenth century. The early demarcation between science and other societal spheres was drawn in the seventeenth-century scientific academies, such as the Florentine *Accademia dei Lincei* (1603) or the *London Royal Society* (1662). Although the seventeenth century was a period of frequent disputes between science, politics and religion (e.g., the appearance of Galileo's *Dialogo* (1632)), the academies provided the first blueprint for scientific communication, operating relatively disengaged from religious and political preoccupations.[13] By mobilising themselves around a concept of distinctive methods for scientific activity (primarily experimentation) and focusing on the production of new knowledge ('innovation') – instead of guarding and commenting on the old one – academic scholars were able to generate a convincing organisational alternative for the hierarchical universities, and could present themselves to the rest of society as a distinct community.[14] The old, imagined community of scholars, the *res publica litteraria*,[15] broke open and gave way to a special scientific community with narrower membership criteria. Even though specific membership criteria differed on a national basis, scientists increasingly saw themselves as 'professionals' – as specialists in a clearly defined area, having little in common with literary 'intellectuals', who addressed a wider public and were politically committed.

Especially in the nineteenth century, science became the province of the professional figure, with a social role of the 'scientist' (a term first used by William Whevell in 1833 to describe the participants at a meeting of the British Association for the Advancement of Science). Science, as a profession, became differentiated more sharply than ever from philosophy, theology and other traditional branches of knowledge. Modern institutional forms for the production and dissemination of knowledge – without which it would be hard to envision research as we know it today – were created. The Humboldtian ideal of the research university provided the main organisational form in which the practice of science could become a full-time career: by providing wages, fusing research with teaching and allowing the historic prestige of universities as centres of scholasticism to valorise the new science. Laboratories were established on a permanent basis and became the predominant setting for everyday scientific practice. While disciplines were relatively unimportant until the end of the eighteenth century,[16] clearly demarcated areas such as 'Biology' – a term first used in 1800 – or 'Physics' now established themselves. Rudolf Stichweh has outlined how research in this period transformed from an activity centred on collecting and organising 'received knowledge' from a plurality of sources, to 'research', the systematic pursuit of 'new knowledge'.[17] Producing 'scientific knowledge' became a more specialised and demanding activity, in which knowledge was only considered valid if produced according to certain methodological constraints of research's own making. In Luhmann's terms, science became an 'autopoietic' system, in which scientific statements could only come about within the science system and under the rules and conditions of the system itself. According to Rudolf Stichweh, 'the novel aspect of an autopoietic system of science seems to be that the system starts to produce all its elements itself and, after having done this for some time, changes its identity: the self-production of new elements seems to become the essence of science'.[18]

A crucial element in the autopoiesis of the modern research system is the role of printing, as it allowed for the regular publication of scientific articles, which could be used as a point of connection for further research.[19] The learned journal, which appeared every two months or so, enabled authors to publicise their scientific findings and observe how other scientists tackled problems in their discipline. Publishing an article (including summarising the current state of research and quoting other publications) hence became the basis of scientific production, the operation of the autopoiesis of science. The scientific journal and its conventions for citation and article acceptance (i.e., through peer-review) turned science into a fully self-referential, autopoietic system of scientific communication. By accepting or rejecting the specific knowledge claims in each paper under review, knowledge claims, taking into account the current state of knowledge, can be sorted under the specific code of science.[20]

Scientific truth is thus not understood as a correspondence to the real world, but as a symbolically generalised communication medium, which makes the production of new, surprising or deviant knowledge more likely. In other words, scientific truth is about unlikely and complex forms of knowledge, 'novelties' that sometimes contradict the self-evident nature of our experienced reality and can deviate considerably from what we consider to be 'true' in everyday life.[21] The code to which truth refers for the production of scientific communication is the difference between 'true' and 'false'. Both values mark communication as scientific, and differentiate it from other communication taking place in society: the first value allows communication to continue in search of new connections, while the second value forces communication to reflect on the conditions that led to an error. This means, of course, that even scientifically untrue knowledge must be treated as scientific, as Popper famously pointed out. If a specific hypothesis proves to be untrue, certain other hypotheses become more probable and can attract research attention as well as resources. By constantly switching between empirically validated and non-validated hypotheses, new research opportunities emerge, and the autopoiesis of the science system is guaranteed.

Yet, while the true/false code differentiates science from other types of communication, it cannot give precise instructions on the topics or the structures that enable and control scientific communication. This is provided by the programs of the science system: theories and methods. They determine the precise (and changeable) conditions under which statements can be considered (scientifically) true or false. They hence limit what is allowed for in science, but also make observable what the research exactly refers to (be it atoms, social systems, etc). Theories are interrelated statements about the world which are based on concepts; they form the external reference of communication, for example to specific 'objects' such as 'protons', 'neutrons' or 'social roles'. Theories and concepts do not guarantee a complete correspondence between scientific truth and the external reality, but rather enable the comparison of different solutions to problems, which are established by scientific communication itself; different theories can be tried out to make sense of scientific observations.[22] The methods then determine the conditions under which the statements can be considered true or false. Only scientific observations that have been gathered in a 'methodologically correct' way can be retained for future scientific communication. While theories represent the 'external reference' and enable an 'asymmetrisation' between scientific observation and the observed objects, methods guarantee the self-reference of science because they have no external reference.[23]

In sum, by skilfully relating theories to methodologically controlled observations, truth claims can be advanced and consecutively evaluated by academic colleagues through formal peer review. Once validated, they can be circulated within the academic community in the form of publications. On the basis of these publications, internal scientific communication can then differentiate between 'old' and 'new' knowledge and construct promising ways to further scientific insight.[24] From the moment science had achieved this autopoiesis by only accepting self-produced knowledge, certified through the peer-review process, and renewed by every new publication, it fully switches towards a routinely operating second-order observation. From Luhmann's point of view, second-order observation implies first and foremost that, with modernity, society – not only science but also other social systems – must forego the traditional external determinants of communication, such as 'nature', 'justice' or 'God'. Instead of directly referring to the pre-given, natural reality, scientists must refer to existing publications and connect to research that has already been conducted, so that science becomes oriented to the self-proclaimed 'accumulation of scientific knowledge'. As Lorraine Daston and Peter Galison have famously argued, 'objectivity' as an epistemic virtue makes its appearance in the mid-nineteenth-century sciences, not as 'truth-to-nature', but as a disciplinary trained judgement, which is oriented towards the scientific 'working objects' (galaxies, skeletons, elementary particles) as they were depicted and visualised in scientific atlases, compendia and other printed material.[25] Just as modern law can only understand the legal meaning or validity of norms, rulings and contracts, by observing existing (i.e., already accepted and published) norms or rulings, the scientific focus of observation is on how reality has been constructed by previous scientific research, and not on observing reality as such.

In the course of modernity, such a shift to second-order observation – the observation of observers – can be witnessed in all function systems. In the modern economy, for instance, markets and prices manifest second-order observation. This means the economic value or price of a product does not depend on the quality of the product itself, but on what the market says it is worth.[26] In the case of the science system, it is only through research observing previously published research that science constructs its own realities and its own values, or 'eigenvalues', to use the mathematical expression often found in Luhmann's texts. This exclusive role of second-order observation in constituting scientific knowledge or 'eigenvalues' implies that 'the critique of research can only be carried out as research'[27], Luhmann points out. As the relevant *eigenvalue* or scientific reality is entirely constructed by scientific research (and its self-observation through publications), the value or credibility of scientific truth-claims, can only be determined, rather tautologically, in a scientific context (and not, for instance, in a religious, economic or political context).

In sum, by observing other (published) scientific observations, the science system self-referentially closes its universe and builds up its own memory and structures of expectations. In the case of science, these are expectations of a cognitive nature, which are changed if they are disappointed. This means that scientific knowledge changes accordingly when research produces new, hitherto unknown results. Generally speaking, every scientific communication produces some new insight – albeit often insignificantly small – and this innovation can be accepted as a prerequisite for further communication, or abandoned if it later turns out to be untrue, or not connectable to further research. In any case, there is no point in doing research unless one aims to find out something which is not yet known; and it will be difficult to publish research which does not (successfully) claim to have something new to say. An understanding of an open-ended future and continuous search for innovation become hallmarks of science and the broader scientific culture, with its problem-oriented, sceptical and critical character.[28]

Disciplines, Interdisciplinarity and Sociology

The establishment of the self-renewing scientific publication machine in the course of the nineteenth century led to an explosive growth of science in terms of the amount of information produced and communicated.[29] Soon, problems of overload and integration arose, which increased the pressure to treat data more selectively. As the scientific mode of gaining knowledge was expanded to ever-increasing subject matters, a certain differentiation between 'scientific objects' emerged. According to the topic of discussion, more specialised frames and knowledge procedures came about, which could be used to sort, reconstruct and produce knowledge in ever smaller fields. This self-referential augmentation of objects of scientific analysis and increasing specialisation are the main drivers behind the internal differentiation of science into disciplines and subdisciplines.[30] Over time, the perception of concrete objects as the initial step of discipline formation (e.g., the molecule, the human psyche, economic transactions, etc) was replaced by the constitution of problems by discipline (i.e., ultimately by a group of scholars who shared common concepts and methods, forming a scientific community, as theorised by Fleck and Kuhn). The scientific discipline also serves as a connection point to the systems of higher education, both as a subject domain for teaching and learning in schools, and as a designation of occupational and professional roles.[31] By the beginning of the twentieth century, the matrix of disciplines and the range of academic subjects that we know today had taken shape, first in Europe and the United States, and a bit later throughout the globe. Already in the interbellum, and more elaborately after World War II, most disciplines took the form of cross-border scientific communities, in which information circulates at great speed, and globally standardised procedures were in place for quality assessment, the allocation of prestige and regulating the impact of research on the broader societal environment.[32]

For our discussion here, the emergence of the social sciences and more specifically the discipline of sociology, is of special interest. While many earlier civilisations might be said to have produced elaborate and systematic descriptions of their respective societies, it was not until the mid-nineteenth century, in the context of accelerated social change in Europe – Luhmann would point here to an intensifying functional differentiation – that a more or less demarcated social-scientific discourse developed, first among intellectuals and philanthropic reformers, and in the closing years of the century among academic sociologists. While European sociology initially thought of itself mainly as a theoretical discipline, toward the end of the nineteenth century, academic sociology everywhere, including in the United States, annexed the field of empirical social studies that had previously belonged to state-sponsored or private surveys (e.g., the early studies of poverty by wealthy entrepreneurs as Charles Booth and Seebohm Rowntree) and started contributing on a large scale to the theoretical and methodical self-observation of contemporary societies. Of course, academic sociology is not the only source of society's self-descriptions. The mass media are probably more important in producing general knowledge about society, yet have different priorities than discussing and testing the truth-value of their propositions (e.g. generating public attention by presenting spectacular information).

While Luhmann explicitly connects his work to the disciplinary history and problematics of sociology, he also – and much more than other major sociologists – has an uneasy relationship with his discipline. Neither the 'tribal' struggles between different 'schools', or between the formalist, quantitative and hermeneutic, qualitative tradition, nor the theoretical orientation towards the 'classics' has been helpful in making disciplinary progress and caused a certain theoretical stagnation in sociology. For solutions, Luhmann looked in other directions. As is well known, he has always paid great importance to cross-disciplinary contacts, and 'imported' into sociology a great number of concepts from other disciplines (cybernetics, biology, information sciences, etc). Over his career, he was an avid reader of general systems theory and second-order cybernetics, and became closely involved with the work of a diverse set of cyberneticians such as Heinz von Foerster, Humberto Maturana, Francisco Varela, George Spencer-Brown, Gregory Bateson and Gotthard Gunther. His major work, 'Social Systems', was introduced as an attempt to reformulate the theory of social systems via the current state of the art in general systems theory.[33] General systems theory should be tested in an encounter with sociological material, and in this way, the advances in abstraction and the new conceptual formations that already exist should be made productive for sociological theory development.

Yet, at the same time, Luhmann also stressed that sociology as a discipline has its own specificity and employed transdisciplinary ideas such as self-referentiality (Von Foerster), autopoiesis (Maturana) or autology (Günther) to highlight this specificity. While sociology shares many aspects with other scientific disciplines, the specificity of sociology consists in the fact that it studies its object (society) within its object (society). Sociology describes the society in which it is generated, and in this way, it also describes itself, that is, sociology discovers itself in its object of study. This circularity demands that a theory of society must also be about itself.[34]

Epistemology and the Constructivist Self-Understanding of Science

Luhmann's sociology hence explicitly includes the constructor of knowledge and describes itself as a self-supporting construction of self-referential observations.[35] His theory of social systems, including the theory of the science system, is a construction that consists of nothing but self-generated conceptual distinctions which refer to each other (e.g., system/environment, operation/observation, medium/form, inclusion/exclusion).

As already indicated, Luhmann's theory also refers back to itself on the sociological level. His theory about science as a specific communicative construction, also realizes that is part of the construction it is about. According to Luhmann, this also goes for science itself. As one function system among others, science hence has to be able to account for its own observation position and reflect on its own singularity and irreplaceability.[36] As other function systems, science does so by developing what Luhmann calls 'reflection theories', self-descriptions that reflect on the specificity, the code and meaning of the function system. Just like political theory and theology serve as the reflection theories of the political and religious system, epistemology or the theory of knowledge is the reflection theory of the science system.[37]

In Luhmann's understanding, epistemology as a reflection theory of science could only emerge once the code and societal function of science systems had differentiated. Questions such as 'What is true knowledge?' or 'How is scientific knowledge to be demarcated from non-scientific knowledge?' can only be reasonably asked when knowledge can be pursued for its own sake, relatively independent from religious, political or economic concerns. Luhmann points out, for instance, that traditional religious semantics only accept one religious and perfect cosmos, which is fully observable or insightful to God only. As there is no godly position within this world, building knowledge of it – i.e., striving for knowledge independently from religious instructions – means breaking away from God, just like Lucifer did.[38] The transition to modernity and functional differentiation, however, implied a repositioning of the individual consciousness – Luhmann terms it 'exclusion' – as the source and the ultimate foundation of all knowledge. In epistemology, this translated into the eighteenth-century debate between the empiricist ('sense-data') and the idealistic interpretation of the concept of the subject, which eventually culminated in Kant's transcendental turn in philosophy. With the emergence of modern science, especially sociology, Kantian transcendental thinking gave way to the insight that all observers are empirical – meaning that they occur in the world, together with their observations, and that observations are observable (and can hence be studied in a theoretical and methodologically controlled way). Stephan Fuchs summarises this nicely:

> Sociology was born with the realisation that there is no view from nowhere. Postmodernists of various persuasions think they have discovered something new because they do not know much sociology. The idea of 'truth' as an unconstrained or 'unsituated' representation of the world as it is, without an observer, is really gone, and gone for good, given the work of Marx, Mannheim, Fleck, and Durkheim. For sociology, observations are made by an empirical observer located in a particular social structure and embedded in a network of related and connected observations that make up a culture.[39]

As part of the world, all observations, including scientific observations, take place at specific locales and times, yet also connect systematically to previous scientific observations. Their empirical status implies that scientific observations, like any other type of observations, can also be observed themselves, by other empirical observers or by an observer who observes himself. Within the scientific 'studies of science', the concepts for carrying out such second-order observation have become available after Kuhn's 'The Structure of Scientific Revolutions' (1962[40]), and its elaboration in empirical science studies. Throughout the work of, for instance, David Bloor,[41] Bruno Latour,[42] or Karin Knorr-Cetina,[43] it has become clear that, for example, objects like neutrons, DNA-chains – or for that matter, social systems – only exist because scientific categories and practices have been developed that allow these objects to be observed. What is observed is the result of how the categories and practices of science construct the object in question and not the representation of this object as a pre-given fact. In Luhmann's terms, this can be explained by the distinction between self-reference (internal reference) and external reference (other reference). While 'science' establishes itself in relation to a world it references as 'outside', by so referencing, it simultaneously deals with a world enrolled in scientific categories and enacted through its methods, tools and procedures.

To designate his own take on constructivism Luhmann preferred the term 'operative constructivism' to other terms such as 'social constructivism' or 'radical constructivism'.[44] Doing so allowed him to emphasize that all observations are real operations of existing systems. Because all scientific knowledge is but a specific scientific observation and is relative to, for instance, the categories and methods of a specific discipline or paradigm, it can always be empirically traced back to a particular operation of a particular observer. Of course, such a constructivist position does not mean that scientific knowledge is arbitrary, relative or denies the existence of 'reality'. Every scientific communication is bound to previous scientific communications, which discriminate between acceptable knowledge and incorrect knowledge and the reality 'outside' always plays a negative role in discriminating between what is (scientifically) valid and non-valid knowledge.

Within Luhmann's constructivist theory of science, the task of epistemology is no longer to provide a foundation for knowledge, but rather to observe observations.[45] Within the framework of 'second-order observation', epistemological observations do not focus on 'what' is observed but on 'how' the observed (first-order) observer observes. Important to note here is that every observation can be observed with reference to its own conditions of possibility, as formulated in the principle of the 'blind spot'. Because observations are necessarily based on a specific distinction, observations are not able to observe the distinction they are themselves using (this is the blind spot of the relevant observation). Only a second-order observation – which observes this observation on the basis of another distinction – can see how the first observation observes, and also see what it doesn't see.[46] While scientific observation within physics, for example, allows one to see external objects like neutrons (because their theoretical categories and technical procedures allow them to observe these), physics itself cannot – at the same time – see how this results from its own operations and distinctions. This can only be observed by a second-order observer, for example, the sociology of science, who can see how physical observation is limited to its own systemic observations. Obviously, it would take a third observer, Luhmannian systems theory for instance, to observe the distinctions of the second-order observer; and yet the same applies for that observer since his or her own observations are based yet again on a distinction that he or she cannot see in the act of observation. Epistemology, in a nutshell, has to account for the unavoidability of blind spots and the fact that we cannot but construct our reality through the distinctions we use in our observations; there is no position from which to observe reality 'as it is'.

While Luhmann's specific type of operative constructivism is not particularly *en vogue* in the interdisciplinary field of science, technology and society studies (STS), many of its assumptions square rather nicely with the empirical study of the scientific production of knowledge. Both approaches agree that science can only know reality by its own operations, that is, by continuously elaborating and testing one's own constructions, and that 'scientific products are "occasioned" by the circumstances of their production'.[47] Yet, Luhmann's systems theory has a slightly different flavour and different concerns than the standard approach within STS.

While the analyses of, say, Bruno Latour[48] or Andrew Pickering,[49] have focused on the minute practices of knowledge production in the laboratory or the broader material world, Luhmann's sociology does not zoom in on everyday scientific practices, although it leaves plenty of room for the materialities of communication such as writing and visualising.[50] Its focus is rather on the general processes of communicative construction of scientific knowledge and its position within modern society. Given Luhmann's focus on communication (with the material world being in the 'environment' of the communicative system) and his ideas about the operational, autopoietic closure of social systems, scientific communication appears as a much 'cleaner' process than is allowed for in STS. The systems theoretical approach also gives room to conceptualise the 'autonomy' of science, which is seen as an old-fashioned conceptual relict within STS. That the reality of science from the systems-theoretical perspective comes into view as a self-produced communicative construction, does not make it less societal or less real, however, as if were a sort of paper construction without genuine consequences for broader society or our daily life. Evidence of the contemporary influence and importance of science is all around us and is undeniable.

The Structural Couplings of Science

Within Luhmann's systems theory, this influence is conceptualised in terms of 'structural couplings' of science to other function systems, such as education (coupled via curricula content in textbooks), the economy (coupled via patents), politics (coupled through research policy as well as policy advice), and last but not least, the medical system (coupled through scientifically tested medicinal knowledge and operative practices).

What is important to emphasise here is, first, that these structural couplings do not imply a loss of the autonomy science acquired in its differentiation processes in the eighteenth and nineteenth century. Luhmann always stressed that functional autonomy and a multiplicity of structural couplings do not exclude each other. On the contrary, the multiplication of structural dependencies or couplings rather increases the capability of a system to switch dependencies and therefore often increases autonomy. It is clear, for instance, that contemporary scientific research is dependent on significant amounts of (public or private) funding and that there is an increased interdependence of science with the economy (for instance, through the pressure to commercialise research findings).[51] On the other hand, economic growth in, for instance, the pharmaceutical sector depends on pharmaceutical research and development, but it cannot simply decree that the research will be successful. We also have to note that, despite the concern with 'scientific capitalism' and the commodification of research,[52] we do not go to Wall Street to discover the structure of DNA, just as we do not attempt to buy stocks or purchase an electron microscope in the laboratory. While money and research are mutually involved, they remain distinct operations, with very different rationales. Furthermore, to the extent that the interdependence between money and research intensifies, it also becomes possible to switch between a plurality of financial sources (private, local, national, cross-national, etc) and even to regulate or encourage the combination of multiple sources, in order to protect scientific autonomy and plurality.[53]

Second, while scientific research at the level of society is just 'loosely coupled' to other systems such as the economy or politics, the coupling becomes tighter at the level of formal organisation. Organisational systems such as universities, hospitals or firms are able to couple different function systems, precisely in their different manner of operation, because they make decisions using the codes of the respective function systems.[54] A university, for instance, establishes a structural coupling between the educational system and the scientific system by simultaneously making decisions in the world of scientific research and the world of education, for instance by deciding on the professional roles in their double function of teaching and doing research. During the process of differentiation of science, organisations such as universities even became necessary to the extent that doing science without organisational backing became an unlikely exception. This process becomes understandable considering the important advantages that formally organised systems provide for doing research. Luhmann summarises the latter as follows:

> Organisations provide motivation. They set the interactive negotiation of results and publications, which more recent scientific research strongly emphasises,

> under restrictions that are not available within interaction, thus neutralizing a certain randomness of purely situational arrangements. [...] Most importantly, organisations allow for periodisation, i.e., the establishment of time-limited projects, with the certainty that the organisation (but not necessarily the individual employment and career) continues after completion. Research is brought into this form, a project that is disconnected from individual life, yet at the same time terminable and unstoppable. In some areas, this project-based research organisation is already so prevalent that research (especially open, theoretical research) that does not conform to it has hardly any chance, while it is undeniable that one would be even worse off if individual researchers, left to their own devices, were to constantly re-evaluate only that in which they once succeeded and made them famous.[55]

Without neglecting the many advantages universities provide for research, Luhmann underlines the difficulties that arise from the strict coupling of research and education. Not only does it lead to a certain bureaucratisation of scientific life, but also 'the direct coupling of teaching and research would, if taken seriously, cause considerable reductions in performance in both areas. Above all but it should be noted that the phase of exponential growth of science, in terms of staff and financial resources, will eventually come to an end (when not already today)'.[56]

Third, it should be emphasised that when autopoietic, operationally closed systems interact with each other, they do this according to their own codes and logic. This means that scientific research cannot simply enter another system without ceasing to be just research. The key factor in the interaction between systems is translation or the 'reconstruction' of meaning engendered in other systems.[57] For instance, when research through experts and policy advice enters the political system, this requires translation of the languages and standards of research and policy. Within scientific policy advice, different organisations and actors specialise in translating scientific data into political or policy-relevant messages, or vice versa. In this process, scientific data are condensed, summarised and simplified for political usage, often to such an extent that the advice can no longer considered to be 'scientific'. On the other hand, the closer policy advice stays to science, the more difficult it will be to provide concrete advice, given that science never provides absolute proof, and is often mired in controversies about how to weigh or assess the evidence.[58] In any case, once research findings cross the boundary between research and politics, they will have become reconstructed in political terms, and from the point of view of the political system, will no longer be scientific but political communication.

Taking into account the incommensurability of these different autopoietic systems, it also becomes clear that Luhmann's systems theory can hardly be looked upon as 'the epitome of technocratic consciousness', as Habermas famously alleged 50 years ago.[59] Habermas' assumption that systems theory implies a direct and linear relationship between the systems of politics and science not only misunderstands social systems theory but also the complexity of operations within these systems. In hindsight, one can notice a reversal of positions. Luhmann's systems theory and not critical theory, is the theory of society which grasps that society has become largely uncontrollable, whether by science, politics or any other function system. Since forms of second-order observation are system-specific and thus incommensurable with one another, Luhmann has indeed sketched a bleak outlook for 'reasonable', 'science-based' or even just coordinated decision-making. Particularly in his studies on ecological communication[60] and risk[61] he emphasised how functionally differentiated society can have no unitary approach to the serious ecological risks we are facing. Instead, the differentiation into function systems means that ecological problems can only find 'resonance' within each different function system. While systems such as law (through environmental legislation), politics (through ecological party programs) and the economy (through internalising environmental externalities in prices) have found ways of dealing with ecological problems according to system-specific criteria, a coordinated approach to issues such as climate change is not within sight and highly unlikely. While functional differentiation has allowed society to scientifically register and visualise this problem, as well as to highlight scientifically backed solutions for tackling it, it has also dismantled other systems' ability to tackle the problem by simply 'following the science'.

Notes

1 Peter Kiefer, 'Vatican City: Pope Backs "Adult" Stem Cell Research', *The New York Times*, 28 June 2007.

2 Niklas Luhmann, *Die Wissenschaft der Gesellschaft* (Frankfurt am Main: Suhrkamp, 1990). All translations from this book are made by the author of this chapter.

3 Ibid., 705.

4 See Niklas Luhmann, *Theory of Society*, Vol. 2 (Stanford: Stanford University Press, 2013), 102 et. seq.

5 Luhmann, *Die Wissenschaft der Gesellschaft* 7. Italics in the original.

6 Niklas Luhmann, 'The Modernity of Science', *New German Critique*, No. 61, Special Issue on Niklas Luhmann (Winter, 1994): 9–23,. Niklas Luhmann, 'Das Erkenntnisprogramm des Konstruktivismus und die unbekannt bleibende Realität', in Niklas Luhmann, *Soziologische Aufklärung 5.Konstruktivistische Perspektiven* (Opladen: Westdeutscher Verlag 1990), 31–58, Translated as Niklas Luhmann, 'The Cognitive Program of Constructivism and a Reality that Remains Unknown', in *Selforganization: Portrait of a Scientific Revolution*, ed. Wolfgang Krohn, Gernot Küppers and Helga Nowotny (Dordrecht: Springer), 64–85.

7 Niklas Luhmann, 'Selbststeuerung der Wissenschaft', in Niklas Luhmann, *Soziologische Aufklärung 1. Aufsätze zur Theorie sozialer Systeme* (Opladen: Westdeutscher Verlag, 1970), 137–46.
8 Niklas Luhmann, *Ecological Communication* (Cambridge: Polity Press, 1989). German version original Niklas Luhmann, *Ökologische Kommunikation* (Opladen: Westdeutscher Verlag, 1986).
9 Niklas Luhmann, *Risk: A Sociological Theory* (Berlin: Walter de Gruyter, 1993). German original Niklas Luhmann, *Soziologie des Risikos* (Berlin: De Gruyter, 1991).
10 Niklas Luhmann, *Universität als Milieu* (Bielefeld: Haux, 1992).
11 Geoffrey Ernest Richard Lloyd, *Early Greek Science: Thales to Aristotle* (New York: Norton, 1970).
12 E.g. Patricia Fara, *Science. A Four Thousand Year History* (Oxford: Oxford University Press, 2009); Luhmann, *Die Wissenschaft der Gesellschaft*, 167–9.
13 Massimiano Bucchi, *Science in Society: An Introduction to Social Studies of Science* (London: Routledge, 2004), 12.
14 Gert Verschraegen, 'Regulating Scientific Research: A Constitutional Moment?', *Journal of Law and Society* 45, no. S1 (2018): 163–4.
15 E.g. Peter Burke, *A Social History of Knowledge: From Gutenberg to Diderot* (Cambridge: Polity Press, 2000), 19–20.
16 Rudolf Stichweh, *Zur Entstehung des modernen Systems wissenschaftlicher Disziplinen. Physik in Deutschland 1740–1890.* (Frankfurt am Main: Suhrkamp, 1984), 14–15.
17 Rudolf Stichweh, 'Self-Organization and Autopoiesis in the Development of Modern Science', in *Selforganization: Portrait of a Scientific Revolution*, ed. Wolfgang Krohn, Gernot Küppers and Helga Nowotny (Dordrecht: Springer, 1990), 195–207.
18 Ibid., 202.
19 Luhmann, *Die Wissenschaft der Gesellschaft*, 432–3, 575 et. seq.; Stichweh, *Zur Entstehung des modernen Systems wissenschaftlicher Disziplinen. Physik in Deutschland 1740–1890*, 394 et. seq.
20 Luhmann, *Die Wissenschaft der Gesellschaft*, 296.
21 Ibid., 175.
22 Ibid., 370, 403–4
23 Ibid., 405.
24 Ibid., 220.
25 Lorraine Daston and Peter Galison, *Objectivity* (New York: Zone Books, 2007).
26 Niklas Luhmann, *Die Wirtschaft der Gesellschaft* (Frankfurt am Main: Suhrkamp, 1988), 91 et. seq.
27 Luhmann, *Die Wissenschaft der Gesellschaft*, 718.
28 E.g., Gert Verschraegen and Frédéric Vandermoere, 'Introduction: Shaping the Future through Imaginaries of Science, Technology and Society', in *Imagined Futures in Science, Technology and Society*, ed. Gert Verschraegen et al. (London: Routledge, 2017), 1–11.
29 E.g. Derek J. De Solla Price, *Little Science, Big Science* (New York: Columbia University Press, 1963).
30 Rudolf Stichweh, 'Differentiation of Scientific Disciplines: Causes and Consequences', in *Encyclopedia of Life Support Systems* (Paris: UNESCO, 2003), 1–8; Peter Weingart, 'A Short History of Knowledge Formations', in *The Oxford Handbook of Interdisciplinarity*, ed. Robert Frodeman and Julie Thompson Klein (Oxford: Oxford University Press, 2010), 3–14.

31 Stichweh, 'Differentiation of Scientific Disciplines'.
32 E.g., Verschraegen, 'Regulating Scientific Research'.
33 Niklas Luhmann, *Social Systems* (Stanford: Stanford University Press, 1995), 1–11.
34 This is one of the main assumptions in Niklas Luhmann, *Theory of Society*, vols. 1 and 2 (Stanford: Stanford University Press, 2012, 2013), Michael Schiltz and Gert Verschraegen, 'Spencer-Brown, Luhmann and Autology', *Cybernetics and Human Knowing* 9, no. 3–4 (2003): 55–78.
35 Luhmann, *Social Systems*, xlix.
36 Luhmann, *Die Wissenschaft der Gesellschaft*, 704.
37 Ibid., 475–80.
38 Ibid., 118–22.
39 Stephan Fuchs, *Against Essentialism. A Theory of Culture and Society* (Cambridge: Harvard University Press, 2001), 29.
40 Thomas Kuhn, *The Structure of Scientific Revolutions* (Chicago: University of Chicago Press, 1962).
41 David Bloor, *Knowledge and Social Imagery* (London: Routledge, 1976).
42 Bruno Latour and Steve Woolgar, *Laboratory Life: The Construction of Scientific Facts* (London: Sage, 1979).
43 Karin Knorr-Cetina, *Epistemic Cultures. How the Sciences Make Knowledge* (Cambridge, MA: Harvard University Press, 1999).
44 Niklas Luhmann, 'The Cognitive Program of Constructivism and a Reality that Remains Unknown', in *Selforganization. Sociology of the Sciences (A Yearbook)*, vol 14, ed. Wolfgang Krohn, Gernot Küppers and Helga Nowotny (Dordrecht: Springer), 64–85.
45 Luhmann, *Die Wissenschaft der Gesellschaft*, 516–22.
46 Niklas Luhmann, 'I See Something you Don't See', in Niklas Luhmann, *Theories of Distinction: Redescribing the Descriptions of Modernity*, ed. William Rasch (Stanford, CA: Stanford University Press, 2002), 187–96.
47 Karin D. Knorr-Cetina, 'The Ethnographic Study of Scientific Work: Towards a Constructivist Interpretation of Science', in *Science Observed: Perspectives on the Social Study of Science*, ed. Karin D. Knorr-Cetina et al. (London: Sage, 1983), 115–40, at 124.
48 Latour and Woolgar, *Laboratory Life*.
49 Andrew Pickering, *The Mangle of Practice: Time, Agency, and Science* (Chicago: The University of Chicago Press, 1995).
50 Bruno Latour, 'Visualization and Cognition: Thinking with Eyes and Hands', *Knowledge and Society: Studies in the Sociology of Culture Past and Present* 6 (1986): 1–40.
51 Verschraegen, 'Regulating Scientific Research', 177–80.
52 Philip Mirowski, *Science-Mart: Privatizing American Science* (Cambridge, MA: Harvard University Press, 2011).
53 For an analogous idea, see Christoph Beat Graber and Gunther Teubner, 'Art and Money: Constitutional Rights in the Private Sphere?', *Oxford Journal of Legal Studies* 18, no. 1 (1998): 61–73.
54 Luhmann, *Theory of Society*, vol. 2, 142 et. seq.
55 Niklas Luhmann, *Schriften zur Organisation. Band 3*. Edited by Ernst Lukas and Veronika Tacke (Berlin: Springer, 2019), 182–3. All translations from this book are made by the author of this chapter.
56 Ibid., 186.

57 E.g. Gunther Teubner, *Law as an Autopoietic System*. Edited by Zenon Bankowski, translated by. Anne Bankowska and Ruth Adler (Oxford: Blackwell, 1993); Kristof Van Assche and Gert Verschraegen, 'The Limits of Planning: Niklas Luhmann's Systems Theory and the Analysis of Planning and Planning Ambitions', *Planning Theory* 7, no. 3 (2008): 263–83.

58 E.g. Naomi Oreskes, 'Science and Public Policy: What's Proof Got to Do with It?', *Environmental Science & Policy* 7, no. 5 (2004): 369–83.

59 Jürgen Habermas, 'Eine Auseinandersetzung mit Niklas Luhmann: Systemtheorie oder kritische Theorie der Gesellschaft', in *Theorie der Gesellschaft oder Sozialtechnologie*, ed. Jürgen Habermas and Niklas Luhmann (Frankfurt am Main: Suhrkamp, 1971), 142–290, at 145.

60 Luhmann, *Ecological Communication*.

61 Luhmann, *Risk*.

Chapter 6

NIKLAS LUHMANN ON RELIGION AND SECULARISATION

Raf Vanderstraeten

Introduction

A central argument in Niklas Luhmann's theory of society is that modern society comprises a variety of function systems. In an early version of his theory, written in the mid-1970s, Luhmann presented a list of ten important function systems: politics, law, the military, the economy, science, the family (and intimate relationships), art, education, medicine and religion. This list was not intended to be exhaustive.[1] Some suggestions for including additional function systems, such as the mass media, social work, sports and tourism, were discussed in later publications.[2] Throughout the different versions of his theory of society, however, Luhmann has continued to underline the idea that modern society is characterised by the primacy or dominance of the form of functional differentiation.

While religion may have contributed to the genesis of modern society, Luhmann argued, it has above all been forced to come to terms with the consequences of its differentiation form. 'Today religion survives as a functional subsystem of a functionally differentiated society. It has gained recognised autonomy at the cost of recognizing the autonomy of the other subsystems, i.e., secularization'.[3] Although, interestingly, Luhmann expressed some hesitations about the usefulness of the concept of secularisation in his late work, he kept using it – if only because it 'calls attention to how religion reacts to the assumption of a secularised society'.[4] While his hesitations have to do with changes in his view on the ways religion adapts to the form of functional differentiation, the challenges associated with secularisation provide a good avenue for analysing and discussing Luhmann's view on the position of religion in modern society.

As is well known, Luhmann was an astonishingly productive author, able to cover a broad variety of topics. He devoted much time and effort to studies on (the evolution of) single function systems. As he remarked in the introduction to the essay collection *The Differentiation of Society*, the analysis of modern society as a functionally differentiated system 'requires a detailed study of each of its single functional subsystems'.[5] He covered religion in a number of papers as well as two books: *Funktion der Religion*[6] and *Die Religion der Gesellschaft*[7]. It should, however, be noted that this second book was published posthumously, and that Luhmann did not have the opportunity to complete it to his own satisfaction. Between the publication of both books, his papers about this function system are also comparatively infrequent and, with one exception,[8] quite short. Yet these publications – about 20 in total – can be used to examine both developments in his theory of society and in his sociological view on religion and secularisation.

The purpose of this chapter is to present an overview of the basic structure of Luhmann's reflections on this subject and some of the revisions that took place in the last decades of the twentieth century. I also want to briefly compare Luhmann's reflections with those of some of his precursors, especially Talcott Parsons. Luhmann indeed worked in many ways 'after' Parsons (in both senses of the word: in the time after as well as inspired by).[9] In order to clarify Luhmann's contributions to the sociology of religion, the chapter focuses on two key Luhmannian conceptual distinctions. First inclusion/exclusion in order to explain the ways in which people participate in the system of religion and second integration/differentiation in order to outline the position of religion vis-à-vis other function systems in modern society. The chapter concludes with a brief discussion of Luhmann's account of the ways in which the function system religion handles the transition to functional differentiation in modern society.[10]

Inclusion/exclusion

Functional specialisation, Luhmann argued in an early programmatic paper begins as a differentiation of specialist roles (soldiers, teachers, priests, monks, etc). It is already possible in previous forms of social order (segmentation and stratification), but 'it gains momentum only if at least two different roles organise their complementary expectations around a specific function – for example, clerics and laymen, politicians and the public, teachers and pupils'.[11] Following Luhmann, functional differentiation is not only dependent on the genesis of specific professional roles but also on the formation of the complementary 'boundary roles'.[12] It is also dependent on the *inclusion* of large populations in *public* roles, which are defined in different function systems.

In Parsons' late work, the notion of inclusion already played an important role. Parsons introduced it in order to adjust and complement the classical sociological thesis, according to which differentiation is related to, and dependent on, demographic changes.[13] Parsons argued, more particularly, that statistical changes in the size and density of populations (including urbanisation) do not suffice to make the difference. Instead, he concerned himself with the *social mechanisms* used to regulate participation in different social systems – thereby directing attention towards the changing forms of membership and of 'acceptance' within society and its subsystems.[14] Parsons listed a number of inclusion mechanisms: the introduction of the poor laws, the beginnings of formal education and mandatory schooling for all, the extension of the franchise, the acquisition of formal citizenship by immigrants.[15] For Parsons, inclusion referred to the assignment of civil rights to increasing parts of the population – eventually to every single individual, irrespective of seemingly natural qualities, such as race, gender, kinship, or ethnicity. In this perspective, increasing inclusion means that increasing parts of the population are expected to 'have developed legitimate capacities to "contribute" to the functioning of the system'.[16]

For Parsons, the institutionalisation of this ideal was to an important degree an achievement of religion (and, in particular, of Christianity). As he argued, the Church of Christ had defined itself as a collective grounded on belief, not on seemingly natural characteristics. From the onset, it was an association 'of those truly in the faith, who by their own commitments had qualified for inclusion'.[17] In spite of its marginal social position and importance, the early Christian Church could therefore adopt an expansive, universalist value system. It could conceive of the universality of membership, of Christian adherence in this world. In Parsons' view, the legitimation of the ideal of full inclusion in the system of religion had gradually paved the way for the institutionalisation of inclusion ideals in the secular subsystems of society. In his writings, he also sketched the 'phases' and 'crucial developments', which could account for the modern forms of inclusion.

Luhmann, in contrast, focused more on the relationship between inclusion and differentiation. His notion of inclusion particularly refers to the formation of the 'boundary roles' in different settings. Following Luhmann, function systems have to specify their own criteria for participation in the boundary roles. Functional differentiation hinges on the institutionalisation of a range of inclusion imperatives. It gains momentum when several function systems start to define their 'clientele' or public in universalistic, totalising terms; it relies on the *differentiation of the rules for inclusion* in a variety of boundary roles. In his early programmatic paper on functional differentiation, Luhmann wrote:

> If the society introduces compulsory school education for everyone, if every person regardless of his being nobleman or commoner, being Christian,

> Jewish, or Moslem, being infant or adult, is subject to the same legal status, if 'the public' is provided with a political function as electorate, if every individual is acknowledged as choosing or not choosing a religious commitment [...] then the whole system shifts in the direction of functional differentiation.[18]

In contrast to Parsons, Luhmann thus lay stress on the decentralisation of inclusion imperatives and practices. In his view, the delegation of inclusion to the single function systems constitutes a distinctive feature of modern society.[19]

In his early work on religion and secularisation, published in the 1970s and the first part of the 1980s, Luhmann paid much attention to the social regulation of inclusion. Like other function systems, he argued, religion has to specify the criteria for participation in its lay or public roles. In many Western nations, the realisation of specific inclusion ideals could count on much support (schooling for all, universal franchise, etc.). Widening access to social services has been the object of numerous state interventions in the 'welfare states', too. The realisation of inclusion in the system of religion has not been an issue of comparable concern, however. In light of the decline in church membership and church attendance, especially in Europe, Luhmann argued that the Christian churches have been forced to develop their own strategies to recruit their public, to motivate the laity to participate in religious communication. They have developed a range of strategies to confront this problem – but with varying degrees of success. Especially in his early publications on religion and secularisation, Luhmann emphasised that these churches had to face the risk that they might fail to attract large populations to worship. He therefore suggested to analyse secularisation in terms of the *problems of inclusion* with which the churches are confronted and of their *reactions* to these problems.

What Luhmann pointed to, more specifically, was that the churches had to react to the relatively sudden confrontation with inclusion imperatives as a result of the transition to functional differentiation. In Europe, the Christian churches kept acting within the norms of a centuries-old tradition. They retained well-established ceremonies of enrolment and admittance (baptism), but also felt pressed to stimulate more active expressions of belonging and religious commitment. The first missionary organisations, for example, were founded around 1800 by Protestants: the *London Missionary Society* (1795), the *London Society for Promoting Christianity amongst the Jews* (1809), the *Basler Missionsgesellschaft* (1815) and many others. Their work was embedded within, and illustrative of a broader movement of awakening, revival or *reveil*, which gained force during the early nineteenth century.[20] For Luhmann, such revivals are a reaction to the differentiation of inclusion imperatives and the corresponding individualisation of decisions about religious commitment.[21] Their degree of success has to be evaluated in light of the new challenges, as it only made sense to specify membership conditions and requirements after the institutionalisation of inclusion imperatives.[22]

Luhmann saw in the 1970s that related issues constituted important challenges for Christianity. These encompassed inclusion problems in professional roles (e.g., the exclusion of women and married men from priesthood in the Catholic Church) as well as increasing demands for internal democracy, for giving the laity a 'voice' in ecclesiastical decision-making bodies.

Luhmann also asked how the churches are able to motivate people to take up a religious role when religious non-commitment does not seem to have important consequences for them.[23] How can churches and religious denominations include large parts of the population when inclusion in religion has little or no consequences for other opportunities or careers? The costs of exclusion from a range of other domains (school education, the labour market, legal protection, and so on) mostly outweigh those of exclusion from organised forms of religion. But the churches forged alliances with organisations in other systems in order to tackle their own inclusion problems. They attempted to establish strong linkages with other, more successful systems. This strategy led, in Luhmann's view, to a reorientation of Christianity – from religious concerns towards worldly activism – and could account for the relatively abrupt transition to a eudemonic and theologically undemanding civil religion.[24] For Luhmann, these reactions to the perceived problem of secularisation came to constitute part of the problem itself. Its numerous worldly commitments directed the system away from its religious *eigenvalues*.[25]

In his late work on religion, Luhmann has fewer doubts about religion's adaptability to modern and world society. In line with broader developments within the sociology of religion, he analysed the shift at the end of the twentieth century from the decline of church membership and the empty-church problem to the rise of new forms of religiosity. At the beginning of the secularisation chapter in his posthumously published, unfinished monograph *A Systems Theory of Religion*, Luhmann points to the many ways in which religion was reacting to the perceived processes of secularisation:

> Today, it is regarded as an established fact that one can speak of 'de-churchification' or [...] of a movement away from organised access to religious behavior – but not of a loss in the significance of the religious as such.[26]

In this light, he also questioned whether the concept of secularisation has to be retained in sociological research. When it is still used, one should not be tempted 'to hypothesise that religion has lost its relevance in modern society'.[27] It is, however, useful to analyse variations in the 'arrangements used to include or exclude members'.[28] 'Secularisation is observed as a provocation to religion, and that is why religion responds to this provocation in several ways – with forms that may be incompatible, culturally acceptable, or perhaps even "strange".[29]

In his late work on social theory, Luhmann had already given more attention to *forms of exclusion* in different function systems.[30] The heightened sensitivity to the distinction between inclusion and exclusion also leads to a different perspective on the condition of religion in modern society. In his *Theory of Society*, Luhmann writes: 'For unlike many other functional systems, religion now has to accept that one can live and die without religion'.[31] In *A Systems Theory of Religion*, he first repeats the point that forms of inclusion are an 'extremely important variable in every function system'.[32] At the same time, however, he puts much emphasis on the relevance of forms of exclusion:

> One can practically not exist without money, and even less without legal protections. And everyone, unless fully unsuited, is sent to school and then forced to answer what they accomplished there [...] But no one is compelled to take part in art, nor really in politics (except passively via the mass media). Tourism is not at all necessary; even if many enjoy it, they don't all have to participate in it. Nor does one have to take part in religion. Certainly this applies only from the standpoint of the individual, without indicating anything about the societal relevance or necessity or these function systems.[33]

Reiterating views articulated in his late work on social theory, Luhmann adds that society is loosely integrated in the domain of inclusion. 'In the domain of exclusion, by contrast, society is strictly integrated. Each deficit reinforces another one; the circulation of disadvantages continues – and is inescapable'.[34] Religion constitutes in his view an exception, however. While this function system has its own inclusion/exclusion arrangements, there are only few interdependencies with the inclusion/exclusion mechanisms of other function systems. 'Being excluded from religion does not, as in the Middle Ages, exclude one from society'.[35] At present, 'religion can blithely ignore any near exclusion from other function systems, such as not having money, an education, an identity card or a chance of being taken seriously by the police or a judge'.[36] What Luhmann sees as a basic fact, viz. 'that religion is independent of the inclusions/exclusions originating in other systems', raises in his view 'important questions for religion in modern society'.[37] Instead of focusing on secularisation problems, Luhmann now underlines the opportunities that this position provides. Functional differentiation thus does not entail a disadvantage or even a loss of function for religion. From Luhmann's perspective, the question rather is 'whether and how religion can take advantage of the ensuing opportunities'.[38] Or formulated somewhat differently: 'How (if at all) can the religion system deploy its own possibilities of inclusion so that persons are included who have been excluded from other function systems?'.[39]

In his late work on religion, Luhmann thus focuses on the potential advantages of differentiation. He still subscribes to the view that (the inclusion/exclusion arrangements of) religion and the different other function systems of modern society do not quite resonate with one another.[40] But he no longer questions whether (and in which forms) the system of religion could survive in modern society, and whether or not it's 'maladaptation' would weaken religion to the point of irrelevance. He rather suggests that religion might make use of its relatively isolated position, of its lack of interdependencies with other function systems. In this sense, secularisation might thus also provide opportunities or chances for religion. Focusing on inclusion and exclusion, Luhmann argues that religion might still fulfil a specific social function – albeit as a kind of counterculture.

Integration/differentiation

In order to complement and deepen our understanding of Luhmann's understanding of religion and secularisation, we now turn to the relationship between the system of religion and other functionally differentiated subsystems of modern society. Parallel with the regulation of inclusion/exclusion for individuals, Luhmann directed attention to the ways in which religion 'responded to the functional differentiation and to the increasing complexity of modern society'.[41] As in the previous section, it is helpful to sketch Luhmann's analyses of the differentiation and autonomy of modern function systems against the background of other approaches on which he built.

The notion of *differentiation* has a longer tradition in sociology, unlike the concept of inclusion. Some highly influential publications in sociology can be interpreted as contributions to this line of research. In his famous study on the Protestant ethic, Max Weber, for example, not only focused attention on the ways in which ascetic Protestantism evolved toward ethical support of the early growth of capitalism, but also maintained that the complex institutions of the modern capitalist economy require(d) forms of regulation framed independently of any directly religious ethic. He introduced the term *Geist des Kapitalismus* (spirit of capitalism) to stand for a differentiated, specifically economic set of regulations. Quoting extensively from Benjamin Franklin's moral instructions, he stressed that this spirit 'has the advantage of being free from all direct relationship to religion'.[42] Moreover, he also argued that a strong, intensified rationalisation of different 'value spheres' depended on the establishment and institutionalisation of boundaries or 'zones of indifference'. In

Weber's view, religion was bound to lose its social significance in an increasingly differentiated and rationalised society. He thought of *Entzauberung* (disenchantment) and secularisation as the inevitable outcomes of increasing differentiation.[43]

Parsons did not question Weber's analysis of the differentiation of secular value spheres in modern society – quite to the contrary. But he did not have much affinity with the pessimism that permeated Weber's analyses of western society and its religious culture.[44] Following Parsons, increasing differentiation and specialisation did not have to signify the loss of religious concerns in favour of worldly interests. In his view, differentiation might even strengthen the impact of religion on modern society. While 'the concept [secularisation] has [...] been widely interpreted to mean a one-way change, namely the sacrifice of religious claims, obligations and commitments, in favor of secular interests', Parsons maintained that 'the other possibility, however, should not be forgotten, namely that the secular order may change in the direction of closer approximation of the normative models provided by a religion, or by religion more generally'.[45]

In Parsons' view, increasing difference does not (have to) bring about indifference. Differentiation allows for specialisation and systemic autonomy. It also prevents religion from being absorbed in a non-religious environment, in this-worldly commitments. As a differentiated subsystem, separated from the world, the Church of Christ has at the same time been able to set ethical standards for life in this world. Gradually, albeit with strong fluctuations over time, it has acquired an 'independent' position from which influence could be exerted on the secular environment.[46] Unlike Weber, Parsons believed that differentiation *from* the world was the condition for intensified commitment *in* the world. Underlining the 'dualism [between other-worldly and this-worldly orientations] inherent in the whole Christian movement',[47] he stressed the interventionist or activistic orientation of Christianity and its 'historic mission' to build the Kingdom of God on earth.

For his own time, Parsons pointed to 'a structural pluralizing in the society as a whole: residence, socioeconomic status, occupation, and political attachment have become increasingly dissociated from religious affiliation'.[48] This 'loose coupling' made it feasible to think of participation in religious collectivities as a matter of free choice and to entitle individuals the right to choose their own religious affiliation, irrespective of other social roles or commitments. But the differentiation of religion *from* other societal subsystems had been met by differentiation processes *within* the system of religion, viz. by the elaboration of a distinction 'between the aspect of devotion and worship on the one hand, and the aspect of the Christian's relation to his fellow men on the other'.[49] From Parsons' point of view, the rise of a generally binding value system – a civil religion – had to counter the centrifugal tendencies inherent in a differentiating society.

Following Parsons, increasing differentiation enhanced the systemic relevance of religion. The differentiation of subsystems leads to increased heterogeneity within the societal system, but this heterogeneity also needs to be regulated. In order to preserve society's wholeness or 'systemness', the influence of the integrative function needs to be strengthened. The differentiated subsystems within society need to be controlled by generalised religious values. 'A true differentiation always involves at the same time an allegiance to common values and norms'.[50] Parsons thus built on the assumption of a law-like relation between differentiation and integration.

In contrast to Parsons, Luhmann argued throughout most of his work that the form of functional differentiation gives precedence to horizontal or heterarchical relations between function systems. He also preferred to use the term *Ausdifferenzierung*. In his view, processes of specialisation and differentiation depend on the formation of boundaries. Specialised systems differentiate *out* within society; they generate their own dynamics; they establish and maintain 'autopoietic' networks of meaningful communication. Correlative with this focus on *Ausdifferenzierung*, Luhmann used a 'negative' definition of integration. In this view, the integration of society depends on the way in which function systems are able to regulate their mutual relationships – on the basis of specific sensibilities and *insensibilities*. Luhmann thus did not comprehend integration in terms of internal cohesion, of wholeness, of coordination between the different parts of the whole. For him, loosely coupled systems can be understood as well-integrated systems, because loose coupling minimises the problems which these systems create for one another.

Integration, following Luhmann, is 'not commitment to a unity perspective, let alone a matter of "obedience" on the part of subsystems to central authorities'.[51] It lies, in Luhmann's view, 'not in the relation of "parts" to the "whole", but in the shifting, also historically flexible adjustment of subsystems to one another'.[52] A key challenge for any complex society is 'to ensure sufficient disintegration'.[53] This point of view is also characteristic of Luhmann's reflections on the conditions and consequences of the differentiation of religion. Luhmann did not link religion with integration in a functionally differentiated society. He did not assume that religion could integrate society any better than any other function system. He rather argued that religion had to find ways to come to terms with the functional differentiation of society.[54] In his view, religion is a special interest at the societal level: one among many function systems and not the one that provides the foundation for the many others. His analyses of the differentiation of religion and secularisation are therefore also closer to those of Weber than those of Parsons.

For Luhmann, the 'differentiation of religion leaves other areas of life without religious support'.[55] It has to find ways to deal with 'the consequences of functional differentiation, which results in religion yielding control of other systems to themselves'.[56] The way in which religious cosmologies did lose acceptability constitutes, for Luhmann, an early indicator of ensuing forms of secularisation. Medieval and early modern theologians could still perceive the social order as an expression of the Creator's will and the reflection of the order God had imposed on all things. They could focus on the harmony or continuity between the work of God and the natural course of the world. From their point of view, to rebel against this order was to rebel against God himself. The underlying idea of the 'great chain of being' made sense in a dominantly stratified society, divided essentially on the basis of rank.[57] It projected the hierarchical social order of the feudal system into the cosmos. With the dissolution of this rank-based order in the eighteenth century, however, the religious cosmologies lost their legitimacy. Instead, the religion system now often opted for negative characterisations of modern society. For Luhmann, 'secularisation' is a description of functional differentiation from the standpoint of religion. It is a description of society, which gained plausibility in a period in which other function complexes (politics, the economy, science, education, and so on) acquired autonomy within society. It is one among many competing descriptions used to characterise our functionally differentiated society.[58] Modernity indeed 'appears to enforce a mode of second-order observation extending to all function systems'.[59]

An advantage of this description (in comparison with religious cosmologies) is that it focuses on difference instead of unity. At the same time, Luhmann questioned in his early contributions to the sociology of religion whether the 'choices made by the system of religion as it was approaching modern times' had made it possible 'to adapt religion to modern conditions'.[60] How the differentiation form of modern society evolves 'is a very complicated story', Luhmann added, but at the moment that this form gains primacy, religion has to 'adapt to this order and has to become a functional subsystem [...]. At least it will be treated as such whether it finds this situation comfortable or not and whether or not it prefers to remain maladaptive to some extent'.[61] As we have already seen, one of the choices, made by the Christian churches, resulted in the rise of its secular activities. These churches could build on a long tradition of providing charity for the poor and indigents, but they expanded their range of activities in the nineteenth and early twentieth century. Religiously committed organisations were established almost everywhere: in education, health care, politics, the mass media, the economy and so on. Often the aim was to ensure that believers could live their entire life in their own circle: from the cradle to the grave. This type of worldly activism may be perceived as a way to control the inclusion of large populations in the system of religion; by investing 'in the world', larger parts of the population could become committed to religious projects. For the Christian churches, however, this worldly activism also had unintended consequences. Religious organisations, which are active in the world, also need to adapt to the world. Whenever they try to make a difference in the world, they have to adhere to other *eigenvalues*, such as educational, medical, political or entertainment interests. As a consequence of the many worldly activities, which the Christian churches tried to pursue, priesthood was thus often transformed into a kind of 'one-man bureaucracy'.[62] In his work from the 1970s and early 1980s, Luhmann was highly critical of the choices made by religion 'as it was approaching modern times' and its ensuing chances in modern society.[63]

In this context, Luhmann again questioned the classical idea that religion is responsible for social integration (or that social integration depends on a broadly shared religious value system). He drew a different conclusion: due to the choices it has made, religion has itself become dependent on social integration. As the churches now heavily rely on their network of secular organisations, the collapse of this network will also have negative consequences for the churches. At the same time, Luhmann saw more potential in other, 'counter-adaptive' choices. With reference to Mikhail Bakhtin, he spoke of a form of 'carnivalisation' that could build the very reason for religion's survival and revival:

> In sociological terms, churches seem to cultivate countermores, depending for their success on being different. Religion may have become counter-adaptive [...]. The Church itself [...] may have become a carnival, i.e. the reversal of normal order.[64]

In his last publications on religion, Luhmann put more emphasis on the revitalisation of religion in world society. 'It has been argued that modern society has not yet found "its religion", a religion appropriate for it, and is thus in a state of experimentation'.[65] But some of the 'crises', which religion had to face in recent decades, might also lead to new options: 'Secularization could then be understood as a cleaning-up project, clearing the terrain so that religious forms adapted to the times can then be developed'.[66] Against this background, Luhmann sketches in the final chapters of *A Systems Theory of Religion* the challenges which ensue when religion is observed as culture.[67]

> While 'secularization' implies that religion is concerned with the increasingly nonreligious directions in modern society, 'culture' exposes a religion to others.[68]

Central to this mode of observation is not the comparison between function systems but between different religions (such as monotheistic vis-à-vis polytheistic religions or animistic religions, religions that affirm the world and those that negate it, differences in relation to the question of life after death and so on). One might suspect, Luhmann adds, 'that such cultural comparisons have a weakening effect on religion. Yet that conclusion may be premature. In the end, a decorated pot is not just less beautiful because other cultures decorate their pots differently'.[69] Following Luhmann, cultural comparisons might help to increase the diversification of forms and the 'micro-diversity' upon which this system might build in our contemporary world society.

World society entails a variety of 'polycontextural descriptions and second-order observations', and for Luhmann 'there is no reason why religion could not be involved in this as well'[70]. But this system 'would obviously have to do without its ontologically based cosmologies'[71]. Looking into 'the possibilities of an evolutionary adaptation to new circumstances'[72], Luhmann also questions the impact of trends towards 'moral or cultural ecumenism'[73]. Somewhat surprisingly, he does not discuss religion in relation to conflict, although the relation between exclusion, religious diversity and violence seems obvious in contemporary world society. He underlines instead the benefits of diversity and pluralism within the religion system.

> A remarkable ability is found to adapt to different local and social-structural demands, different types of audience, and different conditions for inclusion and exclusion. The impression of diversity and liveliness in religious communication is empirically and theoretically justified.[74]

Following Luhmann, religion distinguishes itself in this regard from other function systems (where comparisons typically strengthen tendencies towards isomorphism and homogenisation). And this characteristic creates opportunities for the religion system. From the perspective of Luhmann's late work, there is no real problem for religion as a societal function system. It might rather be said that Luhmann adapted his overall theory of world society to the complexities of this system's *Ausdifferenzierung*.

Against this background, it is fair to add that a feature of both Parsons' and Luhmann's work on religion has been its empirical concentration on Christianity. Parsons had theoretical reasons for this focus: he maintained, building on Weber's work, that modern society was to an important degree an achievement of (Protestant) Christianity.[75] Although Luhmann has always been careful to avoid such kind of statements, the vast majority of the examples, which he provided, was still drawn from this religious tradition. Even in his late work, when he paid more attention to world society, the number of illustrations from other religions is rather small. Luhmann clearly made an effort to broaden the empirical scope of his analyses of religion, but an important and difficult question is whether this Christian bias is accidental (viz. nothing more than a reflection of his own level of familiarity with different religions) or whether his emphasis on the benefits of diversity and plurality could provide impetus to more fundamental revisions of his theory.[76]

Conclusion

Religion constitutes one of the ten or so important function systems within modern society. Implicitly referring to Parsons, Luhmann argued that religion entails 'many examples of preadaptive advances'.[77] He listed three examples: the invention of territorial boundaries 'by church policy and not by secular political rulers during the middle ages', the development of ideals about the 'inward-directed individual' within the context of confessional practice and 'Max Weber might have been right in assuming that urgent concerns for securing salvation by individual action (and not by the institutional mediation of the church) cleared the path for more secular, i.e. economic, insecurities and endeavours'.[78] Building on his own analyses of the religion system, we might add that the forms of inclusion developed within the system of religion predate (and possibly paved the way for) the articulation of forms of inclusion within other function systems. Altogether, however, Luhmann was hesitant to accord the system of religion a privileged position within his theory of society. He analysed this system in a considerable number of publications, but always dealt with it as one of a range of systems (all with their own history, characteristics, problems and so on).

Generally speaking, Luhmann did not question that the comparatively early differentiation of religion had been able to trigger a broad range of other processes of functional differentiation, although he looked much more at the ways in which religion has been able to handle the transition to functional differentiation. An important theme in his work is that religion has had to restructure and reconceive itself as a consequence of this transition. In his early work, he subscribed to the idea (popular among sociologists in the 1970s and 1980s) that modern society posed critical problems for religion which religion had difficulty facing. He argued that religion was 'maladapted' to the conditions of modern society. In his last works, this pessimism seems to have faded significantly. He now underlined the 'outlier' status of the religion system within the contemporary society. He also saw potential in its 'counter-adaptive' choices, although his position remained somewhat undecided. 'Evidently, the form that religion will take on in the new society, the modern one, still cannot be understood and described appropriately'.[79] Luhmann had to leave his work (on religion and other topics) unfinished, as we know, but the direction in which he mainly looked seems quite clear.

In the case of religion, Luhmann presupposes that the distinctions between inclusion/exclusion and integration/differentiation are linked in a specific way. Luhmann links inclusion with differentiation and integration with exclusion. The opportunities for religion, to which he pointed in his late work, ensue from the accumulation of exclusions. A critical note might be added, however. It might, more particularly, be questioned whether Luhmann did not overrate the level of integration in the domain of exclusion. Many empirical examples point in the direction of loose coupling or loose integration in the domain of exclusion, too. 'Illegitimate' or 'undocumented' migrants, for example, are not entitled to political rights in the state to which they have migrated, but they often do take part in economic activities (if only by carrying out undeclared work, which is paid cash-in-hand), while they are obliged to send their children to school.[80] But if our world society is loosely integrated in both the domains of inclusion and exclusion, and if thus the distinctions between inclusion/exclusion and integration/differentiation are orthogonal, the expectations for the system of religion might again be quite different. Under such conditions, it remains an open question whether and how religion might find its social function, and whether and how society might find its religion. If Luhmann would have lived longer, he might have been forced to revise his sociology of religion again. In my view, his early work is as useful as his late work to understand both the history and the current state of the religion system.

Notes

1 Niklas Luhmann, *Systemtheorie der Gesellschaft* (Frankfurt am Main: Suhrkamp, 2017), 793–8.

2 Dirk Baecker, 'Soziale Hilfe als Funktionssystem der Gesellschaft', *Zeitschrift für Soziologie* 23, no. 2 (1994): 93–110; Niklas Luhmann, 'Religion als Kultur', in *Das Europa der Religionen*, ed. Otto Kallscheuer (Frankfurt am Main: Fischer, 1996), 291–315; Rudolf Stichweh, *Inklusion und Exklusion. Studien zur Gesellschaftstheorie* (Bielefeld: transcript, 2005); Tobias Werron, *Der Weltsport und sein Publikum. Zur Autonomie und Entstehung des modernen Sports* (Weilerswist: Velbrück, 2010).

3 Niklas Luhmann, 'Society, Meaning, Religion: Based on Self-Reference', *Sociological Analysis* 46, no. 1 (1985): 14.

4 Niklas Luhmann, *A Systems Theory of Religion*. Translated by David Brenner (Stanford: Stanford University Press, 2013), 205.

5 Niklas Luhmann, *Differentiation of Society*. Translated by Stephen Holmes and Charles Larmore (New York: Columbia University Press,1982), xii.

6 Niklas Luhmann, *Funktion der Religion* (Suhrkamp, Frankfurt am Main, 1977), ch. 2 of this book was published in English as a separate book under the title Niklas

Luhmann, *Religious Dogmatics and the Evolution of Societies.* Translated by Peter Beyer (New York: The Edwin Mellen Press, 1984).

7 Luhmann, *A Systems Theory of Religion.* Original title in German Niklas Luhmann, *Die Religion der Gesellschaft* (Frankfurt am Main: Suhrkamp, 2000).

8 Niklas Luhmann, 'Die Ausdifferenzierung der Religion', in Niklas Luhmann, *Gesellschaftsstruktur und Semantik: Studien zur Wissenssoziologie der modernen Gesellschaft*, Vol. 3 (Frankfurt am Main: Suhrkamp, 1989), 259–357.

9 Luhmann presented both his major theoretical treatises – viz. *Soziale Systeme* (*Social Systems*) and *Die Gesellschaft der Gesellschaft* (*Theory of Society*) – as a critical evaluation and modification of the work of Talcott Parsons, i.e. 'the only systematic sociological theory currently available' Niklas Luhmann, *Theory of Society*, vol. 1 (Stanford: Stanford University Press, 2012), 4. In this regard, his reflections on religion do not constitute an exception; see Raf Vanderstraeten, 'Säkularisierung als Inklusionsproblem', *Soziale Systeme* 13, no. 1–2 (2007): 329–40.

10 Luhmann was a Lutheran protestant by birth and by education. He devoted *Funktion der Religion* to the memory of his deceased wife, for whom, as he wrote, religion meant more than theory was able to express. The grave at the Oerlinghausen cemetery, where Luhmann and his wife are buried, is marked with a Christian cross, but there are no other indicators of a personal religious belief (Rudolf Stichweh, 'Niklas Luhmann', in *The Wiley-Blackwell Companion to Major Social Theorists*, eds. George Ritzer and Jeffrey Stepnisky, vol. 2 (Chicester, England: Wiley-Blackwell, 2011), 287–309.). Of course, the focus on Christianity in his writings might be explained by his own familiarity with this religion.

11 Niklas Luhmann, 'Differentiation of Society', *Canadian Journal of Sociology* 2, no. 1 (1977): 29–54, at 35.

12 Ibid.

13 Émile Durkheim, *De La Division Du Travail Social* (Paris: Presses Universitaires de France, 1930).

14 See Thomas Humphrey Marshall, *Citizenship and Social Class: And Other Essays* (Cambridge: Cambridge University Press, 1950).

15 Talcott Parsons, *American Society: A Theory of the Societal Community* (Boulder: Paradigm Publishers, 2007), 74.

16 Talcott Parsons, 'The Cultural Background of American Religious Organization', in *Ethics and Bigness: Scientific, Academic, Religious, Political, and Military*, ed. Harlan Cleveland and Harold D. Lasswell (New York: Harper, 1962), 141–67.

17 Talcott Parsons, '1965 Harlan Paul Douglass Lectures: Religion in a Modern Pluralistic Society', *Review of Religious Research* 7, no. 3 (1966): 126.

18 Luhmann, 'Differentiation of Society', 40.

19 See Niklas Luhmann, *Theory of Society*, vol. 2 (Stanford: Stanford University Press, 2013), 16–27.

20 Michiel Kagchelland and Raf Vanderstraeten, 'Die Anfänge der protestantischen Erweckung in den Niederlanden: Religionspädagogische Deutungen der Hochwasserkatastrophe von 1825', *Zeitschrift für Pädagogik* 49, no. 5 (2003): 695–717, Martin Petzke, *Weltbekehrungen: zur Konstruktion globaler Religion im Pfingstlich-Evangelikalen Christentum* (Bielefeld: transcript, 2014).

21 Luhmann, *Funktion der Religion*, 232–42.

22 Not everything was new, of course. In the eighteenth and nineteenth century, the churches were increasingly perceived and treated in 'modern' ways – even if they did not (want to) change themselves. They had to 'adapt'; they had to specify their own

rules for inclusion, membership or adherence. The Christian churches retained existing ceremonies of enrolment and admittance, such as baptism, but they were forced to develop more active ways to evangelise, to incorporate large populations into their lay roles.

23 Luhmann, *Funktion der Religion*, 241–2.

24 Parsons, as we have seen, suggested otherwise: the genesis and rise of a generalised civil religion gave in his view support to the institutionalisation of broad, encompassing inclusion ideals. Following Luhmann, religion better emancipates itself from direct external determination of its *eigenvalues* Luhmann, *A Systems Theory of Religion*, 141.

25 Vanderstraeten, 'Säkularisierung als Inklusionsproblem'.

26 Luhmann, *A Systems Theory of Religion*, 201–2.

27 Ibid., 205.

28 Ibid.

29 Ibid.

30 Luhmann, *Theory of Society*, Vol. 2, 16–27. See also Niklas Luhmann, 'Inklusion und Exklusion', in Niklas Luhmann, *Soziologische Aufklärung*, Vol. 6 (Opladen: Westdeutscher Verlag, 1995), 237–64.

31 Ibid, 246.

32 Luhmann, *A Systems Theory of Religion*, 218.

33 Ibid.

34 Ibid., 219.

35 Ibid., 220.

36 Ibid.

37 Ibid.

38 Ibid.

39 Ibid., 255.

40 See Niklas Luhmann, 'Die Weltgesellschaft und ihre Religion', *Solidarität* 9, no. 10 (1995): 11–12; Niklas Luhman, 'Religion als Kommunikation', in *Religion als Kommunikation*, eds. Hartmann Tyrell, Volkhard Krech and Hubert Knoblauch (Würzburg: Ergon, 1998), 135–45.

41 Luhmann, 'Society, Meaning, Religion', 15.

42 Max Weber, *The Protestant Ethic and The Spirit of Capitalism*. Translated by Peter Baehr and Gordon C. Wells (Harmondsworth: Penguin Books, 2002).

43 See Tyrell Hartmann, *Religion in der Soziologie Max Webers* (Wiesbaden: Harrassowitz, 2014).

44 Ibid.

45 Parsons, *Action Theory and the Human Condition*, 240.

46 The most obvious example of the differentiation of religion from the secular world is the development of organised collective monasticism. The religious' withdrawal from the world, symbolised by the vows of poverty and chastity, insured the independence of this form of life from secular ties. The religious' vow of obedience, on the other hand, was an institution which assured 'selective obedience to religious authority [...] and hence protection against nonreligious influences and pressures'. Ibid., 185.

47 Ibid., 196.

48 Ibid., 204.

49 Talcott Parsons, *Sociological Theory and Modern Society* (New York: Free Press, 1967), 393.

50 Ibid., 396. For Parsons, adherence to a Christian framework remained one of America's distinctive features: 'The proper type of this society, broadly called modern society, is widely valued. This is not to say that modern society is acceptable to Christian ethics in all detail and without any critical reservation. Quite the contrary, like any other actually existing human society, it is shot through with elements of "evil," which range from the deplorable to the intolerable [...] There seems, however, to be emerging a consensus on a broad framework of the institutions of the morally acceptable society and on social problems to be solved.' Parsons, *Action Theory and the Human Condition*, 208–9.

51 Luhmann, *Theory of Society*, Vol. 2, 6.

52 Ibid.

53 Ibid., 2:7.

54 See Niklas Luhmann, 'Institutionalisierte Religion gemäß funktionaler Soziologie', *Concilium* 10 (1974): 17–22; Niklas Luhmann, 'Religion und Gesellschaft', *Sociologia Internationalis* 29, no. 2 (1991): 133–9.

55 Luhmann, 'Society, Meaning, Religion', 14.

56 Luhmann, *A Systems Theory of Religion*, 228.

57 Throughout the medieval and early modern era, not infrequently an appeal was made to the order in nature to justify the feudal system as the legitimate form of polity. Ignatius of Loyola, the founder of the Jesuit Order, for example, employed a similar argument in a famous letter on obedience written in 1553. Just as God directs the material world by means of the planets, so he governs the human society with the assistance of those in authority; just as God's commands are gradually passed on from sphere to sphere, so too the divine decrees are made known to the subjects by way of the hierarchy of superiors. See Max Wildiers, *The Theologian and His Universe: Theology and Cosmology from the Middle Ages to the Present* (New York: Seabury Press, 1982), 59–78.

58 Luhmann, *Theory of Society*, Vol. 2, 167–349.

59 Luhmann, *A Systems Theory of Religion*, 227.

60 Luhmann, 'Society, Meaning, Religion', 15.

61 Niklas Luhmann, 'Response to Commentators', *Sociological Analysis* 46, no. 1 (1985): 34–5. In Donald Smith's *Religion and Political Development*, a wide-ranging comparative study, which Luhmann (in *Funktion der Religion*, 256) cited approvingly, one reads: 'The breakup of the traditional system leaves religion with an autonomy which was neither sought nor desired. Thus a largely independent religious system is set adrift, as it were, on a stormy sea of rapid change, without charts and with serious structural weaknesses'. Donald E. Smith, *Religion and Political Development* (Boston: Little & Brown, 1970), 13.

62 Niklas Luhmann, 'Die Organisierbarkeit von Religionen und Kirchen', in Niklas Luhmann, *Schriften zur Organisation* Ed. by Ernst Lukas & Veronika Tacke, Vol. 3 (Wiesbaden: Springer, 2019), 3–54; Raf Vanderstraeten, 'Versäulung und funktionale Differenzierung. Zur Enttraditionalisierung der katholischen Lebensformen', *Soziale Welt 3* (1999): 297–313.

63 Secularisation hence refers to the increasing difference between the function systems of modern society. Following this perspective, Mark Chaves argued that 'the key task [for sociology of religion and secularisation] is to describe and explain variations in religious authority's capacity to significantly influence the functioning of other institutional spheres' Mark Chaves, 'Secularization as Declining Religious Authority', *Social Forces* 72, no. 3 (1994): 749–74, at 765. For a more detailed discussion of the

relation between religion and other function systems, see Vanderstraeten, 'Versäulung und funktionale Differenzierung. Zur Enttraditionalisierung der katholischen Lebensformen'; Raf Vanderstraeten, 'Who Had Faith in Sociology? Scholarly and Ideological Divergences in Belgium around 1900', *Science in Context* 31, no. 4 (2018): 457–75.

64 Luhmann, 'Society, Meaning, Religion', 17.

65 Luhmann, *A Systems Theory of Religion*, 221.

66 Ibid., 222.

67 See Luhmann, 'Religion als Kultur'.

68 Luhmann, *A Systems Theory of Religion*, 225.

69 Ibid., 227.

70 Ibid.

71 Ibid., 227–8.

72 Ibid., 230.

73 Ibid., 255.

74 Ibid., 252.

75 While Parsons stressed that evolutionary changes of the societal system might have been 'caused' by a variety of factors, and that religion itself had not 'produced' modern society, he also stated that Christianity had 'contributed a crucial complex of factors [...] [in] the developmental process' Parsons, *Action Theory and the Human Condition*, 174. This point of view also explains why religion (Christianity) did occupy such an important place in Parsons' late work.

76 See Beyer, *Religions in Global Society*.

77 Luhmann, 'Response to Commentators', 35.

78 Ibid.

79 Luhmann, *A Systems Theory of Religion*, 230.

80 See examples of inclusion and exclusion discussed in Stichweh, *Inklusion und Exklusion. Studien zur Gesellschaftstheorie*.

Chapter 7

HOW IS ART POSSIBLE? LUHMANN'S THEORY OF ART

Paul Buckermann

Niklas Luhmann never claimed to be an expert on the arts. However, the German sociologist offers a highly instructive, comprehensive and theoretically consistent perspective on art in its various dimensions. Luhmann draws on extensive empirical and theoretical insights in order to develop a substantive theory that applies to different branches of art, including visual art, music, poetry and literature, performing arts, and their various subgenres. This approach is deeply embedded both in his general theory of social systems[1] and his theory of society and its evolution.[2] His definitive account on art, *Art as a Social System*,[3] published three years before his death, applies to art major innovations in both of these theoretical fields, intertwining a structural description of the art system with an analysis of its evolution and differentiation as a function system in modern society. In particular, Luhmann sheds new light on core topics in the sociology of arts which include the production, reception and mediation of artworks.

Luhmann's sociological interest in the roots of art poses a seemingly simple question: How is art possible? He rejects both ontological and normative concepts in answering this question. His interest does not lie in improving existing constellations, or realising hidden potentials. Rather, he insists that asking how art is possible requires that a society *has already generated* what sociologists identify as art.[4] Luhmann's method investigates how social processes and structures have shaped what we know as art, assuming, however, that everything is contingent, and developments improbable. Potentially, art (as we know it) could be something totally different, or not existing at all. Starting with such an artificial irritation of supposed givens, sociologists need to understand *how* art has emerged in society. Rejecting teleological and deterministic concepts, Luhmann furthermore explains *why* developments have taken place that led to the evolution of an art system in society. Based on functional analysis,[5] art in its various dimensions is assumed to be a solution (among a virtual multiplicity of functional equivalents) in relation to a problem located in society. This general research strategy leads to Luhmann's comprehensive theory of art, in which art in form of artworks is analysed as a specific mode of communication. For Luhmann, art is ultimately an autopoietic function system in society, whose function is to constantly trigger reflections on the necessary but often invisible contingency of the world.

It follows that art in general, as well as artworks, artists, art genres, art institutions, and art experts, are not defined by pre-social, essential or ahistorical qualities but have emerged and were dynamically stabilised in social processes and semantical apparatuses. Luhmann's theory and analysis of art is carried out at three sociological levels. First, it introduces and applies basic concepts of his social systems theory such as communication, operative closure, medium and form, autopoiesis and second-order observation. Second, Luhmann's analysis of art is conceived as part of his theory of modern society and its social evolution. In this perspective, the operational autonomy of art is not the result of a battle for independence against hostile or colonising forces, but rather the result of functional differentiation. Theorising art with clearly defined, interrelated and abstract concepts like function, code, programme, symbolically generalised communication media and self-description enables systematic investigations and comparisons between art and other function systems. Third, Luhmann's theory of art is a comprehensive sociology of the arts in its own regard and bears considerable inspiration for the sociology of the arts, a discipline in which most studies (exceptions are the works of Pierre Bourdieu[6] and Theodor W. Adorno[7]) are not concerned with a theory, or a concept of society. The comprehensive systems-theoretical framework on production, reception, and mediation of art as well as art's autonomy, aesthetics, cultural classifications, cultural organisations, inclusion/exclusion, and relations to other social spheres provides possible and necessary irritations in a field, which is both heavily predetermined by hegemonic traditions (Howard Becker's seminal work,[8] neo-institutionalism[9] and the production-of-culture perspective,[10] Bourdieu) and constantly looking for slight or paradigmatic innovations.[11]

Luhmann's oeuvre[12] covers an extreme variety of research objects and art is not central. However, his studies on the arts show a remarkable consistency, despite the fact that the theoretical and empirical interests in studying art were influenced by developments in his general social systems theory.[13] As mentioned before, Luhmann's main contribution to art is *Art as a Social System*, published in 1995. The structure and content of this book is shaped by its mission to be a contribution to his analyses of the function systems in modern society. However, he already published several texts on the arts in the 1970s and 1980s; the first was his contribution to a conference on the concept of beauty in 1974[14] and discussed the binary code of art.[15] The following texts on art from this period reflect inspiration by theoretical works of Humberto Maturana and Francisco Varela, Fritz Heider, Heinz von Foerster and George Spencer-Brown. Luhmann discussed these theoretical innovations experimentally for the arts suggesting frames like medium/form and symbolically generalised communication media,[16] the evolution of the arts,[17] the autopoiesis of the art system and its binary code,[18] form theory, observation theory and function.[19] In the main part of this chapter, I shall reconstruct Luhmann's insights on art, followed at the end by a brief comment on the reception of Luhmann's theory of art and possible research perspectives.

Operational Closures: Art as Communication

For Luhmann, art is a form of communication. As communication, it is a self-referential process emerging from various selections in a world of uncertainty that gravitates around the artwork itself and its internal constellations of forms. While all communication is functional but improbable,[20] *communication through art* takes a decisive shape that derives from the artwork.[21] An artwork can be understood as an arrangement of (visual, acoustic, etc.) forms that provoke the unusually attentive perception of selections and deliberately observe them as contingent. Although observations sensitive to contingency are not specific to the arts, they are extraordinarily triggered and conditioned by the object's status as an artwork. While all communicative offers contain a contingent reduction of complexity, artworks as 'compact communication'[22] differ from everyday communication, because they are primarily produced to be observed as contingent in themselves. In this sense, artworks present their selections for observation, which is 'an independent contribution to communication that cannot be translated into any other medium'.[23]

While all purposefully produced things are obviously designed 'in contrast to *natural* objects',[24] artworks have a special status due to their lack of a clear function. Artworks 'serve *no external purpose*'[25] but only refer to their own construction of forms and test their internal fit. This combination of artificiality and lack of external usage provokes a conscious observation of the artwork based on the question: 'What's the point?'.[26] In artworks, forms are materialised that can only be perceived as they are and the artwork is able to be 'orchestrating'[27] an observer's observations of these constellations. This status of an artwork as compact communication 'commits the observer to fixed forms'[28] that are not directly translatable into language.

For Luhmann, communication is not the transfer of a closed package of information from sender to receiver. He conceives it as 'processing of selection',[29] consisting of three components: information, utterance, understanding.[30] In this synthetic concept of communication as a 'three-part unity',[31] *alter* selects an information from a variety of possibilities and s/he selects a way of uttering this information – again from a variety of possibilities. *Ego* must differentiate *alter's* information and utterance, and express this understanding – again a selection from a variety of possible means. Luhmann's concept of self-referential selections in conditions of double contingency is the theoretical key for understanding social systems as chains and networks reproducing themselves.[32] External phenomena (feelings, topics for conversations, research objects, artworks) can be the object of a conversation, but they need to be constructed inside social systems in their autopoietic process producing 'the elements, of which they consist, by means of the elements of which they consist'.[33]

Art is a specific mode of communication that 'makes use of perception'[34] in an exclusive way. Art is a 'functional equivalent'[35] to language, and escapes language's clear 'yes/no code'.[36] In contrast to language, 'communication guided by perception relaxes the structural coupling of consciousness and communication',[37] because, sheltered within the closed psyche, perception gives the observer more time and operational freedom to observe observations without immediately 'subjecting one's perceptions to a test for consensus'.[38] While one can like or dislike what one is perceiving, the uncontrollable perception of immediate existence cannot be doubted.[39]

In contrast to other societal function systems, the arts process second-order observations 'in the realm of perception'[40] that transcends normal communication in social systems. Communication through art roots in the operative distinctions between biological, psychological and social systems. Neuro-impulses (organic systems), perception and thoughts (psychic systems, consciousness) and communication (social systems) operate separately and cannot be translated into other modes. Communication can indeed 'indicate perception'[41] but it cannot make it available immediately in its pure operational form of thoughts.[42]

Art is a specific realm that makes the perception of aspects of the non-social world accessible to society. 'Artistic communication [...] employs perceptions that it prepares exclusively for its own use', and in this 'realizes specific forms of structural coupling between consciousness and society'.[43] 'Art makes perception available for communication, and it does so outside the standardised forms of language',[44] which only reconstructs perception within its own limits and grammar. This specificity of communication through art, and the role of observing contingent selections is the key in Luhmann's theorising of art, not only as a communicative system, but as a function system in modern society.

Observing Contingency: Production and Reception of Artworks

Communication through art elicits the observation of forms. 'Form' is a logical figure for Luhmann. It means an indication that distinguishes a perceivable marked space from a virtual unmarked space. This understanding was introduced by George Spencer-Brown, and Luhmann re-specified it for sociological questions and methods.[45] While this concept of form as the entity of distinction and indication is a highly abstract figure, it is surprisingly accessible in the case of an artwork. Into the 'unmarked state' of the world, a distinction separates a 'marked space' from an 'unmarked space':[46] there is a canvas, and a first line is drawn, which immediately discriminates all other possibilities that have not been realised. Now, other forms may follow or not. The line is perceivable and can be observed as *this line*, and nothing else. Because the artwork triggers this observation of (visual, acoustic, etc.) forms as selective forms with two sides, 'perception encounters contingency':[47] Why this line? Why not another one? Why this colour? Why any form at all? Why not cut the canvas?

Luhmann conceptualises the artwork as a self-referential sequence of forms. Because of its materiality and its durability, an observer can observe single formal elements (a tone, a curve, a material, a movement, a line, a colour, a word) and its complex constellation (a whole painting, sculpture, opera, symphony, dance, play, poem, novel). While all forms only appear on their indicated side, external or second-order observation of this form opens the unmarked space of possibilities and handles the one-sided form as a selective observation. Observing in this way means that 'the other side is perceived as well'.[48] Assessing an artwork from the position of second-order observation means to focus on perceivable distinctions[49] that could have been different but are obviously what they are. However, because no external reason can explain their concrete appearance with certainty, the observer treats them as contingent, and tries to make sense of the selection and use of forms.

This concept of second-order observation modifies traditional roles in the arts.[50] Not only do visitors of museums, theatres or operas observe forms in the artwork, but also the first-order observers, that is, the artists, painters, writers, playwrights, or composers, observe forms during the production of the artwork. Art enables and directs second-order observations continuously, 'on the side of the producer as well as on the side of the observer of art'.[51] The important difference between perception during and after production is that 'production' 'happens *only once*' whereas 'reception' '*repeats*'[52] and asks, 'why this form?' over and over again, from a variety of perspectives and interests.

This emphasis on second-order observations and contingency has theoretical implications for both the autonomy and function of art in modern society. Contingency as 'negation of necessity and impossibility'[53] means that an artwork implies 'the possibility for being different'.[54] However, it appears only 'in this and no other way'.[55]

In an early article on the medium of art, Luhmann introduced forms as tight couplings of elements that refer to a medium, defined as the totality of possible elements and their relations.[56] Referring to Fritz Heider, Luhmann's concept of medium and form emphasises the 'actuality of potentiality' of selections.[57] Luhmann introduced here an innovative perspective on different genres and branches in the arts, including painting, music, poetry, sculpture and theatre. Each tight coupling within a work in one of these genres refers to a possible realm of *this genre's* elements and couplings – its medium as 'an open-ended multiplicity of possible connections'.[58] Every artistic branch has its own range of possibilities which cannot be identified in their totality, but only through a materialised form.[59] For example, a specific musical composition conversely refers to a set of possible sounds and their combination. This perspective on the genre's media offers an instructive perspective on the typical contemporary expansion of a medium (in music e.g., atonality or new instruments); crossings ('multimedia' art and installations); and constant recombinations producing permanent contemporaneity.[60]

Furthermore, Luhmann attributes to the medium of art the establishment of a specific link to society. The medium of art is the guarantor of the 'unity of art'[61] and enables observation of art in society. These reflections on the medium of art are linked to Luhmann's use of the concept of autopoiesis and his understanding of autonomy of art.

Autonomy of Art: Autopoiesis, Code, Programmes

For Luhmann, artworks are self-referential constellations of operations because they emerge only in their own form. These forms must make sense in regard to their own selections within a medium. Producing an artwork is a complicated process, because every new form radically reduces the number of possible forms that can be attached: '[t]he chances of discovering something fitting are dwindling; going on becomes increasingly difficult'.[62] Here, the self-referential nature of a single artwork appears. Autopoiesis in general means 'that the elements of the system are produced within the network of the system's elements, that is, through recursions'.[63] While this description fits a single artwork, theorising a whole art system is something else. Such theoretical investigation needs to transcend the single compact communication, but still be carried out at the level of communication through art (instead of communication about art). Hence Luhmann's claim that a 'differentiated, autonomously operating art system only comes into being when the individual artwork is distinguished from other artworks'.[64] The autopoietic art system consists of artworks as elements in a recursive network of these elements.

Recursive networks of communication are guided by a binary code that has a dual structure of a positive and a negative value (1/0; true/false). Codes are used to decide which communication belongs to the function system. In the case of the art system, they are the means to decide which work is an artwork. Furthermore, programs are required 'that direct the proper choice of one or the other value'.[65]

Luhmann analyses the reception of art with reference to his theory of double contingency. Selections made in an artwork encounter the problem of the improbability of *alter* coding *ego's* communication as art. The probability of accepting specific forms within artworks, and an artwork as whole, ultimately lies in the work itself.[66] Communication through art finds specific conditions for the problem of human encounter in the artwork's use of form and its perception. Double contingency as the problem of two agents selecting from a variety of possibilities and knowing about each selection does not only explain the circularity and inevitable instability of social interaction. It is also a key to understand the solution for this problem: communication as selective processes and the stabilising effects of structures, namely expected expectations to reduce the complexity of possible selections.[67]

A central concern in Luhmann's analysis of art is his contested distinction of beautiful/ugly as the binary code of the social system of art. Luhmann is troubled with the code of beautiful/ugly in all his texts on art, because it blurs the distinction between code and programme.[68] Starting in the 1970s with a discussion of the classical concept of beauty and its philosophical career and deep historical embeddedness,[69] he later (1990) suggests the more abstract binary code of 'fit/lack of fit'[70] *for single artworks* to distinguish between successful and unsuccessful[71] selections made in them. In this sense, every artwork is programming itself, which means 'that the directives for elaborating and evaluating a work of art must be derived from the work itself'.[72] The 'rules that govern the work's own formal decisions are derived from these decisions'.[73] The criteria for identifying fitting and not fitting forms emerge from the work's composition of selections, and not from general aesthetic programmes and concepts of beauty, or external expectations deriving from politics, science, law or religion.

While this conception of code and single works of art matches Luhmann's claims about successive limitations of possible forms in the production of art, the autopoiesis of the art system faces another problem. The code fitting/not fitting is confronted with demands of adequate *novelty*. Novelty always means gradual novelty, unfolding sensitive tensions between 'old' and 'new'. For indicating novelty, different criteria have been developed to identify innovation and tradition such as styles[74] and art historical categories (period, school) that help to identify similarities and differences to already-known art. While artworks isolated from everything else (including other artworks) are programming themselves to show that their constellation of forms is fitting, relations between artworks identify themselves via references located in a spectrum of tradition and innovation. In order to provoke deliberate observations of their own forms, artworks have to surprise, which means that they have to 'distinguish themselves from everything that has been done before'.[75] The concept of style, for example, structures relative sameness and difference. If an artwork shows its style, 'it allows us to recognise what it owes to other works of art and what it means for other, new works of art'.[76] This self-positioning as necessarily different and the same 'establishes lines of connection to other works of art',[77] and simultaneously enables the recursive production of other works in an ongoing autopoietic process.

This constant need for novelty results in a 'self-consummation of forms'[78] at the general level of artistic production. Locating the artwork as gradually new within the history of art provokes novel tight couplings of forms, and possibly an extension of its medium. Forms that identify themselves as internally fitting and adequately new within the art's totality of works constitute the core theoretical argument in Luhmann's analysis of the operationally closed autopoiesis of the art system. 'Fit' or 'novelty' are then not to be understood as essential qualities of objects, but are recursively emerging from everything that has been happening in the art system. This self-referential process needs to constantly produce new forms, which want to be observed as contingent forms. But why? In Luhmann's theory on social differentiation and social evolution, these structures are functional, because they are a particular solution referring to a particular problem, and vice versa.

Art as a Function System in Modern Society

The functional and operational autonomy of the art system is a result of an evolutionary process. Starting in medieval times, art's historical development is closely linked to art's potential and restrictions as communication. In the process of functional differentiation, it became the function of the modern art system to make visible 'possibilities of order' that 'otherwise remain invisible'.[79] This production of potential alternatives is linked to the specific status of the work of art. Because it is produced, perceivable and observable, it appears as real as other objects or communication. However, due to its lack of external utility, it is 'separated from the world of useful or dangerous things'.[80]

In this way, the work establishes a specific 'reality on its own that differs from ordinary reality'.[81] The artwork's enclosed 'imaginary or fictional' reality, exclusively emerging from its arrangement of forms, crucially differs from the 'real reality'.[82] However, this 'split'[83] not only provokes observations of its internal forms, but the fictional reality constitutes itself in this split as an alternative to real reality.

The function of art in modern society is to constantly remind us of the contingency of any order – fictional or real. Through constructing and communicating a fictional reality that begs to be observed as contingent, the world in general appears as a reality set in place by a fictional reality. An observer's irritation is triggered through 'astonishment', which means the artwork 'surprises with information about itself' to unfold 'the self-generated paradox of creating and disrupting illusion'[84]. Luhmann claims that only the 'imaginary world of art offers a position from which *something else* can be determined as *reality* [...]. Without such markings of difference, the world would simply be the way it is. Only when a reality 'out there' is distinguished from fictional reality can one observe one side from the perspective of the other'.[85] Through fictional reality, real reality is actively drawn into a space of conscious reflections. The real reality appearing at this split becomes visible as everyday life and its mostly invisible expectations. On the other side, fictional reality is the space of exceptional reflections of extraordinary and artificial order[86] and art's function is directed at enabling irritations of structures generated *on both sides.*

Art undermines 'the magic of things – that they are, what they are'.[87] However, the function of the art is not limited to a certain (critical/affirmative) attitude towards the real reality.[88] Art does not deliver immediate solutions for the problems of society, or other subsystems. Occasionally art engages in 'performances' for other subsystems[89] or indirectly instigates innovations and creative impulses taken up by industry, fashion design or religious and political propaganda.[90] However, these selections are led by the criteria of political or economic usability, instead of the art's self-reproductive logic of finding fitting forms. This is why art's function is not limited to decisively critical positions towards general social issues (which would also corrupt the artwork's lack of external utility). Irrespective of any particular reference to the world, successful artworks reveal first and foremost the inevitable contingency of any order.

Art's function is not limited to the irritation of order. Although its function implies alternative orders, it is not propagating an 'anything-goes'. The production and recursive compilation of forms is not a random process, but must 'fit' to the artwork's own realm and its 'compelling forces of order in the realm of the possible'.[91] However breathtaking and spectacular, the fictional reality consists of selective forms and challenging interrelations. As soon as forms are selected (and without selections there is nothing), all realities 'no longer happen randomly'.[92] Other (real/fictional) realities are indeed possible, but art shows that 'even in the realm of possibility there is order after all'.[93] If art not only reveals the contingency of order, but also 'makes visible [...] the inevitability of order as such',[94] the function's 'reference problem'[95], which is located at the level of society, can be defined as the quasi-naturalisation of structures and semantics, which at its point of appearing inevitably blocks necessary innovations.

Observing Totality: Self-Descriptions and Reflection Theories

Self-description within the art system as well as external descriptions play important roles in Luhmann's theory of art. In general, a system can be described as an entity through self-descriptions, or through hetero-descriptions by other systems.[96] While hetero-descriptions comprehend the arts using political, economic, religious or other criteria, self-descriptions are orientated at the art's own reproductive logic. Self-descriptions of large systematic patterns offer orientation and memory, which is crucial in identifying traditions and innovations.

Descriptions in form of "indigenous' theories-of-the-system-in-the-system'[97] do not produce novelty on their own, but capture and recognise what has already been processed as new. These 'reflection theories'[98] deal with issues of internal referencing as well as external boundaries. In the arts, there are highly diverse semantics and frames for these reflections, using questions of style, fashion, material, genre, autonomy/heteronomy or the general role of art in society. In this sense, art has established multiple self-descriptions, which occasionally are directly competing with each other.

However, all these theoretical endeavours are not essential for the system's operational reproduction; they only support dynamic stabilisation and destabilisation in evolutionary processes. For art's self-reproduction the distinction between 'communication through art' and 'communication about art' is constitutive.[99] Self-descriptions only observe processes of autopoiesis within the art system after the event. Within their arrangement of forms, styles and other categorical distinctions, artworks already have realised communicative selections – positive and negative references – structured by fitting/non-fitting novelty which are then observed in reflection theories.

Self-descriptions apply their own observational logic and communicate in other media (language, graphs, maps, network models, tables etc.). Self-descriptions reflect on the art's code and programs and as 'secondary communications [...] have their own purpose'.[100] However, they are not art themselves. Self-descriptions can never represent the whole art system; they construct a new reality through their observations. 'Products of self-description must be treated as contingent, even if they resist contingency at the semantic level'.[101] While self-descriptions claim logical consistency and encompassing representation of the totality of art, 'they must be treated as selective choices, incapable of retaining and representing in the system's memory the sum total of what is happening in the system'.[102]

After Luhmann: Reception and Research Perspectives

Luhmann's analyses of art had so far some, although limited, influence on the sociology of the arts and other disciplines.[103] In the English-speaking world, an interesting attempt is David Roberts' assessment of the theory of form and self-reference in literature.[104] In his review of Luhmann's *Art as Social System*, Roberts highlights the problems of binary coding and its relation to aesthetic theory.[105] German discussions of Luhmann's social system theory of art also focus on the binary code and possible alternatives[106] Dirk Baecker has a particular interest in elaborating Luhmann's ideas on form and second-order observations in arts and culture.[107]A number of scholars have introduced and discussed Luhmann's theory on art at a rather general level of sociological inquiry. Although sceptical regarding operational closure and autopoiesis of arts, Erkki Sevänen identifies central research perspectives in Luhmann's theory and highlights Luhmann's discussion of possibilities for marking an object as a work of art.[108] Equally interested in the social circumstances that make a work of art possible is Willem Schinkel, who analyses the institutional field of the art world as an autopoietic system, that underwent crucial shifts in the twentieth century, and demands from Luhmann a profound theoretical scrutiny of the art industry.[109] In a similar fashion, Christian Morgner discusses the role of networks, events, cities, collections and public presentations in a self-organising art system.[110]

There are a few studies comparing Luhrmann with other social theories of art. Matthew Rampley, for example, suggests a deeper system-theoretical investigation of historical changes, co-temporalities and accelerated cultural production, consumption and mediation, thereby comparing Luhmann's approach with those proposed by Pierre Bourdieu and Michel Foucault.[111] Niels Albertsen and Bülent Diken contrast Luhmann's understanding of artworks with network and field theories proposed by Bruno Latour and Pierre Bourdieu.[112]

A canonical topic in the sociology of the arts is the role of institutional and professional infrastructures in regard to artistic production. Numerous studies have researched organisations, institutions and experts residing in the art industry. These studies look at the influences that museums, critics, magazines, art schools, biennales, art critics, curators, art historians and others had on the production of art objects. Luhmann wrote surprisingly little about the art industry, be it single institutions or the institutional infrastructure of art. He is only interested in museums as sites of memories that display past selections; they are discussed as organisations that manage to generate novelty by turning to history.[113] In general, exhibitions, publications and respective specialised institutions (museum, galleries, theatres, magazines, opera houses etc.) increase the probability that an object is perceived as an artwork.[114] Luhmann views art as a result of selections that require certain criteria and expertise. He locates this competence in an 'art specific establishment of more or less significant experts, which is capable of responding positively or negatively to new publications'.[115] For art in modernity, however, this establishment no longer congregates in one institution or under one reflection theory, but is scattered all over the art industry. The historical dispersion and deregulation since the end of feudalism have meant that critical competence is no longer bound to certain organisations.[116] In modernity, the discourse on art is not limited or structured by external resources but has to prove itself within an exclusively art-related discussion about more or less plausible descriptions of what is going on in the arts. Nevertheless, Luhmann identifies art criticism as the 'true source of the art system's self-description',[117] because the systematic methods and terms applied by critics and other observers[118] have the highest capability in generating complex descriptions that inform production or other art-related decisions like curating and collecting.

However, there are developments within the art system that render art criticism, experts and their institutions marginal. In comparison to other function systems, art witnesses a collapse of 'the internal boundary between the self-reflection or theory of the system and the system's productive operations'.[119] For Luhmann, the rich history of philosophical aesthetics led to a multiplication of self-descriptions leading to adopting contingency as a dominant value and ultimately to a situation in which 'reflection theory of the art system presents itself in and through works of art'.[120] In Luhmann's theory of art, every artwork already implies modern polycontexturality[121] and, hence, a multiplicity of perspectives in different contexts. While this argument is highly consistent with Luhmann's theory on art, it seems highly unusual compared to other sociologies of the arts that have been troubled by the role of the institutional and professional art industry, for both society in general and the production of artworks in particular.

Luhmann's writings on art reveal a crucial difference between the most influential sociologies of the arts. Compared to Pierre Bourdieu,[122] Howard Becker[123] and neo-institutionalist approaches, there is a striking gap regarding art industries. There are a number of attempts in the literature sympathetic to systems theory to fill this gap. Dirk Baecker describes the cultural infrastructure as a 'sensitive interface'[124] between society and art that organises mutual interests and limitations: he rehabilitates the notion of culture against Luhmann's dismissive attitude.[125] There are analyses of the art industry as structural coupling between subsystems and analyses of arts' performances for other function systems.[126] Finally, Luhmann's sociology of art could benefit from interdisciplinary studies on museums, galleries, biennales, theatres, opera houses and publishers; these are organisations – a prominent systems-theoretical research field[127] – that play a crucial role in the social infrastructure of the arts and contribute to the system's autopoiesis and evolution of global or world art.[128]

Investigating such organisational types and interrelations leads to questions on the internal structure and differentiation of the art system. First, institutional types in the art industry differ by tasks (exhibiting, commenting, educating, collecting, researching, criticising, relating). Second, museums and exhibition venues, theatres, publishers, festivals, galleries, biennales, magazines, art schools and many more differ in their art-specific reputation established by mutual observations of status. For other function systems, Luhmann introduced a variety of forms of internal differentiations (segmentation, stratification, centre-periphery and functional differentiation). In his sociology of art, he only fleetingly discusses segmental differentiation in art into genres, mainly as a consequence of autonomisation of the art system resulting in the loss of external support of artists (patronage etc) in modernity. For artworks and producers, he mentions the establishment of loose artistic alliances, such as Pre-Raphaelites, Blue Rider, Bauhaus and other, as examples of polycontextural segmentation.[129] Segmental differentiation of art genres enables relatively riskless experiments within one genre, before spreading to others.[130] What is lacking in Luhmann's account is a discussion of differentiation of the art industry and the complex field of professionals and institutions.[131] Research on such questions transcends Luhmann's focus on the artwork and its internal forms (what Schinkel calls 'formalism').[132] However, this research perspective would still be in line with Luhmann's theory of art and exploits immanent potentials. This future work will further provide comprehensive and consistent explanations for why art – as society knew, knows and will know it – is possible.

Notes

1 Niklas Luhmann, *Social Systems*. Translated by John Jr Bednarz and Dirk Baecker (Stanford: Stanford University Press, 1995).
2 Niklas Luhmann, *Theory of Society*, vols. 1 and 2 (Stanford: Stanford University Press, 2012, 2013).
3 Niklas Luhmann, *Art as a Social System* (Stanford: Stanford University Press, 2000).

4 This type of question is well known among sociologists, e.g., 'How is Social Order Possible?' or Simmel's seminal 'How is society possible?' (Georg Simmel, 'How Is Society Possible?', *American Journal of Sociology* 16, no. 3 (1910): 372–91.) Luhmann methodically emphasises the *why* to find explanations for what already has been made possible in a society (Niklas Luhmann, 'Wie ist soziale Ordnung möglich?', in *Gesellschaftsstruktur und Semantik. Studien sur Wissenssosiologie der Modernen Gesellschaft*, vol. 2, ed. Niklas Luhman (Frankfurt am Main: Suhrkamp, 1981); for art, see Niels Werber, 'Nachwort', in *Schriften zu Kunst und Literatur*, ed. Niklas Luhmann (Frankfurt am Main: Suhrkamp, 2008), 467.

5 Niklas Luhmann, 'Funktionale Methode und Systemtheorie', in Niklas Luhmann, *Soziologische Aufklärung 1. Aufsätse zur Theorie sosialer Systeme* (Wiesbaden: Springer, 1970); Luhmann, *Social Systems*, 52 et. seq.

6 Pierre Bourdieu, *The Rules of Art: Genesis and Structure of the Literary Field* (Stanford: Stanford University Press, 1996).

7 Theodor W. Adorno, *Aesthetic Theory* (London: Continuum, 2002).

8 Howard S. Becker, *Art Worlds. 25th anniversary edition* (Berkeley: University of California Press, 2008).

9 Paul DiMaggio (ed.), *Nonprofit Enterprise in the Arts: Studies in Mission and Constraint* (New York: Oxford University Press, 1986); Victoria Alexander, 'Pictures at an Exhibition: Conflicting Pressures in Museums and the Display of Art', *American Journal of Sociology* 101, no. 4 (1996): 797–839.

10 Richard A. Peterson and Narinder Anand, 'The Production of Culture Perspective', *Annual Review of Sociology* 30, no. 1 (2004): 311–34.

11 A good example is the so-called 'new sociology of art', the latest attempt in developing a novel perspectives at a rather general level (Eduardo de la Fuente, 'The "New Sociology of Art": Putting Art Back into Social Science Approaches to the Arts', *Cultural Sociology* 1, no. 3 (2007): 409–25; Eduardo De La Fuente, 'The Artwork Made Me Do It: Introduction to the New Sociology of Art', *Thesis Eleven* 103, no. 1 (1 November 2010): 3–9; Victoria D. Alexander and Anne E. Bowler, 'Scandal and the Work of Art: The Nude in an Aesthetically Inflected Sociology of the Arts', *Cultural Sociology* 12, no. 3 (2018): 325–42). Here, theoretical and methodological findings from science and technology studies and actor-network theory enter sociology of the arts and are combined with approaches of philosophical aesthetics and art history. This calls for a stronger focus on the artworks themselves, respective 'aesthetic properties of art' (de la Fuente, 'The "New Sociology of Art"', 410.), and 'the artwork's agency' (De La Fuente, 'The Artwork Made Me Do It', 7).

12 The archive at the University of Bielefeld provides a comprehensive bibliography (1958–2018): 'Niklas Luhmann Archive', n.d., https://niklas-luhmann-archiv.de/bestand.

13 Werber, 'Nachwort', 465.

14 Ibid., 440.

15 Niklas Luhmann, 'Ist Kunst codierbar', in Niklas Luhmann, *Schriften zu Kunst und Literatur* (Frankfurt am Main: Suhrkamp, 2008), 14–41.

16 Niklas Luhmann, 'The Medium of Art', *Thesis Eleven* 18–19, no. 1 (1987): 101–13; Niklas Luhmann, 'Kunst als Medium gesellschaftlicher Kommunikation', *Artis Observatio. Allgemeine Zeitschrift für Kunstsoziologie und Soziologie der Künste* 1, no. 1 (2022): 7–19.

17 Niklas Luhmann, 'Das Problem der Epochenbildung und die Evolutionstheorie', in Niklas Luhmann, *Schriften zu Kunst und Literatur* (Frankfurt am Main: Suhrkamp, 2008), 100–22.

18 Niklas Luhmann, 'The Work of Art and the Self-Reproduction of Art', in Niklas Luhmann, *Essays on Self-Reference* (New York: Columbia University Press, 1990), 191–214.
19 Niklas Luhmann, 'Weltkunst', in Niklas Luhmann, *Schriften zu Kunst und Literatur* (Frankfurt am Main: Suhrkamp, 2008), 189–245.
20 Niklas Luhmann, 'The Improbability of Communication', in Niklas Luhmann, *Essays on Self-Reference* (New York: Columbia University Press, 1990), 86–98.
21 Luhmann, *Art as a Social System*, 20.
22 Luhmann, 'The Work of Art and the Self-Reproduction of Art', 194; Luhmann, *Art as a Social System*, 35.
23 Luhmann, *Art as a Social System*, 24.
24 Ibid., 44.
25 Ibid.
26 Ibid., 23, 67 et. seq.
27 Ibid., 67.
28 Ibid., 144.
29 Luhmann, *Social Systems*, 140.
30 Ibid., 140 et. seq.; Niklas Luhmann, 'What Is Communication?', in Niklas Luhmann, *Theories of Distinction: Redescribing the Descriptions of Modernity*, ed. William Rasch, trans. Joseph O'Neil, Elliott Schreiber, and William Whobrey (Stanford: Stanford University Press, 2002), 155–68.
31 Luhmann, *Social Systems*, 141.
32 Niklas Luhmann, 'The Autopoiesis of Social Systems', in Niklas Luhmann, *Essays on Self-Reference* (Columbia University Press, 1990), 1–20.
33 Luhmann, 'The Work of Art and the Self-Reproduction of Art', 191.
34 Luhmann, *Art as a Social System*, 13.
35 Ibid., 19.
36 Ibid., 20.
37 Ibid., 141.
38 Ibid.
39 Dirk Baecker, 'Funktion und Form der Kunst', in *Moderne Begreifen, Zur Paradoxie eines sozio-ästhetischen Deutungsmusters*, ed. Christine Magerski, Robert Savage, and Christian Weller (Wiesbaden: DUV, 2007), 13–35.
40 Luhmann, *Art as a Social System*, 74.
41 Ibid., 10.
42 Niklas Luhmann, 'Die Autopoiesis des Bewußtseins', *Soziale Welt* 36, no. 4 (1985): 402–46.
43 Luhmann, *Art as a Social System*, 52.
44 Ibid., 48.
45 Niklas Luhmann, 'The Paradox of Form', in *Problems of Form*, ed. Dirk Baecker (Stanford: Stanford University Press, 1999), 15–26; Dirk Baecker, 'Introduction', in *Problems of Form*, ed. Dirk Baecker (Stanford: Stanford University Press, 1999), 1–13.
46 Luhmann, *Art as a Social System*, 29.
47 Ibid., 30.
48 Ibid., 37.
49 Ibid., 60.
50 Ibid., 37.
51 Ibid., 52.
52 Ibid., 38.

53 Niklas Luhmann, 'Contingency as Modern Society's Defining Attribute', in Niklas Luhmann, *Observations on Modernity* (Stanford: Stanford University Press, 1998), 44–62, at 45.
54 Luhmann, *Art as a Social System*, 67.
55 Ibid., 117.
56 Luhmann, 'The Medium of Art'.
57 Ibid., 107.
58 Luhmann, *Art as a Social System*, 104.
59 Ibid., 109.
60 See Cornelia Bohn, 'Contemporary Art and Event-Based Social Theory', *Theory, Culture & Society* 39, no. 3 (2022), 51–74.
61 Luhmann, *Art as a Social System*, 109.
62 Ibid., 35.
63 Ibid., 49.
64 Luhmann, 'Weltkunst'.
65 Ibid., 193.
66 Luhmann, 'Ist Kunst codierbar', 21.
67 Luhmann, *Social Systems*, 104 et seq; for Parsons' earlier writings of double contingency and Luhmann's changes see Raf Vanderstraeten, 'Parsons, Luhmann and the Theorem of Double Contingency', *Journal of Classical Sociology* 2, no. 1 (2002): 77–92.
68 Luhmann, *Art as a Social System*, 190 et. seq.
69 Luhmann, 'Ist Kunst codierbar'.
70 Ibid., 118; Luhmann, 'Weltkunst', 204.
71 Luhmann, *Art as a Social System*, 193.
72 Ibid., 206.
73 Ibid., 204.
74 Ibid., 208.
75 Luhmann, *Art as a Social Sytem*, 44.
76 Luhmann, 'The Work of Art and the Self-Reproduction of Art', 196 et. seq.
77 Ibid., 197.
78 Luhmann, *Art as a Social System*, 44.
79 Ibid., 96.
80 Luhmann, 'The Work of Art and the Self-Reproduction of Art', 194.
81 Luhmann, *Art as a Social System*, 142.
82 Ibid.
83 Ibid.
84 Ibid., 40.
85 Luhmann, *Social Systems*, 40.
86 Luhmann, 'Weltkunst', 199.
87 Ibid., 201.
88 Luhmann, *Art as a Social System*, 143.
89 On the distinction between function and performances see Niklas Luhmann, *Political Theory in the Welfare State* (Berlin: De Gruyter, 1990), 73 et. seq.; Luhmann, *Theory of Society*, 2013, vol. 2, chap. 4.8.
90 Luhmann, 'Ist Kunst codierbar', 42.
91 Luhmann, *Art as a Social System*, 148.
92 Ibid.
93 Ibid., 146.

94 Ibid., 149.
95 Ibid, 84.
96 See André Kieserling, *Selbstbeschreibung und Fremdbeschreibung: Beiträge zur Soziologie soziologischen Wissens* (Frankfurt am Main: Suhrkamp, 2004).
97 Niklas Luhman, 'Wie ist soziale Ordnung möglich?', in Niklas Luhmann, *Gesellschaftsstruktur und Semantik: Studien zur Wissenssoziologie der modernen Gesellschaft* (Frankfurt am Main: Suhrkamp, 1981), 195–207, 199.
98 Luhmann, *Theory of Society*, 2013, 2:226 et. seq.
99 Luhmann, *Art as a Social System*, 20.
100 Ibid., 22.
101 Luhmann, *Art as a Social System*, 245. Luhmann derives this argument from various contributions by Heinz von Foerster. See Heinz von Foerster, *Observing Systems*. (Seaside, CA: Intersystems Publications, 1984).
102 Ibid.
103 In literary studies, a tradition of systems theoretical research has developed since the 1980s. See the overview in Henk de Berg, 'Luhmann's Systems Theory and Its Applications in Literary Studies: A Bibliography', *European Journal of English Studies* 5, no. 3 (2001): 385–436.
104 David Roberts, 'Self-Reference in Literature', in *Problems of Form*, ed. Dirk Baecker (Stanford: Stanford University Press, 1999), 27–45.
105 David Roberts, 'Paradox Preserved: From Ontology to Autology. Reflections on Niklas Luhmann's the Art of Society', *Thesis Eleven* 51, no. 1 (1997): 53–74.
106 See Sebastian Krauss, *Die Genese der Autonomen Kunst. Eine historische Soziologie der Ausdifferenzierung des Kunstsystems*. (Bielefeld: transcript, 2012).
107 Baecker, *Problems of Form*; Dirk Baecker, 'The Meaning of Culture', *Thesis Eleven* 51, no. 1 (1997): 37–51; For a short English introduction see Rudi Laermans, '"After Luhmann": Dirk Baecker's Sociology of Culture and Art', *Cultural Sociology* 5, no. 1 (2011): 155–65.
108 Erkki Sevänen, 'Art as an Autopoietic Sub-System of Modern Society: A Critical Analysis of the Concepts of Art and Autopoietic Systems in Luhmann's Late Production', *Theory, Culture & Society* 18, no. 1 (2001): 75–103.
109 Willem Schinkel, 'The Autopoiesis of the Artworld after the End of Art', *Cultural Sociology* 4, no. 2 (2010): 267–90.
110 Christian Morgner, 'System Theory and Art: Micro-Diversity and Self-Organisation', *Cybernetics & Human Knowing* 26, no. 1 (2019): 47–71.
111 Matthew Rampley, 'Art as a Social System: The Sociological Aesthetics of Niklas Luhmann', *Telos* 148 (2009): 111–40.
112 Niels Albertsen and Bülent Diken, 'Artworks' Networks: Field, System or Mediators?', *Theory, Culture & Society* 21, no. 3 (2004): 35–58.
113 Luhmann, 'The Work of Art and the Self-Reproduction of Art', 211.
114 Luhmann, *Art as a Social System*, 154.
115 Ibid., 307.
116 Ibid., 307 et. seq.
117 Ibid., 308.
118 Paul Buckermann, 'Ranking Art: Paradigmatic Worldviews in the Quantification and Evaluation of Contemporary Art', *Theory, Culture & Society* 38, no. 4 (2021): 89–109.
119 Luhmann, *Art as a Social System*, 306.

120 Ibid., 307.

121 Ibid., 306 et. seq.

122 Pierre Bourdieu, 'The Field of Cultural Production, or: The Economic World Reversed', in Pierre Bourdieu, *The Field of Cultural Production: Essays on Art and Literature*, (New York: Columbia University Press, 1993), 311–56; Bourdieu, *The Rules of Art.*

123 Howard S. Becker, 'The Work Itself', in *Art from Start to Finish: Jazz, Painting, Writing, and Other Improvisations*, ed. Howard S. Becker, Robert R. Faulkner, and Barbara Kirshenblatt-Gimblett (Chicago and London: University of Chicago Press, 2006), 21–30; Howard S. Becker, *Art Worlds. 25th Anniversary Edition, Updated and Expanded* (Berkeley, Los Angeles and London: University of California Press, 2008).

124 Baecker, 'Funktion und Form der Kunst', 24.

125 On Luhmann and culture see Dirk Baecker, 'Unbestimmte Kultur', in *Widerstände der Systemtheorie. Kulturtheoretische Analysen zum Werk von Niklas Luhmann*, ed. Albrecht Koschorke and Cornelia Vismann (Berlin: Akademie Verlag, 1999), 29–46 and Dirk Baecker, in this Volume.

126 Paul Buckermann, *Die Vermessung der Kunstwelt: Quantifizierende Beobachtungen und plurale Ordnungen der Kunst* (Weilerswist: Velbrück, 2020), 282–9.

127 Niklas Luhmann, *Funktionen und Folgen formaler Organisation* (Berlin: Duncker & Humblot, 1964); Niklas Luhmann, *Organisation und Entscheidung* (Opladen: Westdeutscher Verlag, 2000).

128 Walther Müller-Jentsch, 'Das Kunstsystem und seine Organisationen oder die fragile Autonomie der Kunst', in *Organisationsgesellschaft*, ed. Wieland Jäger and Uwe Schimank (Wiesbaden: VS Verlag, 2005); Walther Müller-Jentsch, *Die Kunst in der Gesellschaft* (Wiesbaden: VS Verlag, 2011), 29–83; Andreas Göbel, 'Weltkunst die Welt der Kunst und die moderne Weltgesellschaft', in *Perspektiven der Kunstsoziologie. Praxis, System, Werk*, ed. Christian Steuerwald and Fabian Schröder (Wiesbaden: VS Verlag, 2013), 13–37; Paul Buckermann, 'Autonome Kunst und frühe Kunstmuseen in Europa: Spuren von Ausdifferensierungsprosessen in der Gründungsphase des alten Museums Berlin', in *Autonomie der Kunst?*, ed. Uta Karstein and Nina Tessa Sahner (Wiesbaden: VS Verlag, 2017), 167–90.

129 Luhmann, *Art as a Social System*, 167, 181.

130 Ibid., 180 et. seq.

131 Buckermann, *Die Vermessung der Kunstwelt*, 309 et. seq.

132 Schinkel, 'The Autopoiesis of the Artworld after the End of Art', 274.

Chapter 8

NIKLAS LUHMANN AND HIS SCEPTICAL NOTION OF CULTURE

Dirk Baecker

The chapter engages with Niklas Luhmann's understanding of the concept of culture, from his critical examination of Talcott Parsons' concept of a normative culture to ideas about a specifically modern notion of culture. It includes discussions of his ideas about culture forms of different media epochs of human society and about culture as memory of society. Luhmann's sociology of culture remains a fragment, but it can provide inspiration for a media-theoretical derivation of culture forms of society, as well as for a social theory of values. Luhmann remained sceptical about the concept of culture throughout his life, since any attempt to 'register' a social phenomenon, for example, religion or art, 'as culture' runs the risk of infringing upon the necessary protection of its latency.

Introduction

Niklas Luhmann tried to get rid of the concept of culture. His relationship to this concept was not only sceptical but also polemical. In the 1980s, he had succeeded in neutralising Talcott Parsons' use of culture as a set of values able to normatively solve problems of double contingency. He pointed out that mere coincidences, that is, time, would do the same. But in the 1990s, he experienced a rebirth of so-called cultural studies, which did not seem inclined to draw their lessons from the failure of cultural studies in the 1920s; when culture was thought to possibly provide the a priori values, by then lacking, ever since ontological metaphysics had lost its grip (Max Scheler, Nicolai Hartmann). Luhmann tried to limit the concept of culture as merely 'historical', as the product of a specific constellation of modern society – belonging to the past more than to any present, let alone future – but in the process of his examination began to conceive of culture as a memory function of society, to which he devoted ever greater attention. Luhmann's description of so-called 'culture forms' of ancient, modern and postmodern society does not lack irony in being highly speculative, but could nevertheless develop into a fruitful paradigm of future research and teaching in cultural sociology.

Culture versus System

Niklas Luhmann had a not-entirely tension-free relationship with both culture and the concept of culture. Culture is 'what one finds in the soil not belonging there'.[1] The concept of culture is 'one of the most detrimental concepts ever to be invented', because – due to its effect of transforming former self-evidence into mere contingency – it has 'disastrous consequences'[2] if something (e.g., religion, art or marriage) is observed as culture.[3] And yet he comments on his essay 'Culture as Historical Concept'[4] in the preface to the volume in which he published the essay, 'that one should further pursue the question of what actually happens when important areas of social communication, including religion and philosophy, are registered as culture'.[5]

Luhmann's difficulties with the concept of culture seem to result from the fact that he sees it as competing with the concept of systems. Both concepts posit the conditions of phenomena they observe and describe, for example, institutions, norms, values or beliefs, as historically and regionally contingent. As being 'contingent' (the term is borrowed from modal logic), they are possible, but not necessary, and may change at any time. However, while the concept of system understands said phenomena as solutions to problems that are both problems as much as solutions, and require sociologically to be appreciated if not outright protected, the concept of culture decries them as contingent without worrying about the consequences. Take religion as an example: the question is not only how one manages to still believe in a God, a concept that, thanks to the 'enlightenment', one has to learn to understand as historically and culturally contingent and to accept that new solutions may be possible to solve the problems a once taken-for-granted religion was able to solve – the problems of grace and mercy, for instance. The concept of system has a sense for the protection of latency of a phenomenon, which the concept of culture lacks. Registering something as culture means exposing it unprotected to comparison, which sets manifest phenomena as contingent, without paying attention to latent functions.

Culture as a Modern Concept

In contrast to a more ancient concept of culture linked to ideas on care, worship, breed and education (cf. Greek *paideia*), Luhmann drew attention to the emergence of a specifically modern concept of culture, in salon discussions of the eighteenth century, when observations on distinctions in culture became a kind of intellectual play, an amusement among connoisseurs. This play consisted in drawing comparisons between regional cultures or historical times.[6] Those comparisons between, say, French and English people regard manners or behaviour in certain situations in which they had to be 'witty', that is, not only surprising but also perceptive and profound.[7] Yet Luhmann pointed out that the notion of culture was soon to lose its wit, when – as a counterweight to almost rampant observations of contingent phenomena – the notion of culture was captured to bolster the still-juvenile concept of nation, and vice versa, the concept of nation was used to lend a culture the feeling of necessity it lacked. In the nineteenth century, identity and substance re-emerged as a twin concept to give weight to both nation and culture. This is true especially of the princely states of Germany, whereas for instance, France and England maintained a more cosmopolitan notion of civilisation (and began to compare races instead of cultures). Kroeber and Kluckhohn note that in World War I, the Allies thought of German *Kultur* as some deeply anchored weapon able to invoke dreadful force – until ethnologists pointed out that *Kultur* is just another word for civilisation.[8]

Yet this peculiar combination of a playful tool to not only observe but produce contingencies, a tool of much use for enlightenment philosophers interested in dissolving seemingly 'irrational' traditions, on the one hand, and the use of culture to produce, if not invent, national identities, on the other, gives the notion of culture its specifically modern twist. Culture 'in its modern emphasis was thereby created in the first place'.[9] The 'devastating consequences' relate to customs and traditions. Yet, they don't stop there. They even relate to old-European philosophy, its ontologies of essence and substance. 'Only from this perspective [within a nation seeking its identity, DB] does culture appear as something that has always been, and is thus able to dissolve and remove the old ontological and categorical world invariants, which were equally valid for past and future'.[10] Of course, this does not happen due to an arbitrary history of ideas, but due to an important change in the material foundations of society. The prerequisite for this double movement – first of comparisons producing contingencies, and then the emphatic revaluation of a contingent culture as an unquestionable national culture – is printing, and the explosion of the written and readable world; knowledge, thanks to the reports of conquering merchants, soldiers, missionaries and ethnologists. It is readers who learn and love to compare. And it is newspapers and journals that propagate images of national identity.

Culture's Translation of Things into Signs

Yet there is still more to it. Culture provides society with a genetic operation producing signs out of things. In order to compare things, one must turn them into signs in the first place. Being signs, they become variable and contingent. And they become signs for something else, some deeper truth nobody expected before. Luhmann speaks of the duplication of things and events as signs and of their use as symbols of their meaning. Only on the level of a double of themselves can things and events be compared with other things and events: 'What one grasps as a cultural phenomenon and exposes to comparison, one can observe and describe a second time whether it is using a knife, praying to God, seafaring, entering a contract, or decorating objects'.[11] This is the formula at work. By comparing knives with chopsticks, it becomes possible (a) to ask what knives or chopsticks tell about the 'culture' of the Europeans and the Japanese, which is only now becoming visible, and (b) to evaluate one and the other as better or worse, including codifying them as 'civilised' or 'uncivilised'. Once observed in this sense, that is, 'registered' as culture, the use of knives or chopsticks is no longer innocent. What was self-evident, perhaps even necessary before this observation, is only contingent afterwards. If table manners, religious beliefs, marriage customs, political authorities or scientific evidence are observed in this way, their self-evident necessity is transformed into historical and regional contingency. The associated impositions on the actors observed in this way are forced and masked as 'enlightenment', in order to be able to communicate them. Culture not only invites but also forces reflection. That reflection may run wild if it is not controlled by some notion of system, which looks not only at contingencies but also at solutions in terms of the problems they solve and the complexities they are able to deal with. Enlightenment 'in the medium of the notion of system' was christened 'sociological enlightenment' by Luhmann.[12] Its focus is not only latency protection but also respect for solutions invented by society.

Double Closure and Memory

Luhmann stays sceptical. Yet this scepticism becomes operational not only in the mind of its author, so to speak, but also in the ideas this author has how society works. What if the mechanism of duplication, comparison and attribution of contingency is operational on the level of society as well? Might it be possible to conceive of culture as adding something specific to the 'autopoiesis' of society? If that 'autopoiesis' consists of operational closure of communication on a first level, the sometimes rather unplayful play of culture may add a closure on a second level. Luhmann borrows Heinz von Foerster's idea of a 'double closure' of autopoietic entities,[13] the first one being operational, bringing in recursion, self-reference and evolutionary drift, the second being the closure of regulations regulating those operations, bringing in reflection, self-description and, indeed, regulation. Both closures together realise the 'cognitive homeostasis' of a system, that is, the calculation of a stable reality in the midst of a turbulent environment, by keeping a kind of inner equilibrium. Luhmann takes up this concept of double closure in order to describe culture in its specifically modern conception, that is, as a result of the effectiveness of regional and historical comparisons made possible by book printing, as one mechanism among possible others of this second closure of society. At the level of its first operational closure, society is the continuation of communication by means of communication ('autopoiesis').[14] At the level of a second closure, society is its own culture, that is, the regulation of its communication from the point of view of a contingent comparison. In this context, Luhmann speaks of culture as the 'memory' of society. Memory is understood as a second version of a system that continuously decides on both remembering and forgetting, that is, has as much sense for tradition as for innovation.[15] Note that there are degrees of freedom between the first and the second level of closure. Reflection, memory and regulation may be at odds with actual operations. Self-description may err. Culture may be biased.[16] Society may be on its evolutionary drift all by itself.

Culture versus Time

Luhmann did not elaborate on the idea of a description of culture as a mechanism of a double closure of society. He had little time in the last phase of his life to investigate alternative mechanisms, given that he was primarily occupied finishing his major project of a theory of society. But apparently both his scepticism and his presumption that culture played a prominent role as a mechanism of double closure, even as memory of society, continued to occupy him until his death in 1998. In the 1980s, Luhmann had primarily dealt with Talcott Parsons' view that the cultural system of action should be understood as its normative system,[17] and that it ultimately is best located in religion.[18] Parsons was of the opinion that only normative values, embodied and practised in the self-evidences of culture could solve the problem of double contingency.[19] Luhmann, on the other hand, holds the view that coincidences, that is, time, are sufficient to solve this problem.[20] The concept of culture thus became redundant within sociological systems theory. Luhmann reconceptualises this by no longer conceiving culture as a supply of norms, but of themes to be employed in society.[21] Parsons' supplementary thought that culture is a normative, albeit variable, code that allows correct or acceptable behaviour to be distinguished from incorrect or unacceptable behaviour is attenuated by Luhmann[22] to the assumption that culture is a code that allows appropriate and inappropriate contributions to communication to be distinguished.[23]

Overflow of Meaning

Luhmann's empirically and historically most important contribution to cultural sociology – namely, his studies on social structure and semantics – examines in four volumes shifts in the use of themes that have accompanied, initiated and made possible the transition from stratification to functional differentiation, and thus from traditional to modern society. These were themes like the individual, self-interest, time, law, education, social order, state and reasons of state, religion, ethics, nature, culture itself, newness, barbarism, knowledge and, in a volume of its own, love as passion.[24] However, the idea of calling this cultural sociology was remote to Luhmann. Instead, he published these studies under the title of a sociology of knowledge.[25] A translation of them into English is badly desired; they can prove that Luhmann was also working as an empirical sociologist.[26]

In the 1990s, Luhmann abandoned his attempts to distance himself from culture. The success of a reinvention of humanities, studies of literature and history as 'cultural studies' was apparently anything but temporary. In view of the growing importance of cultural diversity and cultural conflicts in the world society, oscillating, as it were, between culture clashes[27] and an emerging world culture of a world society,[28] culture could no longer be disqualified as a historically obsolete concept. Apparently, the modern reformulation of culture as a dynamic culture of contingency, vacillating between tradition and innovation, was not only indispensable for the cultural self-understanding of the world society, but also decisive for enabling and balancing processes of globalisation and regionalisation, acceleration and slowdown, and the respectful distance from and critical confrontation with others. Luhmann therefore starts anew and, not atypical for his way of working, finds in his Theory of Society theoretical reasons for his, at first, rather intuitive resistance towards the concept of culture, which becomes explicit on this occasion.

After a detailed appreciation of dissemination media and media of communication, he maintains that these 'considerations leave us with a certain scepticism about the possibilities of a theory of culture', but then presents the idea that

> the combined effect of all communication media – language, dissemination media, and the symbolically generalized media – is to condense what we might overall call 'culture'. Condensation, in this context, means that the meaning used remains the same through reuse in various situations (otherwise there would be no reuse), but is also confirmed and enriched with implications that can no longer be reduced to a simple formula. This suggests that the overflow of meaning is itself the result of the condensation and confirmation of meaning, and that communication is the operation that thus creates its own medium.[29]

Communication once again realises the first closure of society, culture the second. Culture becomes a medium in which communication regulates itself: objectively as a comparison of the one with the other, temporally as a recourse to tradition and anticipation of innovation, socially as a comparison of the native with the foreign, or also of the familiar with the unfamiliar. Culture, however, also becomes a form that, for a space or a time, holds certain possibilities of regulation. Culture distils unity out of a manifold horizon of communication, made possible by media of distribution. And culture shocks arise as new media of distribution of communication (writing in a tribal society, the printing press in early modernity or electronic media in modern society) produce new possibilities of communication – both of action and of experience – which surpasses social structures adapted to the older ones.

Farewell to the Modern Printing Press Society

In a rather speculative chapter of *Theory of Society*, Luhmann tests this idea of overflows of meaning with respect to structures of society calling for new culture forms to control that overflow and thereby generating new meaning.[30] It is his thesis that every society needs to come up with a new 'culture form' in order to deal with an overflow older forms of culture are not able to match. In this sense, Luhmann describes the Aristotelian *telos* as the culture form of antiquity, in dealing with the introduction of writing by taming exploding time horizons, and the Cartesian restless self-reference as the culture form of modernity in dealing with the introduction of book printing by making room for dynamical identities. He was still searching for a culture form of a society that is no longer modern but postmodern, 'next', digital or even post-digital (not Luhmann's words) in dealing with data storage, algorithms and the connectivity of electronic media.[31] It is possible that 'complexity' is a candidate for the culture form of the next society,[32] but others, like Claude E. Shannon's 'information', Gregory Bateson's 'play' or George Spencer-Brown's 'form' may qualify as well. We note his speculation, but also the possibility that he, not without irony, thought of himself and his truly elaborate notion of 'system' as a possible candidate for the author and the culture form of the society of electronic media. Most certainly there are many hints that he considered his *Theory of Society* (2012–2013) as a swan song to the modern printing press society; a swan song, however, which was serious in highlighting the many social problems to which modern, functionally differentiated society had found admirable solutions. All those problems and their solutions would have to be double-checked to make sure that the electronic media society has a minimal understanding, to say the least, of the complexities of society to be dealt with.

An elaboration of Luhmann's cultural-sociological considerations could follow on from these culture forms of media epochs, and ask about culture forms that deal with the meaning overflow not only of newly emerging dissemination media, but also of newly introduced and enforced generalised media of communication, such as power, money, law, faith, truth or beauty.

Values, the Medium of Culture

Whether the culture forms mentioned adequately characterise media epochs, in particular when generalised media and their 'interaction' are taken into account, is currently an open question. Presumably, Luhmann also considered it more probable that the cultural condensation of the interaction of all communication media consists of that loosely coupled 'highly mobile set of viewpoints' which he described as values in modern society.[33] These values are not introduced like truths 'by assertions, which can then be questioned and tested, but by supposition',[34] and can thus accompany conceivable communication more or less suggestively. Values do not apply substantially, but functionally, getting their weight in any concrete situation depending on other values.

Conclusion

Niklas Luhmann's contributions to the sociology of culture have remained fragments, because he never intended to elaborate a sociology of culture. His empirical works on a cultural sociology of the transition from traditional to modern society are presented as a sociology of knowledge, and his approaches to a cultural theory remain sceptical of their possibility of being integrated into his social theory. Luhmann's relationship to the concept of culture, especially that of modern society, tends to be polemical. He accuses the concept of culture of an uncontrolled way of dealing with contingency attributions that do not respect latency protection of society: to 'register' a phenomenon as culture means to set the previously self-evident, perhaps even necessary phenomenon, habit or belief as contingent, without asking about the function of the phenomenon, habit or belief in the context of solving a problem.

Among Luhmann's merits is that he (1) detached the concept of culture from the normative entanglement with the solution of the problem of double contingency introduced by Parsons; (2) formulated a specifically modern concept of culture as memory of society; and (3) nevertheless held the concept of culture in the vicinity of that understanding of a set of values that has always been decisive for cultural sociology. Communication in the 'medium' (here understood in Fritz Heider's sense of a loosely coupled set of elements where 'forms' are to be mould in)[35] of culture, as in the medium of values in terms of cultural sociology, does not mean to discover the substantial basis of society in values, but to understand culture as valuation,[36] to understand this evaluation as selective practise in dealing with ambivalent situations,[37] to consider culture in the sense of Malinowski as a balancing mechanism between body, mind, communication and environment in their conflicting demands on one another,[38] and, for the reconstruction of these values, to look at a complex calculation scheme of not only binary and ternary, but quaternary oppositions.[39] Equally, Marshall McLuhan had pointed out that only a tetrad (a whole consisting of four values) does justice to the complications of a culture that does not exhaust itself in any form, but alternates between forms, that is, links figure and ground at least twice each with each other (by enabling operations of enhancement, retrieval, reverse and obsolescence).[40] And Reinhard Brandt has presented studies that can show that the many orders of the Third (from the Trinity to the separation of powers to the theory of signs) found in European culture all refer to a fourth value that is not specifically designated, yet which defines their unity, and in some way eludes any further distinction (from faith, to power, to meaning).[41] In this way, one would trace the value of culture itself, which in a peculiar way reflects on its values among themselves, yet at the same time refuses to reflect on itself.

Notes

1 Luhmann, personal communication.
2 Niklas Luhmann, *Art as a Social System* (Stanford: Stanford University Press, 2000), 247 and 211.
3 Niklas Luhmann, 'Religion als Kultur', in *Das Europa der Religionen*, ed. Otto Kallscheuer (Frankfurt am Main: Fischer, 1996), 291–315 and 337–40.
4 Niklas Luhmann, 'Kultur als historischer Begriff', in Niklas Luhmann, *Gesellschaftsstruktur und Semantik: Studien sur Wissenssosiologie der modernen Gesellschaft*, vol. 4 (Frankfurt am Main: Suhrkamp, 1995), 31–54.
5 Niklas Luhmann, 'Vorwort', in Niklas Luhmann, *Gesellschaftsstruktur und Semantik: Studien zur Wissenssosiologie der modernen Gesellschaft*, vol. 4 (Frankfurt am Main: Suhrkamp, 1995), 8., translation D.B.
6 E.g. Johann Gottfried Herder, *Reflections on the Philosophy of History of Mankind.* Edited by Frank Edward Manuel (Chicago: The University of Chicago Press, 1968).
7 Jean Paul, *Horn of Oberon: Jean Paul Richter's School for Aesthetics.* Translated by Margaret R. Hale (Detroit: Wayne State U.P., 1973), 152 et. seq.
8 A. L. Kroeber and Clyde Kay Maben Kluckhohn, *Culture: A Critical Review of Concepts and Definitions* (New York: Vintage, 1963), 52 et. seq. See Dirk Baecker, 'Kultur und Schrecklichkeit', in *Krieg und Kunst*, ed. Bazon Brock und Gerlinde Koschik (Muenchen: Fink, 2002), 19–37.
9 Luhmann, 'Kultur als historischer Begriff', 41, translation D.B.
10 Ibid., translation D.B..

11 Ibid., 42, translation D.B.
12 Niklas Luhmann, 'Soziologische Aufklärung', *Soziale Welt* 18, no. 1 (1967): 1–25.
13 Heinz von Foerster, 'On Constructing a Reality', in Heinz von Foerster, *Understanding Understanding: Essays on Cybernetics and Cognition* (New York: Springer, 2003), 211–27.
14 Cf. Humberto R. Maturana and Francisco J. Varela, *Autopoiesis and Cognition: The Realisation of the Living* (Dordrecht: Reidel, 1980).
15 Niklas Luhmann, *Theory of Society*, vol. 1 (Stanford: Stanford University Press, 2013), 354 et. seq.; Cf. Niklas Luhmann, 'Zeit und Gedächtnis', *Soziale Systeme: Zeitschrift für soziologische Theorie* 2 (1996): 307–30; Elena Esposito, *Soziales Vergessen: Formen und Medien des Gedächtnisses in der Gesellschaft* (Frankfurt am Main: Suhrkamp, 2002).
16 Mary Douglas, 'Cultural Bias', in Mary Douglas, *In the Active Voice* (London: Routledge & Kegan Paul, 1982), 183–254.
17 Talcott Parsons and Edward A. Shils, *Toward a General Theory of Action* (Cambridge, MA: Harvard University Press, 1951), 53–109; Talcott Parsons and Neil J. Smelser, *Economy and Society: A Study in the Integration of Economic and Social Theory* (London: Routledge & Kegan Paul, 1984), 69 et. seq.; Talcott Parsons, 'A Paradigm of the Human Condition', in Talcott Parsons, *Action Theory and the Human Condition* (New York: Free Press, 1978), 352–433.
18 Talcott Parsons, 'Evolutionary Universals in Society', *American Sociological Review* 29, no. 3 (1964): 339–57, at 341.
19 Parsons and Shils, *Toward a General Theory of Action*, 15 et. seq.
20 Niklas Luhmann, *Social Systems*. Translated by John Jr Bednarz and Dirk Baecker (Stanford: Stanford University Press, 1995), 123–6; See Dirk Baecker, 'Kulturelle Orientierung', in *Luhmann und die Kulturtheorie*, ed. Günter Burkart and Günter Runkel (Frankfurt am Main: Suhrkamp, 2004), 58–90.
21 Luhmann, *Social Systems*, 163.
22 Talcott Parsons, 'Culture and Social System Revisited', *Social Science Quarterly* 53, no. 2 (1972): 253–66, at 256.
23 Luhmann, *Social Systems*, 163.
24 Niklas Luhmann, *Love as Passion: The Codification of Intimacy*. Translated by Doris L. Jones and Jeremy Gaines (Cambridge: Polity Press, 1986).
25 Niklas Luhmann, *Gesellschaftsstruktur und Semantik: Studien zur Wissenssoziologie der modernen Gesellschaft*, 4 vols. (Frankfurt am Main: Suhrkamp, 1980, 1981, 1989, 1995).
26 A selection of essays from these volumes were recently published in English: Niklas Luhmann, *The Making of Meaning: From the Individual to Social Order*: Selections from Niklas Luhmann's Works on Semantics and Social Structure. Edited and translated by Christian Morgner, Margaret Hiley, and Michael King (Oxford and New York: Oxford University Press, 2022).
27 Samuel P. Huntington, 'The Clash of Civilizations?', *Foreign Affairs* 72, no. 3 (1993): 22–49.
28 John W. Meyer, *World Society: The Writings of John W. Meyer*. Edited by Georg Krücken and Gili S. Drori (Oxford: Oxford University Press, 2009).
29 Luhmann, *Theory of Society*, Vol. 1, 248.
30 Ibid., chap. 2.
31 Ibid., 248–50; see Dirk Baecker, 'Niklas Luhmann in the Society of the Computer', *Cybernetics and Human Knowing* 13, no. 2 (2006): 25–40.
32 Paul Cilliers, *Complexity and Postmodernism: Understanding Complex Systems* (London: Routledge, 1998).

33 Luhmann, *Theory of Society*, Vol. 1, 204.

34 Ibid., 205.

35 Fritz Heider, 'Thing and Medium', in Fritz Heider, On Perception, Event Structure and Psychological Environment. Selected Papers. *Psychological Issues* 1, no. 3 (1959): 1–34.

36 Max Weber, 'Objectivity in Social Science and Social Policy', in Max Weber, *Methodology of Social Sciences* (New York: Routledge, 2011), 49–112.

37 Howard S. Becker, 'Culture: A Sociological View', *Yale Review* 71 (1982): 513–27; Ann Swidler, 'Culture in Action: Symbols and Strategies', *American Sociological Review* 51, no. 2 (1986): 273–86; Harrison C. White and Frédéric C. Godart, 'Stories from Identity and Control', *Sociologica: Italian Journal of Sociology Online* 3 (2007), https://vdocument.in/white-godart-stories-from-identity-and-control.html; Dirk Baecker, 'Kultur', in *Ästhetische Grundbegriffe: Historisches Wörterbuch in Sieben Bänden*, ed. Karlheinz Barck, vol. 3 (Stuttgart: Metzler, 2001), 510–56; Frédéric C. Godart and Harrison C. White, 'Switchings under Uncertainty: The Coming and Becoming of Meanings', *Poetics* 38, no. 6 (2010): 567–86.

38 Bronislaw Malinowski, *A Scientific Theory of Culture and Other Essays* (Chapel Hill: University of North Carolina Press, 1944); Dirk Baecker, 'The Meaning of Culture', *Thesis Eleven* 51, no. 1 (1997): 37–51; Dirk Baecker, *Wozu Kultur?* (Berlin: Kulturverlag Kadmos, 2000); Baecker, 'Kultur'; Dirk Baecker, *Kulturkalkül* (Berlin: Merve, 2014).

39 Kroeber and Kluckhohn, *Culture*, 331 et. seq.

40 See Marshall McLuhan and Eric McLuhan, *Laws of Media: The New Science* (Toronto: University of Toronto Press, 1988), 99, 127 and 129 et. seq.

41 Reinhard Brandt (ed.), *Die Macht des Vierten: Über eine Ordnung der europäischen Kultur* (Hamburg: Meiner, 2013); Baecker, *Kulturkalkül*.

Chapter 9

NIKLAS LUHMANN AND CRITICAL SYSTEMS THEORY

Kolja Möller and Jasmin Siri

Introduction

It is a widespread assertion in sociology and social theory that systems theory is uncritical. This belief is articulated by theories that call upon society to change (itself, its structure, its inner logics). We want to argue that these assertions conceal the critical potentials which are inherent in Luhmann's social systems theory. Admittedly, Luhmann was critical about critical theory and embarked on a controversy with Jürgen Habermas and others about the state of critical theory in the 1960s and 1970s.[1] His point of departure was that critical theory was still indebted to 'old-European assumptions' about how societies are evolving.[2] He sought to demonstrate that critical theory reproduced distinctions – such as between the 'part' and the 'whole' or 'below' and 'above' – which were already melting under an increased functional differentiation of social systems in modern society. Drawing upon Talcott Parson's sociology and evolution theory, he argued that modern society emerged from a rather anarchic social evolution and, thereby, established a plurality of self-referential social systems that are not reducible to a unitary mode of domination.[3] Based on these insights, Luhmann formulates a critique of society which may be deemed less appealing, less self-assured and void of gestures that support a sociologist's self-image of an impressive public intellectual, but – as we argue in the following – it takes up motifs of social critique in the tradition of Hegel, Marx and Adorno and classical sociology such as Simmel and Weber. Not the least, a whole strand of critical systems theory from the 2000s onwards investigated into this potential of Luhmann's theory – be it through clarifying the notion of critique in his work, through combining it with Marxism, post-structural thinking or the legacy of the early Frankfurt School – arguing that modern society calls for different forms of sociological critique.[4]

In this chapter, we focus on a reconstruction of three characteristic dimensions of critical systems theory in order to demonstrate how these resources can contribute to a critique of modern society that operates immanently from within the social. Most importantly, we emphasise how social critique remains connected to a robust social theory instead of collapsing into a free-standing gesture. The first section introduces Luhmann's perspective on voluntaristic approaches to social critique. These approaches, he argues, fall prey to an inappropriate account of functional differentiation. The second section demonstrates that systems theory overcomes these shortcuts through pursuing a functional analysis which allows to criticise social practices. The third section discusses the notion of structural coupling of social systems. It understands this concept as a formalised approach for the diagnosis of processes of social crisis that is able to distinguish between potentially regressive and progressive reaction patterns. The chapter concludes that one of systems theory's most prominent accomplishments has been to uncover relations between social research and critical practices which acknowledge their entanglement in the existing landscape of functional differentiation.

Voluntarism and the Problem of Sociological Critique

Niklas Luhmann insisted that sociological thought often overemphasises an integrated social whole and uses in an excessive manner normative-voluntaristic assumptions that overlook the complexity of societal differentiation.[5] Similar to Theodor W. Adorno's notion that the 'the specifically social [...] consists precisely in the imbalance of institutions over men',[6] Luhmann demonstrates the irrelevance that feelings and diverse states of human consciousness have compared to the inner logics of social systems that shape our society. Humans can raise claims, express outrage, feel humiliated or call for change, but functional differentiation makes it less likely that such communications are taken into account. Rather, it releases humans from the personal limitations of social differentiation in former forms of society such as integration into a family or clan in a segmentally differentiated society.[7]

In modern society, the 'in-dividual' is divided. The function systems of modern society perceive humans not 'as a whole' but in specific systemic roles such as priest and laic (system of religion) or teacher and pupil (education system).[8] The inclusion of humans via these roles is never permanent and is often (besides contexts such as the family system) carried out by organisations that address the system-relevant side of a human's life. The term 'person' addresses this insight in the 'individuality of exclusion':[9] Persons are conceived as a bundle of – depending on the actual systematic stereotype – differently attributed communicative expectations.[10] As much as this form of differentiation produces individual freedom (for example, from specific expectations to follow familial goals or gender roles), it also reduces the 'individual's' chance of influencing social systems. Furthermore, functional differentiation corresponds with the emergence of organisations and complicated structural couplings of systems. This creates problems for a social critique which solely operates on the level of generalised claims: On the one hand, such critique tends to self-referentially reinforce itself and, thereby, loses grip of an adequate analysis of society and its differentiation mechanisms. On the other hand, it loses an addressee. Even if there is a widespread insight in the necessity of reform or change (e.g., the need to fight racism and police violence against Afro-Americans), this goal requires complex social processes to be achieved. Mass protests, kneeling police officers or football players and broad public assurances of the need for change will be hard to sustain over an extended period of time and the question then arises if and how the insights into structural racism will seep into the decision-making processes of institutions and organisations that reproduce racism as a form of intended or non-intended by-product.

At this point, we find again surprising similarities between Adorno's and Luhmann's assessment of human impact on social systems. Of course, Adorno and Luhmann had different motives in observing and commenting on critical thinking, thought and action. Adorno warned the left against self-betrayal by emphasising that critical narratives and gestures can become part of a reactionary scheme. They could be absorbed by systemic logics and therefore fail to have any lasting impact.[11] Luhmann – who also observed the logics of absorbing social protest[12] – aimed at understanding social protest as a social system and deployed a historical interest in social critique. He importantly insisted that functional differentiation tends to marginalise protest on the fringe of the political system. Therefore, protest may unintentionally contribute to stabilise the political system by invoking claims 'from the margins of society' and, thereby, unintendedly affirm the political system as centre of the order. From this perspective, the form of protest is itself a product of bourgeois society with a considerable impact on European democratic publics. Luhmann argued, however, that the impact of critique and other human impact on autopoietic social systems is in general overestimated.[13]

The theories of both Luhmann and Adorno who share a doubt concerning the impact of critical talk and social protest on society are not easily understood in a society based on heroic images of men (mostly, men, much less women) who change the world. The collective imaginary of democratic societies in the twentieth century consists of a promise, enriched with narratives of solidarity, of social thought being able to achieve social change. Hence, social protest seems without alternative, even though it is often oppressed, misunderstood and in many cases without systemic effect. Systems theory does take protest movements seriously and analyses how they are configured. However, it confronts the emphasis on humans' impact on social systems with an observation that is much more complex, much less path-dependent, and relies on the simultaneity of different societal logics. Only on this basis, it will be possible to gain an appropriate picture of social protest and investigate the conditions of its failure and success.

The paradoxical effect of voluntaristic approaches consists in a disregard for the complicated relationship between theory and practice. This amounts to a narrow understanding of how sociological observation, social critique and political struggle are related as well as to the danger of ignoring the difficulties of the collision of scientific, societal and political calculus. As already addressed in the discussion of 'organic intellectuals' by Antonio Gramsci,[14] the role of the critical theorist by Max Horkheimer,[15] and, finally, in Luhmann's emphasis on the differentiation of science and politics, a sound approach to the political role of social research has to focus on the opportunities and restraints of mutual translation rather than on vulgar appeals. Of course, we can only speculate how Luhmann would have reacted to voluntaristic self-understandings of a sociologist's role. Would he have discussed the forms and effects of morality in liberal societies? Or would he have commented on the inner logics of politics and economics, especially capitalist commodity form, to doubt the knightly colleagues' chances of success? He may also have spoken about theory as a 'trojan horse' – and about the fact, that theories (and the sociologists who use them) are not able to control their own interventions.[16]

Functional Analysis as Critical Practice

Luhmann insisted on the fact that sociology has to pursue the pathway of a functional analysis. In our understanding, it is a mode of critique which, by analysing the function of social mechanisms and searching for functional equivalents, allows for replacing, reframing or changing established patterns or institutions. The social institutions of modern society such as 'the state', the 'law' or the 'family' become open to transformation and may be replaced by other institutions that, for example, fulfil the functions 'to take collectively binding decision' (state) or to 'stabilize normative expectations' (law). Luhmann suggested to distinguish between three dimensions of social meaning which can be found in any communication:[17] The social, the temporal and the fact dimension 'in relation to all objects of meaningful intention (in psychic systems) or themes of meaningful communication (in social systems)'.[18] A functional analysis, Luhmann argues, has to take into consideration how these dimensions are entangled and articulated within communications and semantics.[19] It uses relations to understand what enables 'a problem to be solved in one way or another. The relation between the problem and its solution will thus not be grasped for its own sake; rather, it serves as a connecting thread to questions about other possibilities, as a connecting thread in the search for functional equivalences'[20].

The critical implications of functional analysis lie in debating equivalents and investigating why empirical solutions form a practice in one way and not another.[21] In this context, systems theory can discuss alternatives to established social structures by highlighting functional equivalents. It accomplishes this by generalising specific functions and re-specifying them within particular constellations. During this process, alternative re-specification routes become visible and can be investigated for viability.

In this regard, systems theory constitutes an immanent mode of critique: It does not pit external ideals against existing social structures. Instead, it investigates transformative potentials inherently present within social systems. This viewpoint can be extended to a more fundamental inquiry that questions specific functions within the social world. However, in contrast to voluntaristic gestures, systems theory emphasises why these social structures persist. This is a crucial aspect of functional analysis: It does not underestimate the tenacity of social structures. Although systems theory is well-equipped to discuss social alternatives, it is also aware of society's complexity. The empirically overwhelming fact that all communications take place in real time and still form stable structures – for the worse and for the better – has to be processed in every sociological communication that seeks social change or reform. On the one hand, functional analysis pursues a humble pathway: The complexity of social structures makes it much harder to come to a self-assured policy advise, to ideas of social steering or even moral assumptions and condemnations. On the other hand, functional analysis is able to identify the scopes for reform and even for radical transformation in a more reliant and non-voluntaristic manner. And, of course, nobody prevents political actors from taking up these analyses.

In one of his rare interviews, Niklas Luhmann reflected on his own normative compass:

> What I decidedly do not have […] is a normative idea in which direction we should head in order to say: 'You should actually go there'. I lack that, indeed. I don't feel like a schoolmaster for society or someone who knows better where to go, at most as someone who observes changes and then detects deficiencies, for example theoretical deficiencies.[22]

Nonetheless, Luhmann was never apolitical and his works are not free of political assumptions or ideals, as his excursion to programmatic work for political parties demonstrates. It allowed him to discover that party platforms and scientific writing are irreconcilable forms of writing.[23] This nuanced approach to the relation between social research and politics does not imply that systems theory is apolitical. Indeed, it is able to reveal unintended effects of the welfare state[24] or any other structure such as racism or sexism. As a result, functional analysis can be illuminating in detecting hidden logics that conditions a situation and serves as a guide for the search of alternatives to structures that hurt or threaten vulnerable humans.

Evolution of Co-Evolution: Observing Social Crisis with Systems Theory

Luhmann was hesitant to develop a comprehensive theory of social crisis. The concept of social crisis is a key concept in critical theory, exposing societal contradictions and directing the course of history to transformation. But Luhmann has always shied away from all-encompassing gestures. His theory of social evolution and functional differentiation does not allow generalised schemes of social crisis. Using insights from contemporary theories in cybernetics and biology, Luhmann emphasised that social evolution must be viewed as a decentralised, indeterminate process. The paths of social change are chaotic and for him, it is not a central social crisis dimension that motivates society to evolve, but rather a process of recursive communication that transforms, revolutionises or destroys it without following a centralised cathartic movement from crisis to liberation. By demonstrating how the communicative dynamics pursue their own self-referential logics, he argued that there is no unitary process of evolution in his writings on history and social evolution:

> The theory of evolution decomposes […] the image of a unitary process of development, but it establishes a conceptual apparatus […] which serves as the starting point for a reconstruction.[25]

Against this backdrop, it does not seem promising to identify one central crisis dimension which unilaterally explains the course of history. In a comment on Louis Althusser's work on the dynamics of capitalism, Luhmann insists that social evolution is not in the last instance over-determined by a 'determinant' social system (in Althusser's account: capitalism), but remains, on the contrary, 'under-determined'.[26] Evolution is open to a variety of transformative options which range from incremental and technocratic adaption to break-down and revolution. Accordingly, society must be considered as the outcome of non-teleological 'evolution of evolution'[27]. A 'mechanism of multiplication', which recursively applies processes of differentiation to processes of differentiation with uncertain outcomes, sets history in motion.[28] Hence, it remains an open question which 'big bang' incited evolutionary take-offs. Systems theory abides by observing how social mechanisms emerged from the available pool of communications. This approach ultimately affects the possibilities for social critique. According to Luhmann, sociology should retroactively observe the effects of social evolution and trace it back to an interplay of variation, selection and retention.[29] Most importantly, social evolution should not be associated with 'assumptions of progress or growing rationality' because it 'results from contingency and the chaos of multiple, small, uncoordinated micro-events'.[30] However, this rejection of holistic and teleological approaches does not mean that Luhmann is uncritical. He observes negative externalities and risks which accompany differentiation processes.[31] Luhmann was motivated by a hope that sociology becomes able to understand the meaning and implications of functional differentiation and can desist from adhering to old-European methodologies.[32] This includes becoming aware of tensions and collisions between social systems and how society is confronted with a variety of risks that are in need to be addressed.

It is, however, questionable if Luhmann was stringent in his rejection of crisis theory. His focusing on variation and unforeseeable contingency in social evolution ran the risk of not being able to adequately account for selection. The question arises whether systems theory can explain the role of constraints in history and the success or failure of specific differentiation mechanisms. At the very least, the epigenetic turn in modern biology has emphasised the role of enduring in-built limitations that direct evolution from the start.[33] Furthermore, the emphasis on self-referential differentiation tends to fall prey of losing sight of the interaction of social systems and their ossified connection in constellations such as 'the state', 'the subject' and central institutions such as 'marriage' or 'the market'. Luhmann investigated these aspects and the role of inter-systemic relations by using the concept of structural coupling: In the course of evolution, it is not only that social systems undergo self-referential closure, but they establish enduring connections because societal function systems – be it law, politics, the arts or sciences – depend on each other. In fact, social systems presuppose a peculiar environmental set-up which allows them to evolve.

Luhmann defined structural couplings as follows: 'Coupling mechanisms are called structural couplings if a system presupposes certain features of its environment on an ongoing basis and relies on them.'[34] He identified a whole range of structural couplings. Examples include language (structural coupling of consciousness and communication),[35] the modern state budget (structural coupling of politics and economy),[36] or the church (structural coupling between the transcendence of belief and the immanence of the world).[37]

In order to elucidate how these mechanisms of structural coupling operate, it is worth recalling his prominent and widely discussed example of the modern constitution.[38] Luhmann defined the constitution as a mechanism of structural coupling of law and politics: The legal system assists the political system in its function to take collectively binding decisions. Legal provisions of the constitution, in particular procedures, enable politics to take, to apply and to vary political decisions. In return, the function of the legal system, to stabilise normative expectations, is facilitated through legislation adopted in the political system.

Another aspect of constitutional structural coupling is its contribution to the management of foundational paradoxes within law and politics. Both systems are grounded on self-referential communications guided by binary codes: legal/illegal in the case of the legal system and government/opposition in the case of the political system.[39] On a number of occasions, Luhmann discussed the problem of the foundational paradox in both systems.[40]As foundational paradox, he understands that the code cannot be justified by applying the code to itself. For example, it is unclear if the adoption of the legal code is itself legal or illegal. These paradoxical grounds create a certain twilight. On the one hand, social systems invent ways to conceal their paradoxical origins and to stage themselves as necessary and viable. On the other hand, they can explicitly use the paradoxical basic structure to adapt themselves to a changing social environment by revising the meaning of the code.

Constitutionalism as it emerged from the eighteenth century onwards is characterised by both tension and mutual reliance between law and politics.[41] The constitution as a legal document constitutes a higher-ranking law. At the same time, it is a political constitution authorised by a political-volitional act of the 'people'.[42] Luhmann argues that this movement of tension and mutual reliance should be reconstructed as structural coupling that allows each system to conceal its own foundational issues by externalising them to the other system via this mechanism: From the perspective of the legal system, the establishment of the code legal/illegal can be traced back to a political founding act that is (at least partly) external to the constituted powers of law. To be sure, this externalisation also has an inverted direction. From the perspective of the political system, the establishment of its code is stipulated to be a legal construction to prevent excesses of political power and thus relegates its foundation to the legal system:

> Law externalises its paradox towards politics with the aid of the state constitution. [...] The constitution commits politically unconstrained sovereignty to the process of the law. The state constitution, as a structural coupling between the law and politics, is thus characterised by the fact that there is a reciprocal externalisation of the original paradoxes of politics and law.[43]

If we take the observation on the role of structural couplings seriously, the evolutionary approach to society can be combined with notions of social critique and crisis. The evolution of evolution becomes evolution of co-evolution which is characterised by the emergence, transformation and decay of specific structural couplings between social systems. As social systems evolve over time, they constitute broader contexts of societal regulation. In these constellations, social systems 'match' each other through communicative supply chains. This opens up spaces for a theory of social crisis and critique that inquires the historical transformation of structural couplings. The sociologist Paul Bachur used these insights in order to theorise modern capitalism with the means of systems theory:

> It happens through the co-evolution of structurally coupled systems, that inter-systemic asymmetries are historically consolidated. [...]: The relation of politics to law, to economy, to science etc. is different from the relation of law to politics, to the economy, to science etc. and again different from the relation of the economy to law, to politics, to science etc.[44]

Bachur identifies an emerging asymmetry between the various contexts of structural coupling. Given the dominance of the nexus between a market-based growth economy, the law and the state, modern society may be described not only as functionally differentiated but also as a capitalist society. In this specific societal formation, the couplings between the subsystems are not arranged in an egalitarian, but in an asymmetric-hegemonic manner since they rely on the structural dominance of the capitalist economy. Thereby, social systems undergo an ossification which constitutes – at least symbolically – a social whole.

Drawing on these analyses, we can conclude that evolution is not reducible to a differential logic and requires an inquiry into the transformation of co-evolution between social systems.[45] Episodes of overarching stability and regulation are followed by episodes of erosion, decline and change. These developments have root causes that invite an assessment using social crisis theory. The context of regulation undergoes a crisis because the inter-systemic communicative supply arrangement is in such a disarray that regulation fails and, thereby, severely undermines the function of the coupled systems: In order to function, the market requires private law, the state requires money and legal instruments, marriage depends on contract as well as on romantic love. If an element of these arrangements collapses – if there is no private law, no money or no romantic love – it can lead to a crisis that affects the whole context. In such a situation, the context may no longer be able to be re-regulated by technocratic means. Foundational issues and paradoxes resurface:

If social systems are encountering an enduring and severe mismatch, the avenues for social transformation, break-down or revolution are opening up.

Such a systems-theory approach to crisis is accompanied by a substantive account of social environments. Their status cannot be reduced to an idiosyncratic construction of the respective system which is used to separate itself from what it is not. To stabilise the regulatory context, social systems must exhibit a certain degree of fitness to the substantive framework of their environment as it has evolved in history. Approaches within critical systems theory emphasise the dual role of social environments as both an internal construction of the system and a substantive social substrate. Georg Klaus, a GDR-based forerunner of critical systems theory and cybernetics, argued that in order to explain systemic reactions to social change, one must delve into 'the historical past of the social system'.[46] In his seminal work on cybernetics and epistemology, he stressed that social system's internal models of the outer world have to match it at some point, otherwise they become unable to adapt themselves to changing societal conditions.[47] In his view, the central mechanism which allows for a sound reaction to these circumstances are feedback loops that reflect on the difference between system and environment. In this way, they are able to match the existing social substrate and block the tendency towards an exaggerated excess of systemic self-referential closure.[48]

Ultimately, for Klaus, this struggle for adequacy between the internal 'constructed' and the external substantive environment (between the *unmarked state* and the *unmarked space* in Luhmannian parlance[49]) can serve as the starting point for learning processes. They can be observed when social systems succeed in overcoming constellations of crisis and re-establish relations of fitness so that they are able to regulate inter-systemic arrangements. Internal reflexivity plays a pivotal role in dealing with the differences between the unmarked space and the social system. Using these insights, a central concern of critical theory, the distinction between progress and regress, can be reformulated within critical systems theory: Regressive reaction patterns to societal crisis are distinguished by their inability to adequately process the distinction between system and environment and, as a result, tend to misconstrue their respective historically constituted social substrate. In contrast, progressive reaction patterns attempt to avoid regressive short-cuts and approximate the given social substrate through reflexivity.

Conclusion

Systems theory can be used to reclaim the possibilities for an immanent critique of modern society. Beginning with Luhmann's rejection of voluntaristic approaches to social change and his distance to idealised or principal-based approaches to understanding society, we demonstrated how a functional method and a unique analysis of social crisis processes based on systemic co-evolution can revive social critique. Luhmann's emphasis on the difficulties that arise when translating social research, social critique and politics in relation to one another should not be interpreted as a retreat from the public sphere. Rather, we argue that acknowledging competing systemic rationalities is a necessary precondition for fruitful interventions in public discourses and organisations. It is worth noting that Luhmann drew heavily on the insights of social research in his time (1960s to 1990s), but remained committed to the connection between social theory and social critique. Instead of staging critical gestures, for him social critique remains linked to an all-encompassing social theory that demonstrates how society actually operates. On this basis, it may be possible to explain and, possibly, overcome the challenges and contradictions of contemporary world society rather than merely scandalising them.

Notes

1 See also Gorm Harste, *The Habermas-Luhmann Debate* (New York: Columbia University Press, 2021).

2 Niklas Luhmann, 'Sytemtheoretische Argumentationen', in Jürgen Habermas and Niklas Luhmann, *Theorie der Gesellschaft oder* Sozialtechnologie (Frankfurt am Main: Suhrkamp, 1971), 291–405 at 372.

3 Ibid., 399 et. seq.

4 Dirk Baecker, *Studien zur nächsten Gesellschaft* (Frankfurt am Main: Suhrkamp, 2007); Dirk Baecker, 'Wahr ist nur, dass alles falsch ist. Zur Kritik der nächsten Gesellschaft', in *Systemtheorie und Gesellschaftkritik. Perspektiven der Kritischen Systemtheorie*, ed. Kolja Möller and Jasmin Siri (Bielefeld: transcript Verlag, 2016), 223–39; Armin Nassehi, *Der soziologische Diskurs der Moderne* (Frankfurt am Main: Suhrkamp, 2006); Armin Nassehi, 'Systemtheorie und Kritik. Ein Interview mit Armin Nassehi', in *Systemtheorie und Gesellschaftkritik. Perspektiven der Kritischen Systemtheorie*, ed. Kolja Möller and Jasmin Siri (Bielefeld: transcript Verlag, 2016), 207–22; Andreas Fischer-Lescano and Marc Amstutz, eds., *Kritische Systemtheorie. Zur Evolution einer normativen Theorie* (Bielefeld: transcript Verlag, 2013); Jasmin Siri and Kolja Möller, 'Kritische Theorie und Systemtheorie – eine Einleitung', *Soziale Systeme* 20, no. 2 (2015): 223–6.

5 Niklas Luhmann, *Social Systems* (Stanford: Stanford University Press, 1995), 74 and 80–4.

6 Theodor W. Adorno, 'Society', *Salmagundi* 10–11 (1969/1970): 144–53 at 144.

7 Niklas Luhmann, *Die Politik der Gesellschaft* (Frankfurt am Main: Suhrkamp, 2002), 70 et. seq.

8 Niklas Luhmann, 'Die Form "Person"', *Soziale Systeme* 2, no. 2 (1991): 166 et seq., 211–13.

9 Niklas Luhmann, *Theory of Society*, Vol. 2 (Stanford: Stanford University Press, 2013), 17–18. See also Niklas Luhmann, 'Individuum, Individualität, Individualismus', in Niklas Luhmann, *Gesellschaftsstruktur und Semantik*, Vol. 3 (Frankfurt am Main: Suhrkamp, 1989), 149–258 at 160.

10 Christine Weinbach, 'Die systemtheoretische Alternative zum Sex-und-Gender-Konzept: Gender als geschlechtsstereotypisierte Form "Person"', in *Frauen, Männer, Gender Trouble. Systemtheoretische Essays*, ed. Ursula Pasero and Christine Weinbach (Frankfurt am Main: Suhrkamp, 2003), 144; Luhmann, *Die Politik der Gesellschaft*, 20.
11 Max Horkheimer and Theodor W. Adorno, *Dialectic of Enlightenment* (Stanford: Stanford University Press, 2002), 94 et. seq.
12 Niklas Luhmann, *Protest. Systemtheorie und Soziale Bewegungen* (Frankfurt am Main: Suhrkamp, 1996).
13 Maren Lehmann, 'Das "Altwerden funktionaler Differenzierung" und "Die nächste Gesellschaft"', *Soziale Systeme* 20, no. 2 (2015): 316 et. seq.
14 Antonio Gramsci, *Prison Notebooks* (New York: Columbia University Press, 2011).
15 Max Horkheimer, *Critical Theory* (New York: Continuum, 2002).
16 Luhmann, *Protest. Systemtheorie und Soziale Bewegungen*, 74.
17 Luhmann, *Social Systems*, 74 et. seq.
18 Ibid., 77.
19 Ibid., 54 et. seq.
20 Ibid., 54. For a detailed interpretation and adaption to qualitative sociological methodologies see Jasmin Siri and Katharina Mayr, 'Management as a Symbolizing Construction? Re-Arranging the Understanding of Management', *Historical Social Research* 36, no. 135 (2011): 160–79 at 163.
21 Niklas Luhmann, *Trust and Power* (Chichester, Toronto: Wiley, 1979), 2.
22 Luhmann, *Protest. Systemtheorie und Soziale Bewegungen*, 70, translation by the authors.
23 Niklas Luhmann, 'Probleme eines Parteiprogramms', in *Freiheit und Sachzwang*, ed. Horst Baier (VS Verlag für Sozialwissenschaften, 1977), 167–81.
24 Niklas Luhmann, *Political Theory in the Welfare State* (Berlin: de Gruyter, 1990).
25 Niklas Luhmann, 'Geschichte als Prozeß und die Theorie sozio-kultureller Evolution', in Niklas Luhmann, *Soziologische Aufklärung 3* (Opladen: Westdeutscher Verlag, 1981), 192–3, translations by the authors.
26 Niklas Luhmann, 'Evolution und Geschichte', in Niklas Luhmann, *Soziologische Aufklärung 2* (Wiesbaden: VS Verlag für Sozialwissenschaften, 1973), 156. Luhmann criticises Althusser's social theory in this passage. In contrast to Luhmann, Althusser developed a scheme of social evolution that displayed an inverted relationship of variation and selection: While existing social systems select and evolution varies contingently according to Luhmann, social instances within capitalism vary, but social evolution is determined 'in the last instance' by a dialectic of productive forces and production relations as a selection pattern, according to Althusser. However, Althusser noted that the 'lonely hour of the last instance never comes', emphasising that this dialectic roughly directs history (Louis Althusser, *Für Marx* [Frankfurt am Main: Suhrkamp, 2011], 139). In order to accentuate this type of causality through absence, he referred to Sigmund Freud's conception of over-determination.
27 Luhmann, 'Geschichte als Prozeß und die Theorie sozio-kultureller Evolution', 193. For a critical reconstruction of this approach cf. Barbara Kuchler, 'Das Problem des Übergangs in Luhmanns Evolutionstheorie', *Soziale Systeme* 9, no. 1 (2003): 39.
28 Niklas Luhmann, *Theory of Society*, Vol. 1 (Stanford: Stanford University Press, 2012), 301.
29 Luhmann, *Social Systems*, 41 et. seq.

30 Kuchler, 'Das Problem des Übergangs in Luhmanns Evolutionstheorie', 28.

31 Luhmann, *Die Politik der Gesellschaft*, 421–9, 432–3.

32 Luhmann, *Social Systems*, 211–13.

33 For an attempt to make use of these resources for a critical systems theory see Hauke Brunkhorst, *Critical Theory of Legal Revolutions* (London and New York: Bloomsbury Publishing, 2014); Fábio Portela L. Almeida, 'The Emergence of Constitutionalism as an Evolutionary Adaptation', *Cardozo Public Law, Policy, and Ethics Journal* 13 (2014): 1.

34 Niklas Luhmann, *Law as a Social System* (Oxford: Oxford University Press, 2004), 382.

35 Luhmann, *Theory of Society*, Vol. 1, 63.

36 Luhmann, *Die Politik der Gesellschaft*, 384.

37 Niklas Luhmann, *A Systems Theory of Religion* (Stanford: Stanford University Press, 2013), 167 et. seq.

38 Luhmann, *Law as a Social System*, ch. 10 and Niklas Luhmann, 'Verfassung als evolutionäre Errungenschaft', *Rechtshistorisches Journal* 9, no. 1 (1990): 180. For an elaboration of the law/politics/society-nexus from a critical systems theory perspective see Darrow Schecter, *Critical Theory and Sociological Theory. On Late Modernity and Social Statehood* (Manchester: Manchester University Press, 2019), 34 et. seq.

39 Luhmann, *Social Systems*, 242 et. seq.

40 See, for example, Niklas Luhmann, 'The Third Question: The Creative Use of Paradoxes in Law and Legal History', *Journal of Law and Society* 15, no. 2 (1988): 153–65. For an inquiry into the role of paradox in systems theory see Urs Stäheli, 'Politik der Entparadoxierung. Zur Artikulation von Hegemonie- und Systemtheorie', in *Das Undarstellbare der Politik. Zur Hegemonietheorie Ernesto Laclaus*, ed. Oliver Marchart (Wien: Turia/Kant, 1998), 52–66.

41 See Chris Thornhill, *A Sociology of Constitutions: Constitutions and State Legitimacy in Historical-Sociological Perspective* (Cambridge: Cambridge University Press, 2011).

42 Kolja Möller, 'Das Ganze der konstituierenden Macht. Zur politischen Soziologie verfassungsgebender Gewalt', in *Systemtheorie und Gesellschaftkritik. Perspektiven der kritischen Systemtheorie*, ed. Kolja Möller and Jasmin Siri (Bielefeld: Bielefeld Verlag, 2016), 39–56; Kolja Möller, 'Drohung und Verfahren', in *Prozeduralisierung des Rechts*, ed. Tatjana Sheplyakova (Tübingen: Mohr Siebeck, 2018), 245–64.

43 Gunther Teubner, 'Exogenous Self-Binding: How Social Systems Externalise Their Foundational Paradox in the Process of Constitutionalisation', in *Sociology of Constitutions: A Paradoxical Perspective*, ed. Alberto Febbrajo and Giancarlo Corsi (London: Routledge, 2016), 30–48.

44 João Paulo Bachur, *Kapitalismus und funktionale Differenzierung* (Baden-Baden: Nomos, 2013), 112, translation by the authors. For similar perspectives see Uwe Schimank, 'Die Moderne: Eine funktional differenzierte kapitalistische Gesellschaft', *Berliner Journal für Soziologie* 19, no. 3 (2009), 327–51; Bob Jessop, 'Zur Relevanz von Luhmanns Systemtheorie und von Laclau und Mouffes Diskursanalyse für die Weiterentwicklung der materialistischen Staatstheorie', in *Der Staat der bürgerlichen Gesellschaft. Zum Staatsverständnis von Karl Marx*, ed. Joachim Hirsch, John Kannankulam, and Jens Wissel (Baden-Baden: Nomos, 2008), 165–92.

45 There are obvious similarities to contemporary crisis theory based on pragmatism and critical theory. Cf. Rahel Jaeggi, *Critique of Forms of Life* (Cambridge, MA: Belknap. Press. Imprint of Harvard University Press, 2018), 114 et. seq.

46 Georg Klaus, *Kybernetik und Erkenntnistheorie* (Berlin: VEB Deutscher Verlag der Wissenschaften, 1966), 87.
47 Ibid., 34 et. seq.
48 Ibid., 259 et. seq.
49 On the difference between unmarked state and unmarked space in Luhmann's writings, Cf. Urs Stäheli, *Sinnzusammenbrüche. Eine dekonstruktive Lektüre von Niklas Luhmann's Systemtheorie* (Weilerswist: Velbrück Wissenschaft, 2000), 82 et. seq.

Chapter 10

LUHMANN, ON ALGORITHMS, IN 1966

Elena Esposito

Problems of Automation in the 1960s

In the 1960s, what did Luhmann know about digitisation and algorithms? It may sound like a rhetorical question, but Luhmann already knew a surprising amount of information about these subjects, which I should like to demonstrate by way of analysing the 1966 text *Recht und Automation in der öffentlichen Verwaltung* (*Law and Automation in Public Administration*).[1] I use quite a few direct quotations from Luhmann's text, which is unusual for me, but I hope that the quality of the citations will speak for themselves. Of course the argument in the end is my own, yet it has been inspired by and constructed with material from Luhmann's text.

Big data and self-learning algorithms obviously did not yet exist, but Luhmann was already anticipating them, as various passages show. For example, he suggested that the idea that machines cannot solve system problems through other than purely logical means:

> [...] will probably one day be unhinged with the counterargument that you can teach a machine leaps of logic and that it can clarify the admissibility of such leaps better than humans. The Carnegie Institute of Technology, Pittsburgh, is already working on computer programmes for problems which are unclearly defined and [these programmes are] designed to imitate and perhaps even surpass the human approach [...] And every time that those advocating the use of human beings precisely formulate their reasons, at the same time they create the basis for the formulation of new equivalent machine programmes.[2]

The current competition/cooperation between humans and machines in the development of game algorithms (and machine-learning in general) could hardly be better described. For example, there is the famous case of DeepMind's 'AlphaGo' programme that plays the Chinese board game Go, in which the machine learned from humans how to beat the best human players, who then learned from the machine how to improve their strategies, leading to a further improvement in the programmes.[3] Luhmann was also informed about attempts to build 'a general problem-solving computer programme with learning possibilities',[4] which is what we have today with self-learning algorithms.

The acuity of Luhmann's text, however, lies not only in his foresight, but above all in his approach. Although Luhmann refers to two precise fields – administration and law – his text offers ideas about some of the most puzzling general questions in the current debate on the proliferation of intelligent algorithms. To this purpose, it is unnecessary that a sociologist knows the latest developments in technology, because this can even be misleading. Luhmann was aware that sociological problems first arise on another level. As early as 1966, he could see that 'it is not simply a question of choosing a new remedy [...] but a structural decision whose rationality cannot in essence be adequately determined by cost comparisons'.[5] 'The revolutionary effect of administrative automation will emanate from its preconditions and implications for thinking',[6] and this also is the case outside the bounds of administration. The problem in 1966, and even more so today, is that 'there is no comprehensive theoretical comparative framework, no conceptual language'[7] to deal with these problems. Luhmann's considerations 'are based on the central idea that questions of this kind are neither posed nor answered within the conventional frame of reference of legal thought, nor by the economic, probabilistic, statistical models of action rationalisation, nor by computer logic'.[8] They would require a 'comprehensive theoretical frame of reference'[9]. The challenge of automation (today we would say digitisation) lies in the fact that it produces a 'refreshing pressure to think', which leads us to reconsider many categories that would otherwise be taken for granted – and this is precisely thanks to the 'fortunate circumstance [...] that machines are so expensive'.[10]

At this level, Luhmann is extraordinarily enlightening. The whole book is a treasure trove of ideas. Here, I present only certain issues which address the most contested and problematic points in the current debate on digitisation and algorithms – which goes to prove that we still need more reflection at the level of social theory. Even if the 1966 text does not provide full-fledged answers, we can already find the starting points to make the debate more fruitful and avoid many of the dead ends in which we are still stuck.

Machine Logic and Human Thinking

I start with the issue of 'singularity',[11] which dreads a situation where machines are increasingly capable of performing tasks previously reserved only for humans (communicating, independently producing information, deciding and predicting), which now they can develop autonomously and with full operational control. In 1966, Luhmann was engaged in a debate with Karl Zeidler, who asked 'whether, under what conditions and with what legal consequences it is permissible to transfer administrative acts from humans to machines'.[12] The fear, then as now, was that 'if data-processing machines cannot be sufficiently dominated and controlled by humans [then] they secretly produce nonsense'.[13] Luhmann's objection is that if the purpose of automation is 'to relieve conscious human activity', the output of machines cannot be 'precisely controlled and incorporated into human consciousness and cannot even be predicted in its details'.[14] Machines are used precisely to abdicate total control in a controlled way. 'The extent to which machine activity is monitored by conscious processes is in essence randomly variable',[15] and cannot be the criterion.

The reason for Zeidler's worries is based on a logical error: 'The fact that legal norms can only be addressed to humans in no way means that only human action can be legally relevant'.[16] There are also many examples of this outside technology – 'think of the falling roof tile'.[17] Zeidler had already pointed out the difficulty of abandoning the idea that actions 'must be borne by the consciousness and will of human beings',[18] albeit the notion of will is inchoate, and tends to be identified acritically with a psychological concept.[19] According to Luhmann, however, '[I]n the last analysis there are no rational reasons for preferring human performance to machine performance'.[20]

Machines work differently than humans, and that is why they are useful. They follow a logic which is not based on thinking.

> [The machine] accomplishes a work with symbols that can be implemented without having to consider the meaning of the implementation or even the meaningful background of the decision rules (just as one can correctly calculate in a schematic way without considering the mathematical sense of the calculation rules or the practical sense of the calculation task).[21]

Just as automatic translation programmes of today work without understanding the translated texts and languages. Algorithms translating from Chinese into English know neither Chinese nor English, nor their grammar – and not even the programmers who designed the algorithms necessarily know these languages – which is why they work so well.

That machines don't think isn't a problem, but rather an advantage. The difficulties that must be tackled are different, and result from their operating principle: 'The machine works step by step according to the individual instructions of the programme'.[22] It is an algorithm. The machine, therefore, has very little flexibility, and requires 'decision analysis in microscopic refinement,[23] much beyond what is otherwise necessary in communication. This detailing is connected to the 'transition from a material to a temporal order';[24] the material complexity of the correlations must be dissolved into a temporal sequence of simple signals – which is the main difficulty. In many cases, one does not know how the complexity of information can be reduced to a format compatible with machine processes. One must relinquish ambiguity, yet ambiguity is often necessary for the performance of a certain function.

Luhmann deals with legal communication, whose performance for society is termed 'absorption of uncertainty'.[25] In this case, the ambiguity of legal concepts and situations provides the necessary space for legal justification, which is convincing not because all its various stages are controlled: 'The rationality of legal problem-solving lies [...] not in the logical correctness of its conclusions'[26] but in 'that it convinces everyone that it has convinced its author'.[27] This is no longer the case with inflexible algorithms.

Responsibility and Accountability

Here we encounter – a half century ago – one of the topics most vehemently discussed in the current debate on the spread of algorithms, namely the controversial question of 'algorithmic accountability'.[28] Now that algorithms seem to function as social actors, produce information and take decisions, who should be accountable for their actions? This is the very subject of the discussion concerning the 'right to be forgotten' by such entities as Google.[29] Who should be addressed regarding the requirement that the Web makes inaccessible the private data of those who request such and meet certain conditions, if the personal information is generated autonomously by an algorithm, which neither Google nor its programmers know or control? Or more dramatically: who is accountable for accidents involving self-driving cars that autonomously decide how to deal with contextual circumstances – whether and when to brake, turn around, pass another car and the like?

What does Luhmann have to say about this? The fact that the actor is a human being or a machine is of relative indifference to the law. 'The kind of "equipment" on which programmes are carried out, the machine or the human brain, is irrelevant to the "logic" and correctness of the conclusion'.[30] 'Transfer of the decision to machines does not change the legal situation itself'.[31] As we know today, machines are often much safer than human drivers with regard to the risk of accidents, because – as Luhmann remarks – the machines 'allow for much fewer errors in the processing of data'.[32]

But what arises when the autonomously deciding machine *does* make errors – for example, when the self-driving car has an accident? How can the law accomplish its social performance of uncertainty absorption? The problem in these cases lies in an 'incongruence of responsibility and accountability'.[33] The attribution of responsibility takes place in all cases of uncertainty absorption, and is not solely the concern of 'human data processing' – although the uncertainty to be absorbed, of course, pertains to people and not cars.[34] Similar to the relationship between doctor and patient, the responsibility is shared between people and machines:

> [A]s it cannot be said that the patient alone bears responsibility for his health – because he trusts the doctor for well-considered reasons – the person who, for well-considered reasons, accepts the results of a computer system cannot be said to bear sole responsibility. If we define responsibility in our sense as a function of communicative processes, it no longer makes sense to attribute it individually.[35]

This is precisely why there arises a discrepancy between responsibility (*Verantwortung*) and attributable accountability (*zurechenbaren Verantwortlichkeit*), thus complicating the issue of algorithmic accountability.

Algorithms certainly bear responsibility. But does it make sense to say that they are accountable? And most importantly, would this accountability provide the required uncertainty absorption? In the case of errors, one must know who is accountable, and cannot dodge this expectation with a perpetual 'I don't know'.[36] With algorithms, however, it is much more difficult to determine accountability. When it comes to people, it suffices to regulate 'the representation but not the production of the decision'[37] and the secrets of uncertainty absorption are respected. The attribution is compatible with some degree of opacity regarding the decision-makers' processes and thoughts. Yet, given the way algorithms work – they faithfully follow (and must follow) the instructions in the programme – the attribution would require a detailed study of all steps in the procedure generating the decision. Due to the impenetrability of the most advanced algorithms,[38] this is not only virtually impossible but would not even serve to absorb the uncertainty.

Once responsibility has been established, how do we proceed? The purpose of automation, as we have seen, is to consciously relinquish the need to control all aspects of the process. The result is a kind of 'de-individualisation of errors'.[39] How can the person in charge prevent the error from repeating, if the advantage of the procedure is that he or she need not control it? The only form of prevention would be private insurance, which does not absorb the uncertainty of other observers.

The problem is that in these cases, 'the threat of imprisonment effectively fails as a motivational tool',[40] not only because there is not much that can be done, but the errors in most cases do not depend on motivation, or a lack thereof – for example, an interest in comfort or in reducing the workload.[41] The motivation of those responsible has little to do with the settlement of damages, so their possible sanctioning would do little to help in absorbing the uncertainty of the audience. Tesla's punishment for an accident caused by a self-driving car would not increase confidence that there will be no more such accidents in the future.

Digitisation highlights a difficulty that is still open, and invites sociological reflection: the reference of the meaning of communication to a person's thoughts and motives is a fiction.[42] We, therefore, need a general theory that shifts the reference to the social meaning of the processes, in this case to the communicative effects of digitisation. In 1966, Luhmann proposed a 'novel theory of administration'[43] – in the next 30 years, he delivered a novel theory of society.[44]

Notes

1 Niklas Luhmann, *Recht und Automation in der öffentlichen Verwaltung* (Berlin: Duncker & Humblot, 1966), all translations from the Luhmann text are by the author of this contribution.
2 Ibid., 59–60, fn. 24.
3 David Silver and Demis Hassabis, 'AlphaGo: Mastering the Ancient Game of Go with Machine Learning', *Google AI Blog* (blog), 27 January 2016, https://ai.googleblog.com/2016/01/alphago-mastering-ancient-game-of-go.html; Cade Metz, 'In Two Moves, AlphaGo and Lee Sedol Redefined the Future', *Wired* (blog), 16 March 2016, https://www.wired.com/2016/03/two-moves-alphago-lee-sedol-redefined-future/; Cade Metz, 'What the AI Behind AlphaGo Can Teach Us About Being Human', *Wired* (blog), 19 May 2016, https://www.wired.com/2016/05/google-alpha-go-ai/; Paul Taylor, 'The Concept of "Cat Face"', *London Review of Books* 38, no. 16 (2016): 30–2.
4 Luhmann, *Recht und Automation in der öffentlichen Verwaltung*, 40.
5 Ibid., 130.
6 Ibid., 141.
7 Ibid., 11.
8 Ibid., 13.
9 Ibid.
10 Ibid., 9.
11 E.g., Ray Kurzweil, *The Singularity is Near* (New York: Viking Books, 2005).
12 Karl Zeidler, *Über die Technisierung der Verwaltung. Eine Einführung in die juristische Beurteilung der modernen Verwaltung* (Karlsruhe: Müller, 1959), 30.
13 Ibid.
14 Luhmann, *Recht und Automation in der öffentlichen Verwaltung*, 31.
15 Ibid.
16 Ibid., 31–2.
17 Ibid., 32.

18 Ibid., 30.
19 Ibid., 32.
20 Ibid., 60.
21 Ibid., 45.
22 Ibid., 49.
23 Ibid.
24 Ibid.
25 Ibid., 56–7.
26 Ibid., 59.
27 Ibid., 55.
28 For an insightful and up-to-date discussion, see Anna Beckers and Gunther Teubner, *Three Liability Regimes for Artificial Intelligence: Algorithmic Actants, Hybrids, Crowds* (Oxford: Hart, 2022).
29 Meg Leta Jones, *Ctrl + Z: The Right to Be Forgotten* (New York: New York University Press, 2016); Elena Esposito, 'Algorithmic Memory and the Right to Be Forgotten on the Web', *Big Data & Society* 4, no. 1 (2017), https://doi.org/10.1177/2053951717703996.
30 Luhmann, *Recht und Automation in der öffentlichen Verwaltung*, 55.
31 Ibid., 47.
32 Ibid., 80.
33 Ibid., 105.
34 Ibid.
35 Ibid, fn. 7.
36 Ibid., 106.
37 Ibid.
38 Jenna Burrell, 'How the Machine "Thinks": Understanding Opacity in Machine Learning Algorithms', *Big Data & Society* 3, no. 1 (2016), https://doi.org/10.1177/2053951715622512.
39 Luhmann, *Recht und Automation in der öffentlichen Verwaltung*, 110.
40 Ibid., 111.
41 Ibid., 112.
42 Ibid., 115.
43 Ibid., 142.
44 Niklas Luhmann, *Theory of Society*, 2 vols. (Stanford: Stanford University Press, 2012/3).

Chapter 11

NIKLAS LUHMANN OBSERVED IN A LUHMANNIAN PERSPECTIVE

Klaus Dammann

Introduction

The chapter asks what kind of biography in writing about Niklas Luhmann as a person is compatible with Luhmann's own theory. In contrast to most other canonical authors in social science, with whom Luhmann was well acquainted,[1] his biographical writings are characterised by an 'ambitious modesty' (to use Michael King's and Anton Schütz' label[2] and reveal a sceptical distance to information on the non-scholarly person. By adopting a Luhmannian perspective and using his theoretical distinctions the chapter introduces Luhmann as a divided person. A central concern of the chapter resumes in an effort to reconstruct a Luhmannian perspective on biography and to use his view on methodology and empirical research. In the last part, the chapter debunks allegations of Luhmann's involvement in Nazi Germany and demonstrates instead the usefulness of Luhmann's theories for studies of Nazi violence.

Niklas Luhmann Individualised and Divided

We need both names, Luhmann and Niklas, to refer to the phenomenon that has become recognised in the discipline of sociology. Luhmann insists throughout his work that sociology should not speak of 'the' individual, but refer to addresses (billions) when conceiving individuals: Which individual? Sometimes it is necessary to use bureaucratic data, like 'born in 1927 in Lüneburg, died 1998 in Oerlinghausen' in order to identify and address him, because there are fake Niklas Luhmann (not only on Facebook) and other Niklas Luhmann (real, named after him?).

Not only the rise of individuality in the Western world is a topic in Niklas Luhmann's work, but we also find a theory of 'personal division', dividuality.

Luhmann's distinction between social communication and psychic processes, which he derived in part from US role theory, suggests the distinction between social and psychic Luhmann. The latter is visible for a sociologist only by observing the psyche in its communicative academic and lay versions. In Christian faith the soul, and in sociology the psyche (in Luhmannian parlance: consciousness), can be conceived of as individual, that is: indivisible. Non-sociological academic analysis does not think in this way: the psyche (observed by psychology) and the body (observed by biology) must be seen as divided as Luhmannian sociology conceives the person in communication as being divided.[3]

Luhmann when googled is sometimes individualised (e.g., 'married to Ursula von Walter, three children', 'The Hegel of the 20th Century' or 'The Popstar with a card index', my translations). More often we find labels that describe fixed roles or can be applied to others as well, like 'brilliant' and 'one of the most important sociologists of his century'.

For the purpose of this chapter, Luhmann will be conceived of as a person who is known for his scientific and scholarly publications in sociology, law and the humanities as well as other works, such as art reviews, talk show appearances and interviews. We will call this person in an author's role NL, a brand he used when referring to publications signed with his name.[4] We will not, however, divide this NL further, for instance through time dimensions into an early and a late author, or through social dimensions into a politically red, a black and a green author. The remaining person will be marked Niklas Luhmann. We can investigate the links that are formed between the two using this distinction: Did Niklas Luhmann have any influence on NL, or is NL unaffected by other personal expectations, as texts suggest that claim the 'death of the author'.[5]

How to Do Biography?

The early NL, from his first publication in 1958 onward, presents himself only using a short curriculum vitae containing some bureaucratic data. Around his 60th birthday, he began to answer biographical questions, but he was sceptical on the value of such kind of communication.[6] To counter this biographical reluctance, I sketch some events in Luhmann's history and describe them with a little help from his theories.

In the following, I wish to ascertain which aspects of Luhmann's theory can be used for his biography. In his analysis of modernity in contemporary society, Luhmann operates with a distinction between social structure and semantics.[7] This distinction replaces previous attempts to double reality and to theorise relationships, such as superstructure/basis or ideas/their realisation, culture/structure, or discourse/other structures. Social structure in NL's late work is defined by using the distinction operation/observation and occurs when 'communication just happens' and does not describe itself. Applied to biographical analysis this means that the data which historians find about Luhmann in archives or in transcriptions of interviews are data that contain semantics of all kinds (juridical, economical, popular etc.), and there is difficulty in identifying social structures in NL's sense. This undermines the conventional distinction between (objective) trajectories (individualised life paths) and (subjective) biographical writing as a real or fictional account of this. For example, 'from jurist to sociologist and beyond' is semantically loaded biography, not a (hidden) life path that has been discovered and subsequently described. Almost all known communication from and about Luhmann which we know contains such (non-academic) semantics.

Can the concept of life course be applied to his biography? In NL's theory, it is neither a standardised pattern nor an individualised path, but rather a medium into which the function system of education inscribes forms. In this sense, it belongs to the social structure, especially the educational function system.[8]

NL's work provides few guidelines for the writing of history in general and even fewer suggestions for doing biography. First: We could use the three meaning dimensions present in NL's theoretical work for reviewing Luhmann's life events and trajectories. In the time dimensions, we can distinguish 'before/after NL'. Some observers tell us that after NL everything has changed in their discipline. Before, in the humanist tradition, the factual (some translate 'material') and the social dimension of meaning have been confused by constructing subjects and intersubjectivity. In the factual meaning dimension, one has to divide Luhmann by means of roles (as I already did in a simple way: NL and Niklas Luhmann), function systems, selected theoretical predecessors, careers and ageing. Both the expectations, forming the bundle called person, and their fulfilments and disappointments, that is deviance/conformity (normative expectations) and knowledge/ignorance (cognitive ones), can be used as topics. Of course, an unperson, as NL calls it, being transformed into a person is of special interest for some audiences. Was something concealed that may become attached to his person? For NL, this can be shown only with data from publications because this person is defined by published texts.[9] In the social dimension of meaning, alter ego is added to ego. The question arises: Who becomes the observer? Dissent/consent may be explored.

Second: One of NL's short biographical dictums is 'My thought is primarily historical'[10], indicating that NL is interested in long-term change in both social structure and semantics. The caesurae most frequently mentioned by

NL are the emergence of new primary forms of differentiation. His theory of social change is an evolutionary theory of neo-Darwinian origin[11] and he does not find much in conventional historical research that may be a contribution to this and the other theories he embraces.[12]

One of NL's contributions to the theory of history, inherent in evolutionary thinking, is his insistence on contingency. For biography, both opportunities that arrive by chance and a readiness to grasp them are important. This idea has been applied in a historical study on the German 'social history' school. It is necessary to emphasise that this school refrains from using the concept of contingency, unlike other works by conventional academic history, popular history writing and fiction.[13]

Third: From NL's theory of meaning (leading distinction: actuality/potentiality) and his view on chance follows that in the history of semantics (scientific or not) missed opportunities can be found and newly selected. Trajectories not chosen remain latent and can be made manifest by research. He demonstrated this in the case of Vauvenargues.[14] However, I am not aware of latent opportunities in this sense in the evolution of NL's work. He is familiar with the work of Weber, Parsons and Goffman and consciously distances himself from it in many ways.

Fourth: The leading distinction of the academic study of history seems to be dis-/continuity. In order to avoid continuity bias when writing the history of scientific or other theories, NL recommends decomposing unities into their constituent parts.[15] Applied to writing the history of Modern Systems Theory (the Bielefeld School), which began in the 1960s and has continued to the present day, this 'Systems theory' must be understood as a collection of theories, each with their own leading distinctions; these include not only system/environment, but also information/utterance/understanding (communication theory), as well as variation/selection/retention (evolutionary theory) and a few other distinctions. And these half a dozen sub-theories can be decomposed into distinctions (not just the most important ones) as their elements. When studying the history of sociological approaches, one may come across discontinuity of distinctions and hypotheses with empirical content that ended to a significant extent in graveyards. There are already renowned studies of the itineraries of NL's distinctions.[16] Since 1965, NL investigated, through a variety of empirical case studies, the relationship between the formation of scientific distinctions and social structure.[17]

Fifth: Another advice of NL is to be aware of what linguists call antonym substitution and not rely on terminology rather than on concepts. Most concepts can be re-described as distinctions with two sides. When terminology evolves, it may be that one term remains the same but the distinction has changed. NL's use of the concept person is an example of this kind of substitution. In his early writings, person (and personality) is sometimes conceptualised as a system, a psychic system. Later, at least from 1984 onward, persons are identified in communication and no longer conceptualised as systems.

Sixth: Reality is in sociological and historical research produced ('constructed') when communication resists other communication.[18] Hypotheses regarding NL's and Niklas Luhmann's life trajectories can be tested against what is found in archives, scholarly works, and, in the case of journalism, other reliable texts.[19]

To conclude: The elements of science are publications, and reputation is a key factor in selecting publications. Both the reception of older pieces of work by NL and the reception of NL's work by others form additional key themes in biography. In fact, there are not only theories and distinctions that form the contents of science and other academic work. Nevertheless, there are several distinctions from NL-Theory which can be found in his own texts on Luhmann-biography: careers/ageing, motives and networks, sometimes coming together by chance and in seizing opportunities.

Careers, Motives and Contingencies

Using the distinction between career and age,[20] we can see that Luhmann's and NLs calendar ages influenced crucial career decisions. After paramilitary service as an anti-aircraft auxiliary, he is forced to become a German soldier at the age of 17, and his life is endangered by the US Army's progress in liberating Germany from Nazi rule and by German military justice. Due to his age, he is not forced to work in a French prisoner-of-war camp (which would have been in French mines). Furthermore, due to his age, he becomes an emeritus professor at 65, 'retired but not tired', and is able to accept invitations from around the globe without being required to teach.

Not only deviance (from norms) but more generally disappointment with expectations attracts attention. Some of NL's and of Niklas Luhmann's careers seem to have disappointed normative or cognitive expectations. NL is one of a minority of social scientists being educated in law and practising law (as a law clerk before and after a second law degree between 1949 and 1955, and as a civil servant between 1956 and 1962, on leave for study at Harvard University in 1961–62) before becoming an academic. After completing his university studies at the age of 21, there were no attractive academic career opportunities for people with his degree. He therefore had to look for other ways of making a living. NL is one of the few sociologists among the German postwar cohort who does not enter the academic world by teaching or by assisting a professor, but who holds instead of this senior research positions

(1962–66). Another irregularity: Niklas Luhmann becomes a single parent to their three children born between 1961 and 1965 after his wife dies in 1977.

Unexpectedly, the career of his publications reaches 28 languages (Arabic, Georgian and Korean included). English is not the most frequent foreign language.[21] Except for natural sciences and mathematics, nearly every academic discipline shows interest in his writings, from educational studies, legal studies, political science, theology and comparative literature to sociology. There are sociologists who have created the impression that the sociologist NL is least known in his own discipline. But he is one of the few German sociologists who is awarded local honours (one honorary chair and eight honorary degrees in five countries), and international awards (membership in two academies of science, Hegel and Amalfi prizes, many special editions of journals and conferences on his work).

As to other careers, there is a sense of irritation because Niklas Luhmann's known political career crossed lines that may be no other sociologist ever crossed; his contributions have been popular with Marxist and Catholic journals and were picked up by several German politicians, excluding only extreme right-wingers and those of the minor liberal party in Germany who were satisfied with Sir Ralf Dahrendorf as their intellectual figurehead. Luhmann's career as a media star, equipped with a fan base and Facebook addresses, continues after his death. Conferences on NL have attracted speakers from various continents and have flourished since then. However, the interest in the careers of Niklas Luhmann, the person formed outside the expectations observable in NL's publications, seems to have become stagnant since his death.

Niklas Luhmann's narratives refer to contingency, especially chance, and to career opportunities that were seized. It was by accident that his army comrade was killed by an American grenade close to him (springtime 1945 in Southern Germany) and that Niklas Luhmann survived. Contingency and a chain of random events characterise the career of the sociologist NL as we know him. Let us sketch three versions: (1) From 1949 to 1955 he works on a doctoral dissertation (comparative political science, for a law degree). His supervisor Wilhelm G. Grewe leaves university, however, to pursue a diplomatic career (negotiations with the allied countries about the status of occupation; then ambassador inter alia at Washington, DC) and does not succeed in continuing his right to participate in doctoral examinations as other professors did.[22] NL abandons his dissertation. Would he have attempted, armed with a law doctorate, to work as an assistant to a professor of law before pursuing a tenured academic career in law? (2) After passing his second law examination in 1953, entitling him to enter any legal job in Western Germany outside of academia, Niklas Luhmann attempts to become a lawyer working for the aviation industry. His closest friend, having participated in the Anti-Hitler plot of July 1944 together with Otto John, an aviation lawyer (*Lufthansa*), tries to get him a job at the re-established *Lufthansa* via this Otto John, then chief of Western Germany's domestic intelligence service. John, however, a former secret agent for the German resistance and American and British secret services and an ardent antifascist, disappeared in Communist Berlin (and then Moscow) on the day of the 10th anniversary of the coup against Hitler. Seven days after having lost Otto John as a possible agent, Luhmann applies for the civil service of his native federal state of Niedersachsen.

After the two losses of possible agents, other chances arise for this man who can be proud to have a strong talent for picking up opportunities. He obtains the job of a clerk at the Higher Administrative Court in Lüneburg where he meets Carl Hermann Ule, then a judge and later a professor of administrative law. Ule becomes an important figure for NLs career, providing a reference for NL's Harvard scholarship and assisting him in his job and publication careers that contributes to NL's enormous productivity in his early years and finally to two offers of a chair at Speyer School of Public Administration. Entering the Speyer Research Institute was indeed a 'crucial decision' for NL. It is there that he produces, in less than five years (1962–1965), several books and scholarly essays, including the typoscript and the publication he uses for his first and second doctorate (*Habilitation)* at Münster University in 1966. NL is offered the position of university professor of sociology at Bielefeld University as a result of this. NL has a low non-scholarly workload in Bielefeld because the sociology department has a large staff and supports him to schedule teaching around his publications with just minimal administrative work.

It is standard biographical procedure to inquire about the motives of the person in question as well as their mentors. In the case of NL, the candidates for being mentors are the lawyer Ule and sociologists Dieter Claessens and Helmut Schelsky who help in finding a job and assist at graduation at Münster University; Philosopher Jürgen Habermas has an unofficial role; he is the Goliath in the story of NL's reputation having won the David versus Goliath debate in 1971. NL adopts the 'vocabulary of motives' concept from C. Wright Mills; it enables motives to be chosen from vocabularies and presented when it is expected.[23] In this vein both, NL and Niklas Luhmann, are able to adapt motives to special situations when asked for motivations, and can later even maintain that they are not sure to have a correct memory of their past motivation. Concerning the mass media's revelation that many left and liberal celebrities in West Germany had been made members of the Nazi state's party on the occasion of Hitler's birthday in 1944,[24] Niklas Luhmann provided a number of arguments, among them one motive. He mentioned on the British military government's questionnaire that there was an allied amnesty for the youth, and further that he did not receive any membership confirmation (which was required by civil law, even in Nazi times, as well as the consent of his father). He remembered later that his school class, all of them anti-aircraft auxiliaries on airports in northern Germany during RAF bombing, had been threatened by being locked up in an aeroplane hangar until they and him agreed to join the party.[25]

Networks, the Why-Question and the Luhmannian Analysis of Nazi Violence

There are three uses of a simple network concept (consisting of units and ties) in NL's work. First: networks of operations form a system, using a system/environment distinction. There are second networks of concepts (distinctions). Linking and not inventing these concepts may be the merit that can be attributed to NL individually (and not to a role).[26] The third use is that of a network of addresses, that is, of organisations or persons. The impact of personal networks on system differentiation varies from one region of world society to another. We may distinguish these social networks from social systems by identifying if they use the distinction system/environment. For example, what is called strong ties, for example, intimate dyadic or triadic relations,[27] are forms of system building too.

A scholar gains a special reputation if recognised as the founder of an academic school. So far there is no study of a NL-School (Modern System Theory (MST), Bielefeld School or Critical Systems Theory School). There are two journals associated with the thoughts of NL: *Soziale Systeme* (established 1995) and *Sistemas Sociales* (since 2013). However, it is unclear if they contribute to forming a school and if a system/environment distinction is used in selecting contributions by these reviews created by this NL system. There are attempts to place NL into three other schools of thought, named after the city of Leipzig (sociologist Hans Freyer as its leading figure), the philosopher Joachim Ritter (specialist on Hegel) and Talcott Parsons. However, there is no convincing evidence of sufficient ties (intellectual or otherwise) to NL.

Was NL a member of a personal network that included (former) Nazis? When Theodor W. Adorno (1903–1969) returned from his forced emigration in 1949 and became a professor at Frankfurt University in 1953, he wrote to a friend that he had to shake many bloody hands.[28] As for Luhmann, there were few 'bloody hands' in this broader sense that he encountered. And nearly all of his 'Nazi' contacts were persons who had converted (or reconverted) from fascism to liberal democracy. The only man he meets who is accused of still being a fascist (for his racism) was the British psychologist Hans Jürgen Eysenck. NL negates and even ridicules Eysenck's biological (in this case:

neurological) style of thought.[29] Furthermore, in a lecture commemorating Edmund Husserl's epochal 1935 book *The Crisis of European Sciences and Transcendental Phenomenology*, NL does not reveal any sympathy with Husserl's eurocentrism[30] that led this man, who had to give up teaching due to racist Nazi persecution, to claim white cultural supremacy over 'gypsies' and 'Indians'.[31]

Looking at the networks and organisations in which Luhmann operated, there is no Nazi naming and shaming of most of the colleagues whom NL meets at his permanent workplaces. There is no convincing criticism for recruiting practices of these local organisations in which he worked (court, administrative agency, academic units). A small number of his students (including distance-learning students) are considered to have become toxic right-wing political activists. However, if you review their publications, there is no NL-concept tied to right-wing semantics.[32] I suggest that right-wing political theory is not compatible with Luhmannian theory.[33]

General questions of 'why?' are found in NL's work in two forms: asking for genesis and asking for the persistence of phenomena. However, concerning biography, it seems not helpful to look for causal links but more suitable to use the problem/solution scheme that underlies NL's functionalism: What are the problems that can be tackled by biographic writing?

Some see a problem of 'better' understanding NL's texts. An old device of literary criticism, applied to the problem of linking NL to Niklas Luhmann, is said to lead to 'better understanding': using biographic details.[34] The examples I know do not seem to correct the current understanding of NL's work. Education and practice as a lawyer, overseeing Hannover city's planned motorways when first conceiving systems theory, having become a (fictive) Nazi-party member in 1944, saved from death by chance in 1945 – these and some other events mentioned in biographic sketches on Luhmann do not help explain any part of NL's theoretical work. One of NL's more fundamental objections seems to be: Why stick to an author's intentions that you cannot know? Occasionally, while analysing NL's case-related studies historical examples for understanding concepts that frame the case are needed. You may in searching cases profit from looking at Niklas Luhmann's past, including the news he is supposed to have consumed.[35]

Second, the evolution of NL's terminology and concepts sometimes led to older ones becoming obsolete. Histories of terms and distinctions can help to follow this evolution and to avoid an older framework that does not fit anymore.[36]

Third, reputation has been shown to be an effective substitute for truth in science. However, reputation is fragile. It can be endangered by gossip when a discipline like sociology is divided along political lines. There is no empirical data for a political label that places NL outside the majority of his West-German colleagues who are widely considered as having supported left and liberal politics in the decades since 1970.[37] Nevertheless, because Luhmann did not present himself as a socialist (in US terms: liberal), neither in academic life nor outside it, he was accused by about a dozen colleagues and in some mass media (including online media) of having been a young Nazi until 1945, showing a theoretical bias to 'technocratic fascism' or military regimes, citing toxic pre-fascist and fascist scholars (Darwin, Nietzsche, Heidegger, Arnold Gehlen, Schelsky) and using Nazi jargon ('selection'). Being aware of this kind of argument, other people miss an adequate analysis of what NL calls the 'fascist movements of the interwar period' or 'Auschwitz-like' permanent 'silencing'. It is assumed by them that his theory is not able to contribute to any debates about fascism.[38] This kind of biographical political interest is not confined to theorist NL. Max Weber and Talcott Parsons encounter attacks that are similar.

To focus on naming and shaming and to defy it would result in a grossly disbalanced biographical discussion. Instead of this, I want to show the utility of NL's theory for analysing fascist rule and Nazi violence by showing how NL uses one of his frameworks for case studies of German fascism and how one of NL's students does a case study of fascist murder using NL-theory.

NL's reputation stems from his role as a 'King of Theory' and his input to functionalist research designs, in particular, focusing on comparison and functional equivalents. His other contributions to designing research and collecting/analysing data are less known. For instance, he criticised a method that merely collects data and then uses them to construct a self-created reality; he promoted instead 'describing unchallenged facts with various theories and other distinctions'[39].

Numerous undisputed facts exist regarding serial mass killings during the violent twentieth century and before. NL provides case studies and frames for such studies[40] on elements and consequences of German fascism, including two lengthy and several brief accounts. The case framework I want to examine is found in two pages of an influential 1965 essay on the constitutional debate on conscientious objection and a sociological concept of conscience. It is concerned with the definition, use and non-use of conscience in different situations, especially how society offers paths for people to avoid recourse to conscience. Even for physicians and civil servants, who are obliged to help or follow orders, there are ways to avoid raising their conscientious objections by resorting to 'non-personal, nearly routine action. In this way we can understand that so many National Socialists did not involve their conscience and today claim to be the most helpless victims of National Socialism, because they remain identified with something which they do not accept as their own'.[41]

Routine refers to NL's theory of organisational decision-making that is based on the work of Herbert A. Simon and the Carnegie School. Routine, that is, conditionally programmed decisions, take the form 'if x happens y follows'. We find decision-making conditioned in this way inside the Nazi annihilation bureaucracy; examples come from Shoah, military justice and eugenic killings. What does 'nearly' routine mean? NL's concept of routine decision-making allows for flexibility; there are various forms of discretion in the procedure, in fact-finding activity and in the interpretation of texts. Helplessness refers to situations in which motives have to be presented from vocabularies of motives. It may be impossible to show motives accepted by one's significant others.

If we accept NL's theoretical framework of organisational routine, we have to ask: Which National Socialist decision-makers exhibited this combination of (flexible) routine, lack of conscience and helplessness? At the time of NL's essay, the German translation of Hannah Arendt's famous account of the Eichmann trial in Jerusalem was available. At a first glance, NL's theoretical framing seems to fit Arendt's view on Adolf Eichmann's behaviour during his supervision of the logistics of the Shoah mass murders. But did Arendt's description of the trial make Eichmann's helplessness visible? Eichmann presented motives that were acceptable to his reference group, that is, his and Hitler's followers. During the trial, he did not create the subsequent image of a fervent anti-Semite but of an obedient functionary, one of the proverbial cogs in the machinery.

There are other data that fit NL's theoretical frame, in particular, dividuality. One jurist, with whom Luhmann was well acquainted since his early career, is easily identified for a hate act in 1940 (publication) and a killing act in April 1945 (decision as a military judge). This civil servant, judge and professor is a good example for NLs notion of a person divided in time dimensions. Sometimes this is called a conversion. After the war, being converted to social democracy (having been a left liberal party member before 1933) and having become an ardent adherent of the rule of law, he found himself among relevant colleagues (NL included), who could not accept possible motives for his national socialist almost routine behaviour.[42]

Violence in an NL-framework has to be studied by reviewing the systems in which it occurs. NL distinguishes four types of social system: interaction, organisation, societal function system or protest movement and Stefan Kühl's analysis of one Shoah-killing unit, 'Polizeibatallion 101', revisiting the case studies of the US historian Christopher Browning and the political scientist Daniel Jonah Goldhagen, demonstrates how NL's typology of social systems helps to frame descriptions and even possible explanations[43].

Two genocide research questions are elucidated in Kühl's study and discussed by him:

(1) How much of the mass murder of Jews during the Holocaust can be attributed to individuals' respective organisations? Kühl assumes that only a small portion of victimisation can be attributed to individuals, with the vast majority being the result of collaboration. This appears distinct from the tsarist-era pogroms in Russia, for which organisational attribution is controversial.[44] As Raul Hilberg and others[45] have revealed, the Holocaust consisted of organised violence. Excesses and special cruelty beyond the organisational expectations may be attributed to individuals. This is what Goldhagen focuses upon to have data for a 'German' specialty: 'eliminationism'.[46] (2) How can member's participation in organisational killing be explained? Kühl links this question to their membership role into which NL-theory binds together what in other approaches are just various factors, neither explained nor weighted. And he uses widely NL's communication theory and not lay psychology as Goldhagen does.

Some other questions treated in a Luhmannian framework by others remain implicit in Kühl's book: (3) How did organisations decide to be involved in the Shoah? We may suppose that NL (and Kühl) would not focus on Hitler and other chiefs to look for explanations.[47] (4) Was Shoah violence part of a military function system or at least part of a conflict system called war, 'war of annihilation' as some historians say? Kühl insists that wars facilitate intentional violence against civilians.[48] (5) What about a 'fictional consensus' (a Luhmannian notion discussed by Kühl) about killing Jews, that resides in societal communication, not only in its organisations? Fiction, in this concept, means not absence of reality but tacit assumptions in communication. Kühl studies a consensual dictatorship and fictional consensus about excluding Jews from Germany. To reconcile NL's and Goldhagen's perspectives on consensus, it is necessary to demonstrate a fictional consensus not only about spatial exclusion but also about eradication, and this for function subsystems that can be called German.

Violence that stems from protest movements, NL's fourth type of social systems, is rarely cited to explain the Shoah, perhaps because the 'movement era' of Nazism was finished by the time the Shoah began, after the pogroms on German soil. NL gives a hint by citing an essay by Richard Gale that studies the incorporation of movements into non-movement organisations, for example, that of states.[49] Is there any organisational mass murder during the Nazi era that did not result from the incorporation of hate movements into various countries' state organisations (including Vichy-France and authoritarian Bulgaria): departments or single officers specialising in 'Jewish Affairs' or in the persecution of mentally handicapped people, Gypsies, male homosexuality and so on?

Is NL's theory 'to be adopted either completely or not at all'? Kühl combines multiple components, but not the most recent. We can conclude that the vast majority of theories and distinctions of NL are loosely coupled, that almost none have become obsolete, and that research, for example on Nazi violence, may select those that appear useful.

Notes

1 Luhmann published essays on the sociology of Durkheim (1977), Weber (1964) and Parsons (1980), which are reprinted in Niklas Luhmann, *The Differentiation of Society*. Translated by Stephen Holmes and Charles Larmore (New York: Columbia University Press, 1982). Karl Marx, Herbert A. Simon, Erving Goffman and other eminent sociologists were equally important and are cited throughout his work.

2 Michael King and Anton Schütz, 'The Ambitious Modesty of Niklas Luhmann', *Journal of Law and Society* 21, no. 3 (1994): 261–87.

3 See Hans-Georg Moeller, *Luhmann Explained. From Souls to Systems* (Chicago: Open Court, 2006), 89. There is a discussion in German sociology, whether individuality is to be ascribed to consciousness or to body, see Rudolf Stichweh, 'Körperindividuum oder Bewusstseinsindividuum? Der Mensch der funktional differenzierten Weltgesellschaft: Symposiumsbeitrag zu: Gesa Lindemann, Strukturnotwendige Kritik. Theorie der modernen Gesellschaft. Band 1', *Soziologische Revue* 43, no. 2 (2020): 153–9. NL looks on the body of human and non-human animals as divided into different system types, e.g., cells, brains and immune systems, observed today by different scientific disciplines: 'physical, chemical, and organic systems', see Niklas Luhmann, *Social Systems*. Translated by John Bednarz Jr and Dirk Baecker (Stanford: Stanford University Press, 1995), 244. Unless cited separately, the chapter uses Luhmann's concepts as defined in 'Social Systems'. They can be found in this book's index, Ibid., 619–27.

4 'N.L.' or 'NL' appear for example in: 'Luhmann, *Social Systems*, xliv and lii, and in William Rasch, *Niklas Luhmann's Modernity. The Paradoxes of Differentiation* (Stanford: Stanford University Press, 2000), 171–94.

5 See Seán Burke, *The Death and Return of the Author: Criticism and Subjectivity in Barthes, Foucault and Derrida* (Edinburgh: Edinburgh University Press, 2008).

6 There is an online bibliography of NL- publications: 'Niklas Luhmann - Gesamtbibliographie (1958-2018)', 20 April 2020, https://niklas-luhmann-archiv.de/person/nl-bibliographie. Interviews that contain aspects of what is conventionally called 'biography' are (in order of interviewing): Luhmann 1987_IB08 (1985, Erd/Maihofer); Luhmann 2000_IB02 (1991, Guibentif); 1993_IB02 (1991, Hudson); Luhmann 2017_IJ01 (1994, Kluge); Luhmann 1997_IB01 (1996, Horster) und Luhmann 2004_IB01 (1997, Hagen).

7 For the citation on modernity, see Niklas Luhmann, *Observations on Modernity* (Stanford: Stanford University Press, 1998), 2; and for citation on social structures, see Rasch, *Niklas Luhmann's Modernity*, 195. A well-known account of NL's doubling of reality is Rudolf Stichweh, 'Semantik und Sozialstruktur. Zur Logik einer systemtheoretischen Unterscheidung', *Soziale Systeme* 6, no. 2 (2000): 1–14.

8 Claudio Baraldi and Giancarlo Corsi, *Niklas Luhmann: Education as a Social System* (Cham: Springer, 2017), 57–60, 71, 118.

9 NL added the form person/unperson to the older fourfold distinction person/role/program/value in Niklas Luhmann, 'Die Form "Person"', *Soziale Welt* 42, no. 2 (1991): 166–75. There are Italian and Japanese translations. Both concepts are compatible.
10 Niklas Luhmann, '"Ich denke primär historisch": Religionssoziologische Perspektiven', *Deutsche Zeitschrift für Philosophie* 39, no. 9 (1991): 940–1.
11 Rudolf Stichweh, 'Die Rolle des Zufalls in den Funktionssystemen der Weltgesellschaft', in *Contingentia. Transformationen des Zufalls*, ed. Hartmut Böhme (Berlin, Boston: De Gruyter, 2015), 173–85.
12 One of NL's early students and colleague at his department applied a kind of evolutionary theory to the history of NL's thought in his introduction to NL's theory. See Gábor Kiss, *Evolution soziologischer Grundbegriffe. Zum Wandel ihrer Semantik* (Stuttgart: Enke, 1989). If a history of books and essays introducing NL were to be written, it would be interesting to ask how many sociologists were among the authors? And how successful have sociological introductions been, see, for example, Daniel B. Lee and Achim Brosziewski, *Observing Society: Meaning, Communication, and Social Systems* (Amherst: Cambria Press, 2009).
13 See Arnd Hoffmann, *Zufall und Kontingenz in der Geschichtstheorie: mit zwei Studien zu Theorie und Praxis der Sozialgeschichte* (Frankfurt am Main: Klostermann, 2005).
14 See Niklas Luhmann, 'Zeit und Handlung - Eine vergessene Theorie', in Niklas Luhmann, *Soziologische Aufklärung 3. Soziales System, Gesellschaft, Organisation* (Opladen: Westdeutscher Verlag, 1981), 101–25.
15 See Niklas Luhmann, 'Epilog 1994', in Niklas Luhmann, *Funktionen und Folgen formaler Organisation* (Berlin: Duncker und Humblot, 1995), 398–405; Stichweh, 'Semantik und Sozialstruktur. Zur Logik einer systemtheoretischen Unterscheidung'.
16 Andreas Göbel shows in a general way how NL's distinctions follow a career of problems, see Andreas Göbel, *Theoriegenese als Problemgenese. Eine problemgeschichtliche Rekonstruktion der soziologischen Systemtheorie Niklas Luhmanns* (Konstanz: UVK Verlag, 2000). On the other hand, Rudolf Stichweh describes the career of the distinction of semantics, see Stichweh, 'Semantik und Sozialstruktur. Zur Logik einer systemtheoretischen Unterscheidung'.
17 See in particular Niklas Luhmann, *Gesellschaftsstruktur und Semantik: Studien sur Wissenssoziologie der modernen Gesellschaft*, Vols. 1 to. 4 (Frankfurt am Main: Suhrkamp, 1980, 1981, 1989, 1995).
18 See e.g., Rasch, *Niklas Luhmann's Modernity*, 177.
19 From the very few biographical sketches on Luhmann whose communication resists that of the archives, I recommend autobiographical sentences in 1993_IB02 (Interview with Wayne Hudson) and Eva Knodt's foreword, in Luhmann, *Social Systems*, XIII–XIV, even if some minor misunderstandings may occur from this (law degree not 'from the University', but the state; NL did not 'follow Schelsky' to Bielefeld University, but was its first professor; not two 'publications' accepted for degrees: one text was not yet published). There are four frequent mistakes in another well done text; namely, Luhmann was not prisoner as an anti-aircraft auxiliary but as a soldier; did not 'lecture' at the Speyer school, but was only engaged in research; did not begin a career in 'Lüneburg's' public administration, but in a state court located in this town; lectured at Frankfurt/Main not before, but after being appointed at Bielefeld, see 'Dr. Niklas Luhmann Architect, Jurist and Theoretican', *ArchINFORM* (blog), 22 April 2020, https://www.archinform.net/arch/43195.htm.
20 Developed by Giancarlo Corsi, 'The Dark Side of the Career', in *Problems of Form*, ed. Dirk Baecker (Stanford: Stanford University Press, 1999), 171–9.

21 See the NL- bibliography, supra note 6.

22 See Ruth Lambertz-Pollan, *Auf dem Weg zu Souveränität und Westintegration (1948-1955): Der Beitrag des Völkerrechtlers und Diplomaten Wilhelm Grewe* (Baden-Baden: Nomos, 2016).

23 C. Wright Mills, 'Situated Actions and Vocabularies of Motives', *American Sociological Review* 5, no. 6 (1940): 904–13.

24 Kate Connolly, 'Elderly Germans Discover Hitler Made Them Nazi Party Members', *The Guardian*, 17 July 2007.

25 I heard this in an interview with one of his family members. Its name cannot be disclosed for legal reasons.

26 Niklas Luhmann, 'Ich nehme mal Karl Marx'. Interview with Walter van Rossum, in *Niklas Luhmann: Archimedes und wir. Interviews*, ed. Dirk Baecker and Georg Stanitzek (Berlin: Merve, 1987), 14–38.

27 Mark S. Granovetter, 'The Strength of Weak Ties', *American Journal of Sociology* 78, no. 6 (1973): 1360–80.

28 This letter has been shown in an exhibition at Frankfurt/Main in 2009/10, see the comment on the problems of dealing with academic Nazis after remigration Arno Widman. 'Frankfurter Schule. Schwierige Heimkehr', *Frankfurter Rundschau*, 17 September 2009.

29 See the debate between Luhmann and Eysenck in '*Wie halten Sie's mit Außerirdischen, Herr Luhmann? Nicht unmerkwürdige Gespräche mit Niklas Luhmann.* Edited by Klaus Dammann (Berlin: Kadmos, 2014), 39–63.

30 Niklas Luhmann, 'Modern Sciences and Phenomenology', in Niklas Luhmann, *Theories of Distinction. Redescribing the Descriptions of Modernity*, ed. William Rasch (Stanford: Stanford University Press, 2002), 33–60 at 38.

31 There is now a broad discussion of Husserl's eurocentrism, see Dermot Moran, '"Even the Papuan Is a Man and Not a Beast": Husserl on Universalism and the Relativity of Cultures', *Journal of the History of Philosophy* 49, no. 4 (2011): 463–94.

32 See e.g., the work of an 'ethnopluralistic' activist which had got an award for her philosophical dissertation using Kantian and Luhmannian theory of morals: Caroline Sommerfeld-Lethen, *Wie moralisch werden? Kants moralistische Ethik* (Freiburg/München: Alber, 2005); on her political activism, see Katrın Bennhold, 'A Very German Love Story: When Old Left and Far Right Share a Bedroom', *The New York Times*, 1 May 2018.

33 NL has been accused advocating a minimal state and thus revealing a 'neoliberal' bias. However, this criticism is misplaced because his interest is in evaluating the outcome of state activity and to eschew an illusion of steering; see Niklas Luhmann, *Political Theory in the Welfare State* (Berlin: De Gruyter, 1990). In this translation of original German book of 1981 the clear concluding chapter is missing. Luhmann's views on the economy do not resemble 'Reaganomics' or 'Thatcherism' but are sociological analyses of both state failure and market failure.

34 In German and Spanish, the device is discussed under the name of biographism, see Tom Kindt and Hans-Harald Müller, 'Was war eigentlich der Biographismus—und was ist aus ihm geworden? Eine Untersuchung', in *Autorschaft: Positionen und Revisionen*, ed. Heinrich Detering (Stuttgar/Weimar: Metzler, 2002), 355–75.; this discussion is linked to that on authorship, see supra note 5.

35 See the Nazi case-study frame discussed below.

36 For checking obsolescence, see Göbel, *Theoriegenese als Problemgenese. eine problemgeschichtliche Rekonstruktion der soziologischen Systemtheorie Niklas Luhmanns.*

37 See Perry Anderson, 'A New Germany?', *New Left Review* 57, no. 5/6 (2009): 5–42.

38 Such accusations by use of false data continue today; see the refutation of several kinds of blaming by a colleague in Frankfurter Allgemeine Zeitung 2022 in Klaus Dammann, 'Warum "Grenzen der Verwaltung"?', *Soziale Systeme* 25 (forthcoming).

39 See Luhmann, *Observations on Modernity*, 5; Niklas Luhmann, *Theory of Society*, vol. 1 (Stanford: Stanford University Press, 2012), 13–18. Methodology for empirical research that suits NL's theory is discussed in René John, Anna Henkel, and Jana Rückert-John, *Die Methodologien des Systems: Wie kommt man zum Fall und wie dahinter?* (Wiesbaden: Verlag für Sozialwissenschaften, 2010).

40 The case study methodology that fits NL's cases and was probably known to him can be found in Robert K. Yin, *Case Study Research: Design and Methods*, 2nd ed. (Thousand Oaks: SAGE, 1994).

41 Niklas Luhmann, 'Die Gewissensfreiheit und das Gewissen', *Archiv Des Öffentlichen Rechts* 90, no. 3 (1965): 257–86, translation KD.

42 For these data see Sebastian Wolf, 'Nachkriegsgründung und doch angebräunt. Die Hochschule für Verwaltungswissenschaften Speyer und der Fall Erich Becker', *Forum Recht* 3 (2007): 98–9 (hate act), Carl Hermann Ule, *Beiträge zur Rechtswirklichkeit im Dritten Reich* (Berlin: Duncker und Humblot, 1987), 179 (violent act) and for personal *dividuality* and the whole case, see Klaus Dammann, *Wie werden aus Tätern 'hilfloseste Opfer des Nationalsozialismus'? Dis-/Kontinuitäten von Rechtslehrern in einer Soziologie des deutschen Faschismus* (Universität Bielefeld: Bielefelder Arbeiten zur Verwaltungssoziologie, 2022).

43 Stefan Kühl, *Ordinary Organisations: Why Normal Men Carried Out the Holocaust* (Cambridge: Polity Press, 2016).

44 Klaus Dammann and Hanna Rychlewski, *Genocidation of Serial Mass Killings. Saving the Concept of Civil Society from Racist Social Movements* (Universität Bielefeld: Bielefelder Arbeiten zur Verwaltungssoziologie, 2000).

45 Raul Hilberg, *The Destruction of the European Jews*, Rev. and expanded ed. (London: Holmes & Meier, 2012); Zygmunt Bauman, *Modernity and the Holocaust* (Cambridge: Polity Press, 1989).

46 Daniel Jonah Goldhagen, *Hitler's Willing Executioners. Ordinary Germans and the Holocaust* (New York: Vintage, 1997).

47 My work, Klaus Dammann, *Garbage Can Decision Processes? A Sociological Redescription of the Functionalist Research Programme in Shoah Historiography* (Universität Bielefeld: Bielefelder Arbeiten zur Verwaltungssoziologie, 2002), shows how theories of the middle range, compatible with NL's theory, resemble theories implicit in the 'structural' approach of Shoah history writing.

48 For a differentiation of military and genocidal violence, observing different codes of a military and a political, economic etc. system, see Klaus Dammann, 'Women, Children, Older People. Genocide, Warfare, and the Functional Differentiation of Society', in *The Moral Fabric in Contemporary Societies*, ed. Grazyna Skapska and Ana Orla-Bukowska (Leiden: Brill, 2003), 291–308; Klaus Dammann, 'Vernichtungskrieg, Kampf und Volksgemeinschaft.' Empirische Studien zur urfaschistischen Begriffswelt mit relationaler Soziologie, *Soziale Systeme* 26 (forthcoming) - with data on fascist violence around Leningrad, in Yugoslavia and Ethiopia.

49 Richard P. Gale, 'Social Movements and the State: The Environmental Movement, Countermovement, and Government Agencies', *Sociological Perspectives* 29, no. 2 (1 April 1986): 202–40. Luhmann uses this essay in his *Theory of Society*, vol. 2 (Stanford: Stanford University Press, 2013), 163, note 477.

Chapter 12

THREE ENCOUNTERS WITH NIKLAS LUHMANN

Gunther Teubner

A New Tone

In 1968, when I worked as a court clerk and was writing my dissertation, I suffered from acute symptoms of *horror vacui*. My somewhat naïve hopes in the rationality of legal arguments, but also in the potential of the social sciences to enlighten them, had been disillusioned. I had worked my way through the relevant literature on law and the social sciences, but, of course, without finding a solution to my problem. I doubted the scientific quality of legal scholarship, equated legal doctrine with absurd conceptual acrobatics, and found in legal sociology nothing but irrelevant fact-gathering or artificial theory exercises. In those days, the critique of law as an instrument of brute power was en vogue and I agreed wholeheartedly. My own experience in the courts contradicted what I had learned in law school about the inner persuasiveness of law when it came to solving social conflicts. I realised that in day-to-day practice, legal arguments would neither determine judicial decisions, nor produce plausible reasons for the parties concerned, nor satisfactorily resolve social conflicts. Likewise, as a doctoral student, I had to learn that legal arguments are neither participating in an interdisciplinary debate nor realising social values, not to speak of producing discursive rationality.

Suddenly a new tone! *Norms in sociological perspective* – a short but brilliant article by a still unknown Niklas Luhmann which radicalised the usual critique of law in a cool and distant language. He showed that legal methods of attribution are untenable in scientific terms. So far, so not astonishing. But what impressed me was that starting with this critique of law, Luhmann developed sociological arguments for legal autonomy which he later transformed into a whole theory of law's autopoietic self-production. When social or moral conflicts seem to be unresolvable, the law still finds an additional perspective that makes these conflicts resolvable and thus endurable in social life. The argument contradicted the *Zeitgeist* of these days. Law is not supposed to mirror social communities' shared understanding of conflicts – but the opposite, to alienate drastically social conflicts is law's well-founded stubbornness.

Suddenly the absurd legal doctrine made sense. It translates otherwise non-resolvable conflicts into a highly artificial web of legal topoi, concepts, norms, principles, constructs so that they are almost no longer recognisable as social or moral conflicts, but appear as genuinely juridical problems which can be argued and decided via legal fictions and without a counterpart in social reality. In those days when it was en vogue to mock legal arguments, this was a new serious tone. At the same time, this kind of analysis seemed to formulate a categorical imperative for the critique of law: Criticise only according to that maxim whereby you can, at the same time, discover alternative possibilities of construction.

Cool Distance

Years later, when I met Niklas Luhmann in person, I was taken aback by his cool distance which I felt always to be behind his friendly smile. In personal encounters, I experienced this distance intensely. I observed his almost physical aversion against what he called the 'stickiness of people's gazes'; how he was greeting colleagues only to turn away from them as fast as possible, and how he refused his disciples to create a Luhmann school (but could not avoid its self-organisation). I encountered the distance he kept from any fraternisation, his dislike of chummy communication. Should one find here the biographical motive for the often described, and often criticised, piercing coldness of his theory?

Today I see things differently. It is the painful, even traumatic experience of the inaccessibility of the other's inner life which created, almost in a Demosthenes-effect, the greatest insight of Luhmann's theory – the duplication of meaning production, the clear-cut separation of social and psychic life. The starting point was the insight that inner experiences are in principle not communicable, even more, that inner meaning will be destroyed by its verbalisation and communication. He liked to cite the German romantic poet Novalis: 'Much is too tender to be thought of, even more, to be spoken'. From the insurmountable distance between human beings followed Luhmann's construction of psychic monads, the autopoietic closure of inner experience, and the famous double contingency, which is the mutual inaccessibility of their minds when people encounter each other.

What impressed me most was Luhmann's insistence that any attempt to overcome this closure will always end in the solitude of psychic life. But what made his analyses so fruitful is the insight that the energies of overcoming the closure will have effects in a totally different direction. Luhmann's reaction to the closure of inner worlds was different from the usual escape routes: no sentimental stylisation of communitarian yearnings, no straitjacket of intersubjectivity, no mystical transcendence of alterity, no substitution of the subject by *différance.* At the same time, no farewell to the individuals' inner experience, no contempt for the philosophy of consciousness, no prohibition of private language, no reduction of meaning to sheer sociality.

Luhmann undertook a radical deconstruction of former concepts of intersubjectivity, but he did it with sufficient subtlety so that the new theory could arrive at a world of meaning beyond individual experience: the autonomous world of communication. What is hidden in the duplication of meaning, in the emergence of autonomous communication, in the crystalline structures of social systems, is the compensation for the painful impossibility of meeting of minds.

Contrapuntal Textures

My third encounter with Luhmann's work had to do with its *Stimmungsgehalt*, its *ambience*, its atmospheric content. Here I have always been struck by its elective affinity to the contrapuntal compositions in the old masters' music. In its formal rigour which expresses at the same time a high affective intensity, Luhmann's theory composes contemporary society as one single theme in multiple variations, making use of distinctions in various social contexts, searching for isomorphies as well as for fundamental differences. I experience Luhmann's masterpiece *Social Systems* in close kinship to Johann Sebastian Bach's *Art of the Fugue* or the *Musical Offering.* Luhmann wrote his series of books on different social systems in a fashion analogous to Bach's fugues and canons, each using some variation of a single principal subject, and generally ordered to increase in complexity. Luhmann's monumental theory seems to me like a great project of *ars musica – ars mathematica,* a systematic passage through the rich possibilities of rigorous techniques of contrapuntal composition, which combines high formality with strong emotions. *Theory as Passion* – the title of a collection of essays dedicated to Luhmann, is pertinent.

In the perspective of such an austerely constructed theory, its object, society itself, appears as the result of a contrapuntal composition, namely as the self-application of a chain of differences in numerous variations. Social differentiation is the single theme that is reflexively applied to itself with increasing complexity. The polyphony of communications in various social systems is similar to the autonomy of voices in a musical piece, which are at the same time disciplined by the constraints of canonical composition – yet with the decisive difference that the confidence in *harmonia mundi* is today superseded by the frightening experience of infinite contingency.

It is said that Bach's music – in its formal rigour, its remarkable expressivity and in its sober seriousness – became possible only after the experiences of the Thirty Years War (1618–1648). I think that Luhmann's theory – in its formal rigour, its remarkable expressivity and its sober seriousness – has been possible only after the 30 years with two World Wars in the twentieth century (1914–1945). This might sound implausible in the light of Luhmann's affective asceticism, his irony toward moral entrepreneurs, his distance toward nice and helpful social theories and his refusal to participate in the normative turn of sociology.

But there are hidden passages in his work:

> The experience of national socialism had widely expanded the imagination of what is possible. Horrible crimes had been permitted in politics, even had been committed by politics, and had not been impeded by the law. [...] One had to raise the question whether these acts had been permitted by the law and, more radically, whether they had been proscribed by the law.

However, Luhmann did not search to re-vitalise natural law, nor to re-moralise the law, but rather to activate political resistance within society against political totalisation. This meant to re-interpret constitutional rights and to understand them not only as legal rules but rather as a social institution, which has the potential to strengthen the civilising effects of social differentiation.

In my view, Luhmann thought that particularly after the historical experience, German society had been sufficiently immunised against political totalitarianism so that he directed his attention to ecological endangerments, to new sorts of fundamentalism and tendencies of social exclusion in the emerging world society. Sociological enlightenment – again in the sense of Luhmann's categorical imperative – means not only to analyse in-depth the dark past but also to become aware of new social exclusion problems and ecological dangers.

And one can find numerous allusions and enigmatic wordings in Luhmann's *Theory of Society* dealing with structural problems and endangerments of world society. They will have to be deciphered in a contrapuntal composition analysis, similar to the inventive puzzles in the *Musical Offering* which the old Bach had pointed to in a handwritten invitation: *Quaerendo invenietis*.

INDEX

www.ingramcontent.com/pod-product-compliance
Ingram Content Group UK Ltd.
Pitfield, Milton Keynes, MK11 3LW, UK
UKHW041831100926
8556IPUK00002B/119

9 781839 984884